lonely

PARIS

Mary Winston Nicklin, Jean-Bernard Carillet,
Eileen Cho, Fabienne Fong Yan, Catherine Le Nevez,
Jacqueline Ngo Mpii, Danette St. Onge

Meet Our Writers

DIETER MÖCKLI/500PX ©

Mary Winston Nicklin

@MaryWNicklin

Based on the left bank of Paris, Mary Winston is a Franco-American writer and editor. She loves going on urban hikes across the city and beyond the *Périphérique,* looking for street art and stories.

Jean-Bernard Carillet

@jb.carillet_photography

Jean-Bernard is a Paris-based freelance journalist, photographer and filmmaker. He studied in the 5e and 16e *arrondissements,* lived in the 13e and 14e, and has been riding his bike throughout the city for more than 20 years.

Eileen Cho

@yo_cho *@eileenwcho*

Eileen W Cho is a Korean American writer and photographer from Seattle, Washington, based in Paris.

Fabienne Fong Yan

@a.fab.journey

French-Chinese born and raised on Réunion Island, Fabienne has travelled between Europe and Asia for the past 15 years. She now works in Paris as a digital content strategist. Her passions include Asian food, awesome nature and mysterious stories.

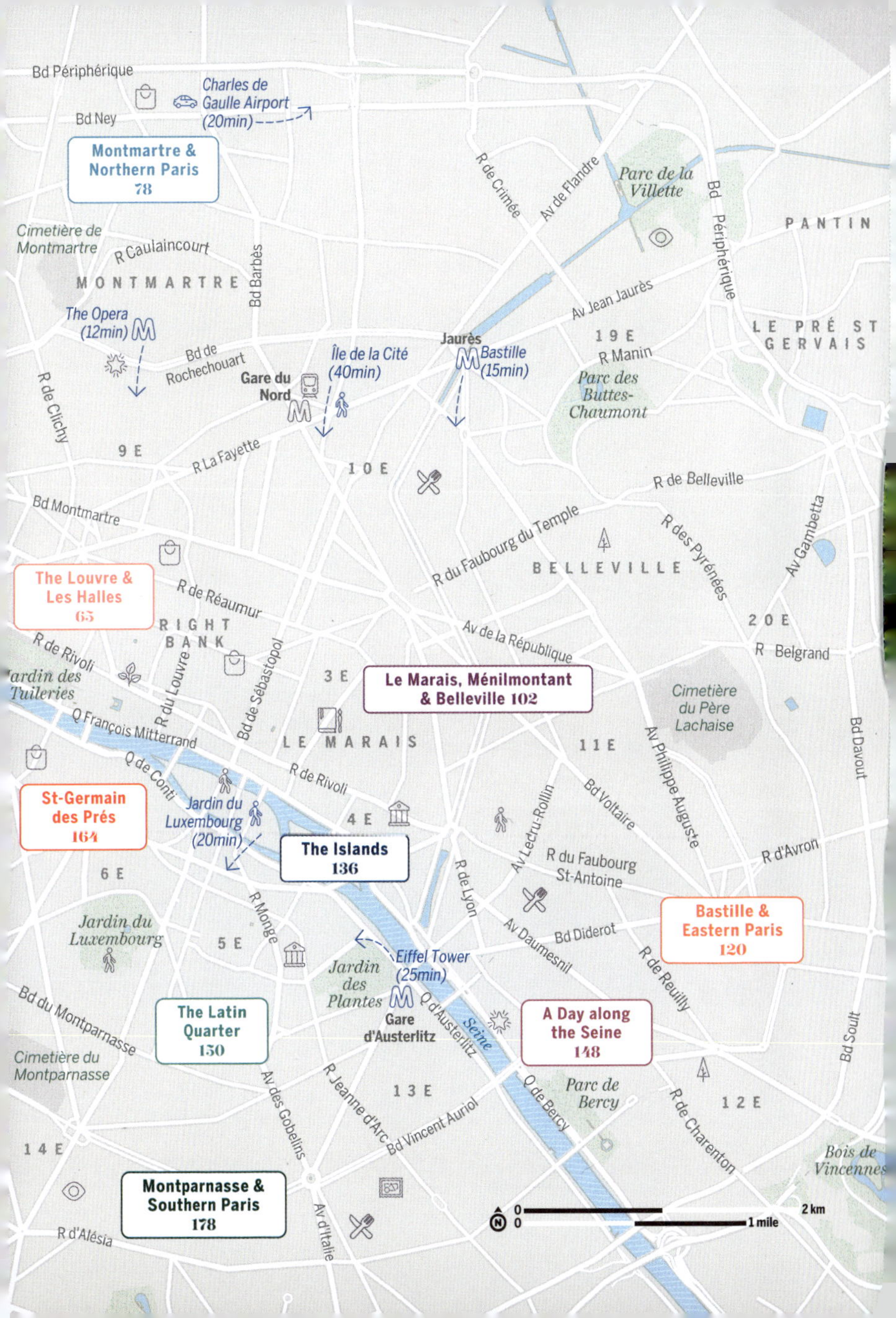

Bd Périphérique
Charles de Gaulle Airport (20min)
Bd Ney
Montmartre & Northern Paris 78
Cimetière de Montmartre
R Caulaincourt
MONTMARTRE
Bd Barbès
The Opera (12min)
Bd de Rochechouart
Gare du Nord
Île de la Cité (40min)
Jaurès
Bastille (15min)
R de Crimée
Av de Flandre
Parc de la Villette
Bd Périphérique
PANTIN
Av Jean Jaurès
19E
R Manin
LE PRÉ ST GERVAIS
Parc des Buttes-Chaumont
R de Clichy
9E
R La Fayette
10E
R de Belleville
Bd Montmartre
R du Faubourg du Temple
R des Pyrénées
Av Gambetta
BELLEVILLE
The Louvre & Les Halles 65
R de Réaumur
RIGHT BANK
Av de la République
20E
R Belgrand
R de Rivoli
Jardin des Tuileries
R du Louvre
Bd de Sébastopol
3E
Le Marais, Ménilmontant & Belleville 102
Cimetière du Père Lachaise
Q François Mitterrand
LE MARAIS
11E
Av Philippe Auguste
Bd Davout
Q de Conti
R de Rivoli
Av Ledru-Rollin
Bd Voltaire
St-Germain des Prés 164
Jardin du Luxembourg (20min)
4E
The Islands 136
R de Lyon
R du Faubourg St-Antoine
R d'Avron
6E
R Monge
Bd Diderot
Av Daumesnil
Bastille & Eastern Paris 120
Jardin du Luxembourg
5E
Eiffel Tower (25min)
Jardin des Plantes
Gare d'Austerlitz
Q d'Austerlitz
Seine
A Day along the Seine 148
R de Reuilly
Bd du Montparnasse
The Latin Quarter 150
Cimetière du Montparnasse
Bd Soult
Av des Gobelins
R Jeanne d'Arc
13E
Q de Bercy
Parc de Bercy
R de Charenton
12E
Bd Vincent Auriol
14E
Bois de Vincennes
Montparnasse & Southern Paris 178
Av d'Italie
R d'Alésia
0
2 km
0
1 mile

Savour classic French cuisine in a buzzy bistro. Listen to live music on a boat floating on the Seine. See a trove of art at museums and galleries and in the city streets. Uncover historical secrets through enduring architecture. Shop for stylish fashion and striking accessories. Escape to secluded parks and gardens. Wander along photogenic backstreets to discover hidden villages. Shop with locals for bountiful produce at lively street markets. Get blown away by pigeon's-eye panoramas of the urban landscape.

This is Paris.

TURN THE PAGE AND START PLANNING YOUR NEXT BEST TRIP →

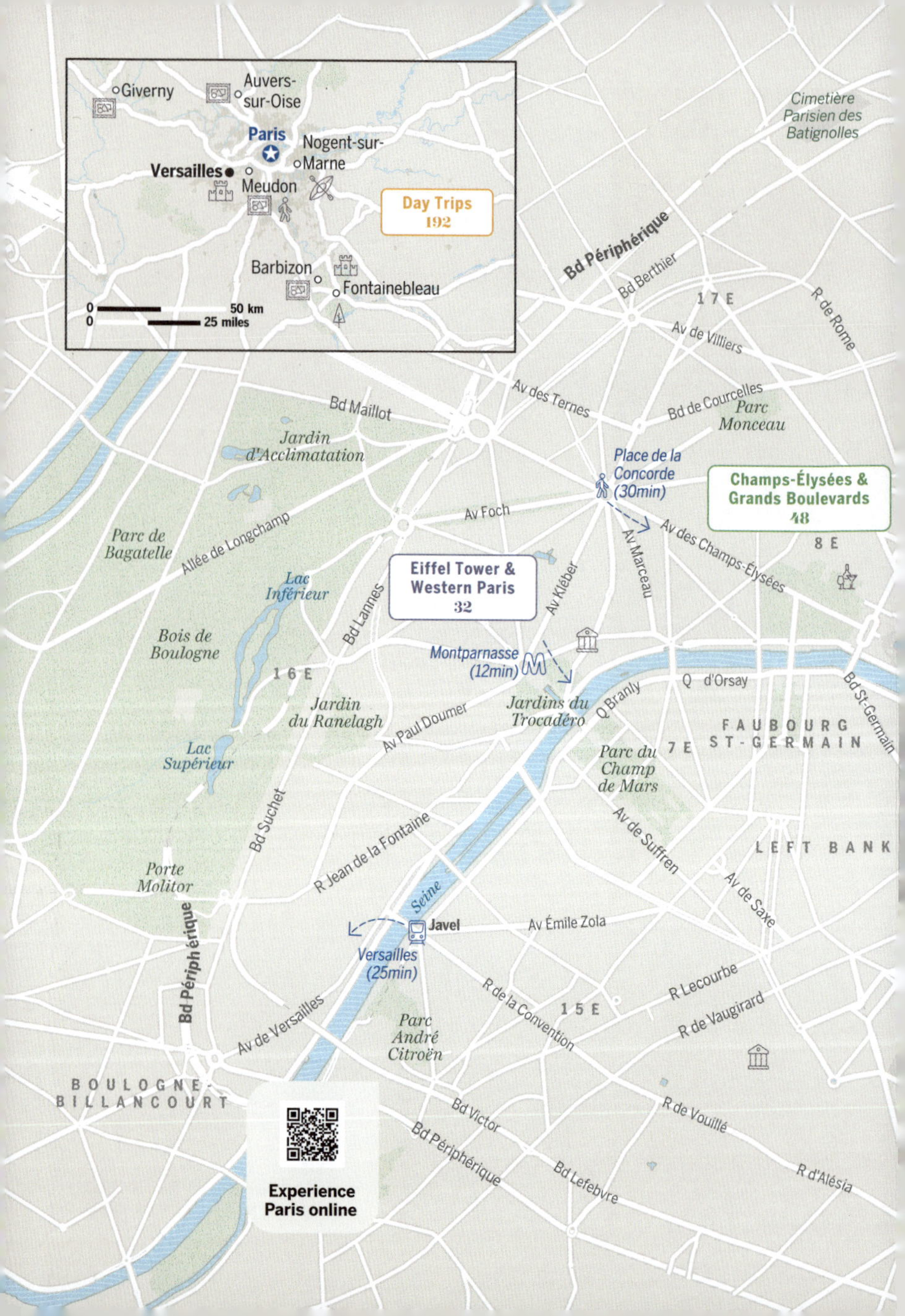

Giverny
Auvers-sur-Oise
Paris
Nogent-sur-Marne
Versailles
Meudon
Day Trips
192
Barbizon
Fontainebleau
0
50 km
0
25 miles
Cimetière Parisien des Batignolles
Bd Périphérique
Bd Berthier
17E
R de Rome
Av de Villiers
Av des Ternes
Bd de Courcelles
Parc Monceau
Bd Maillot
Jardin d'Acclimatation
Place de la Concorde (30min)
Champs-Élysées & Grands Boulevards
48
Av Foch
Av des Champs-Élysées
8E
Parc de Bagatelle
Allée de Longchamp
Eiffel Tower & Western Paris
32
Av Marceau
Av Kléber
Lac Inférieur
Bd Lannes
Bois de Boulogne
Montparnasse (12min)
16E
Q Branly
Q d'Orsay
Bd St-Germain
Jardin du Ranelagh
Av Paul Doumer
Jardins du Trocadéro
FAUBOURG ST-GERMAIN
7E
Lac Supérieur
Parc du Champ de Mars
Bd Suchet
R Jean de la Fontaine
Av de Suffren
LEFT BANK
Porte Molitor
Seine
Av de Saxe
Bd Périphérique
Javel
Av Émile Zola
Versailles (25min)
R de la Convention
R Lecourbe
15E
R de Vaugirard
Av de Versailles
Parc André Citroën
BOULOGNE-BILLANCOURT
Bd Victor
R de Vouillé
Bd Périphérique
Bd Lefebvre
R d'Alésia
Experience Paris online

Previous page rue des Thermopyles (p185) **Above** *Bouquiniste* (p15)

Catherine Le Nevez

see lonelyplanet.com/authors/catherine-le-nevez

Writing for Lonely Planet since 2004, Catherine first road-tripped across Europe from Paris aged four. She's visited 60-plus countries, completing her PhD, master's degree, and editing and publishing qualifications along the way.

Jacqueline Ngo Mpii

@yaquimpii *@yaquelinah*

Born in Cameroon and raised in France, Jacqueline is the founder and CEO of multimedia and cultural agency Little Africa, a resource for creatives and entrepreneurs from the African diaspora. She is also the author of *City Guide: Afrique à Paris,* the first guidebook highlighting Afro-Parisian culture.

Danette St. Onge

@globalgastronomiste

Danette St. Onge is a freelance food and travel writer. Originally from California, she's now based between London and Paris and has also lived in Italy and Thailand.

Contents

Best Experiences 6
Calendar 18
My Perfect Day..............26
7 Things to Know
About Paris....................28
Read, Listen,
Watch & Follow............. 30

Eiffel Tower & Western Paris 32

Eiffel Tower Outing.........36
Garden Follies................42
Museum Hopping 44

Champs-Élysées & Grands Boulevards 48

The Charms of the Champs...............52
Ghost Hunting at the Opéra 56
Drinks in a Palace..........58
Trendsetting Shopping 60

The Louvre & Les Halles 65

Love at the Louvre..................... 68
Coffee at the Palais Royal 72
Food Shopping in Montorgueil................74

Montmartre & Northern Paris 78

A Night in Pigalle............82
Vintage Clothes & Jazz 88
Boating & the Buttes......90
Dancing on Train Tracks 92
La Goutte d'Or.............. 94
Secret Canal Corners......................... 98

Le Marais, Ménilmontant & Belleville 102

Royal Intrigue in Le Marais 106
Jewish Culture in the Pletzl.................. 110
Sunset in Belleville........112
Gravestones & Greenery 116

Bastille & Eastern Paris 120

Green Line Rambles 124
Saint-Antoine's Artisans 128
Market Finds at Aligre........................132

The Islands 136

Exploring the Islands...140
Silver Tower Magic.......144

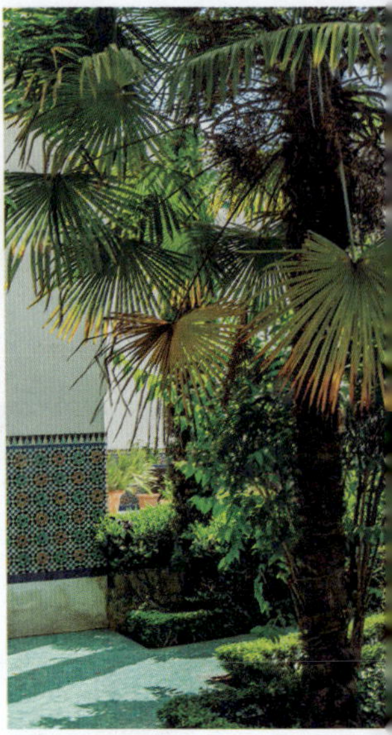

FRANCK LEGROS/SHUTTERSTOCK ©

A Day along the Seine 148

The Latin Quarter.... 150

Arab Allure....................154
Exploring the Latin Quarter................156
The Roving Cinephile....160

St-Germain des Prés 164

The Chicest Shopping 168
Left Bank Magic 170
Painters & Paint 172
Sweets on Rue du Bac....174

Grande Mosquée de Paris (p155)

Montparnasse & Southern Paris............ 178

Massive Murals 182
Secret Villages.................184
Asian Flavours.................188

Day Trips 192

A Costumed Affair...........196
Parisian Paddleboarding.............200
Suburban Culture & Nature............ 202
A Forest Hike & Palace.........................204

Practicalities............. 206

Arriving 208
Getting Around...............210
Accommodation 212
Safe Travel 214
Money 215
Responsible Travel 216
Essentials 218
Language........................220

ESSAYS

Women of Montmartre.... 86
Noire Paris....................... 96
The 100 Nationalities of Belleville 114
The Urban Farms of Paris.............................126
Notre Dame Splendour........................142
Bistros, Brasseries & Bouillons 186
Artist Villages 198

VISUAL GUIDES

Don't Leave Paris Without................... 40
A Brief Guide to Cheese.........................130

HOURS & RESERVATIONS

Restaurants generally open from noon to 2pm and 7.30pm to 10.30pm.

Most restaurant shut at least one day of the week (usually Sunday). Many close for summer holidays in July and August.

Reserve *well* ahead for popular and/or high-end places.

BON **APPÉTIT**

As a world food capital, Paris is a bastion of French culinary tradition, drawing chefs from across the globe to sharpen their knives in Michelin-starred kitchens. This is where baguettes are judged in an annual contest and *pâtissiers* compete with artful pastries almost too pretty to eat. It's also a multicultural hub incorporating the full spectrum of global flavours – not to mention the tasty street food shaking up the scene.

→ PASTRY REVOLUTION

Forget macarons. There's never been a better time to find pastry nirvana in Paris. Culinary maestros such as Cédric Grolet draw lines to their jewellery-box shops.

Left Oysters and rosé **Right** Pastries by Cédric Grolet **Below** Marché d'Aligre (p132)

MENUS

For the best-value dining, forgo ordering à la carte (from the menu) for daily *prix-fixe* menus (fixed-price, multicourse meals). Lunch can be a fraction of the dinner price at high-end establishments.

↑ TO MARKET, TO MARKET

The vibrant *marchés* (markets) are a cornerstone of local life. From Bastille to bd Auguste-Blanqui, produce-laden street markets are staged at least once a week in every *quartier*.

Best Food Experiences

- **Slurp sublime oysters in the vestiges of Paris' former wholesale markets around rue Montorgueil.** (p75)
- **Fire up the spice at the noodle shops and family-run restaurants of Paris' biggest Chinatown.** (p188)
- **Taste the flavours of Africa in Paris' northern neighbourhoods.** (p95)
- **Partake in tradition at bustling bistros and historic brasseries.** (p186)

ALTERNATIVE ART SPACES

Les Frigos is housed in a former refrigerated storage depot in the 13e.

59 Rivoli was once an artists' squat on one of the city's most prominent streets.

La Ruche is a historic 'beehive' of studios on the Left Bank.

REINVENTING **PARIS**

The French capital ignites imaginations around the world. Iconic sites such as the Louvre Museum, Arc de Triomphe and Eiffel Tower are instantly recognisable. But Paris is also full of unexpected treasures that reflect its cosmopolitan spirit and new-wave creativity. Forget the stereotypes and see the city through a new lens.

→ MICROBREWERY REVOLUTION

Multiple craft-beer entrepreneurs have followed the pioneering Brasserie de la Goutte d'Or. A scenic spot is the Paname Brewing Company (p100) on the Bassin de la Villette.

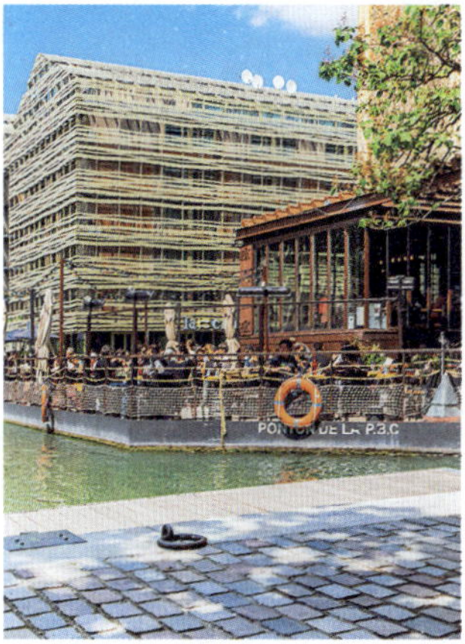

KIEV.VICTOR/SHUTTERSTOCK ©

Left Les Frigos **Right** Paname Brewing Company (p100) **Below** Ground Control (p125)

EXPLORE PARIS

The Explore Paris website (exploreparis.com/en) offers tourism activities and guided tours that break away from the Paris classics, with an emphasis on meeting locals.

RIGHT: FREDERIC REGLAIN/ALAMY STOCK PHOTO ©
LEFT: GUICHAOUA/ALAMY STOCK PHOTO ©

↑ CULTURAL CENTRES

Some of the most happening places today are hybrid cultural venues that host diverse programs of events, often in previously disused industrial spaces, such as Ground Control (p125).

Best Unusual Experiences

- **Party in a former train station at Le Hasard Ludique.** (p92)
- **Pilot an electric boat on the Canal de l'Ourcq.** (p91)
- **Admire photography exhibits in a former public bathhouse.** (p99)
- **Shop for trendy African-inspired fashion at Maison Chateau Rouge.** (p95)

SEE THE SIGNS

The city's 700 historic markers were created by designer Philippe Starck in the shape of an oar – a reference to the ship in the Paris coat of arms.

Plaques on buildings detail the famous residents who lived there.

LIVING HISTORY

Spanning more than two millennia, the city's multi-layered history is present at every turn. Remarkable vestiges and architectural monuments are packed into a surprisingly compact area. In Paris, you can picnic in an ancient Roman amphitheatre, marvel at a medieval alchemist's house, climb a flamboyant Gothic tower and see a WWII bunker – all in one day.

Left Le Procope (p171) **Right** Sarcophagus, Notre Dame **Below** rue Saint-Jacques

→ NEW DISCOVERIES

During the Notre Dame restoration, two mysterious sarcophagi were found buried under the nave. In April 2023, an ancient necropolis was unearthed during construction at the Port Royal train station.

JULIEN DE ROSA/AFP VIA GETTY IMAGES ©

THE OLDEST CAFE

Dating back to 1686, Le Procope (p171) serves French classics surrounded by rich relics of its past. Napoleon left one of his signature bicorne hats – allegedly to pay a bill.

RIGHT: PETER FORSBERG/EUROPE/ALAMY STOCK PHOTO ©
LEFT: HEMIS/ALAMY STOCK PHOTO ©

↑ A ROMAN RUE

Once an ancient Roman road, the rue Saint-Jacques is the oldest street in Paris. It's part of the pilgrimage route to Santiago de Compostela in northwestern Spain.

Best History Experiences

- **Discover the Resistance bunker at the Musée de la Libération de Paris.** (p191)
- **Peek behind the scenes of Paris' historic opera house, the Palais Garnier.** (p56)
- **Admire some of Paris' oldest buildings in Le Marais.** (p106)
- **Stand in awe of Notre Dame, restored by 1000 artisans after the 2019 fire.** (p142)
- **Revel in the palatial surrounds of Château de Versailles.** (p196)

Parisians of all walks of life use the efficient and affordable metro system.

A variety of contactless Navigo passes are available.

The RATP app provides itinerary recommendations and live traffic updates.

LIKE A LOCAL

Paris might be one of the world's most popular destinations, but it's not just a playground preserved for tourists. The city is home to a vibrant population of more than two million, swelling to 11 million when you include Greater Paris. Unlock the secrets of Paris by hanging with the locals in offbeat neighbourhoods.

Best Local Experiences

- **Shop at the Marché d'Aligre.** (p132)
- **Explore southern Paris' charming villages.** (p184)
- **Drink an apéritif on the Canal Saint Martin.** (p98)
- **Picnic in the Parc des Buttes-Chaumont.** (p90; pictured above)

JEROME LABOUYRIE/SHUTTERSTOCK ©

FANTASTIC & FREE

Paris might be the capital of culture, but you don't have to spend a centime to enjoy its wealth of offerings. Catch a concert in a garden pavilion, attend a literary event at a bookshop and admire street art in the *rues* and boulevards. You'll even find museum freebies – from the modern art museum to the Maison Victor Hugo, the city operates a selection of museums with free-to-access permanent collections.

→ ARCHITECTURE

A cobblestone's throw from the Seine, the Pavillon de l'Arsenal shows the city's architectural evolution in a free permanent exhibition that includes a giant digital map of Paris.

Best Free Experiences

- **Spot massive street-art murals while exploring the unique 13e.** (p182)
- **Follow the trails blazed by some of Montmartre's lesser-known female figures.** (p86)
- **Stroll through Père Lachaise cemetery's leafy byways.** (p116)
- **Traverse an elevated park atop a 19th-century viaduct.** (p124)

← CULTURE FIX

Paris Musées oversees 12 museums, some of which offer free access to their permanent collections. A few favourites are Petit Palais (p54), Musée Cognacq-Jay (p119) and Musée d'Art Moderne de Paris (p45).

Above left Musée d'Art Moderne de Paris (p45)
Left Pavillon de l'Arsenal

THE FLOOD SENTINEL

Locals use the 5.2m-high statue of Le Zouave on the Pont de l'Alma as an unofficial gauge for water levels.

Covered feet mean the river is flooded.

Covered knees mean the quays are closed and river traffic stopped.

FOCUS ON **THE SEINE**

Flanked by famous monuments, the river is Paris' lifeblood. The Left and Right Banks are connected by 37 majestic bridges, and the quays – perfect for promenades – are a Unesco World Heritage Site. It's also a place of pageantry: Parisians party on houseboats, dance on the quays and picnic at the water's edge. In a historic first, the Seine will be the stage for the opening ceremony of the 2024 Olympic Games.

Left Joséphine Baker swimming pool (p190) **Right** Seine *bouquinistes* **Below** Île aux Cygnes (p47)

→ LES BOUQUINISTES

Likened to an open-air bookshop, the riverbanks are lined with 900 traditional green-metal stalls where booksellers showcase antiquarian books, old advertising posters and other treasures.

JUST ANOTHER PHOTOGRAPHER/SHUTTERSTOCK ©

A COLOSSAL CLEANUP

The city has invested €1.4 billion to stem pollution and make the river swimmable again. This pharaonic project includes a giant storage tank for rain runoff near the Gare d'Austerlitz.

RIGHT: PAGE LIGHT STUDIOS/SHUTTERSTOCK ©
LEFT: GAUTIER STEPHANE/ALAMY STOCK PHOTO ©

↑ ÎLE AUX CYGNES

Ideal for strolls, this little-known artificial island was created in western Paris in 1827. A Statue of Liberty replica stands tall near the Port de Grenelle.

Best Seine Experiences

▸ **Listen to a concert at the Petit Bain.** (p149)

▸ **Play a game of *pétanque* at Paris Plages.** (p148)

▸ **Go for a dip in the floating Joséphine Baker swimming pool.** (p190)

▸ **Peruse photography and urban art in floating museums.** (p149)

▸ **Cruise the waterway while enjoying a gourmet meal.** (p38)

FAVOURITE PARISIAN PARKS

Jardin du Luxembourg (pictured; p171)

Parc de Belleville (p113)

Parc Montsouris (p191)

Parc des Buttes-Chaumont (p91)

URBAN **OASES**

Paris' beautiful parks and gardens are its apartment-dwelling residents' communal backyards. Green squares, rooftop gardens and other secluded pockets are complemented by sprawling parks with old-fashioned children's activities such as puppet shows and modern sporting facilities, and – at the eastern and western edges of central Paris – its two rambling forests.

Best Park Experiences

- **Smell the roses at the untouristed Parc de Bagatelle.** (p43)
- **See the Seine close-up at the tiny, triangular Square du Vert-Galant.** (p147)
- **Discover the natural treasures of the Jardin des Plantes.** (p159)
- **Explore secret oases in Le Marais such as Jardin des Rosiers – Joseph Migneret.** (p118)

VIBRANT VISTAS

The magnificent cityscape of Paris is best admired from above. As the capital's tallest building, the Eiffel Tower offers pinch-me panoramas, but other vantage points abound: rooftop restaurants, hotel terraces and a bevy of bars where you can drink in the views along with a killer cocktail. The highest bar hangout is at the TOO Hotel, located inside the Jean Nouvel–designed Tours Duo.

→ MONTPARNASSE MONSTER

When the Montparnasse Tower opened in 1973, it was considered an eyesore. But as the city's second-tallest building, its 56th-floor observation deck overlooks all the sights, including the Eiffel Tower.

Best Sky-High Experiences

- **Admire Haussmann's boulevards from atop the Arc de Triomphe.** (p54)
- **Get a bird's-eye view of Paris from the top of the Eiffel Tower.** (p36)
- **Lunch on the terrace at the Galeries Lafayette Haussmann department store.** (p61)
- **Toast the sunset overlooking the city from the Parc de Belleville.** (p113)

★ PRIME PERCHES

Le Perchoir first opened atop an industrial building in Ménilmontant and has since expanded to a number of trendy rooftop bars at the Paris Expo, Gare de l'Est and more.

Above left View from the Arc de Triomphe (p54) **Left** Observation deck, Montparnasse Tower

Demand for accommodation peaks in the warmer months. Book ahead when possible.

Nuit Blanche

Kicking off the summer cultural season, this popular all-night arts festival brings art installations and concerts to the streets in early June.

↖ Fête de la Musique

This national music festival welcomes summer on 21 June with live performances at outdoor stages citywide.

↓ Bastille Day

France's national day (14 July) features a morning military parade along av des Champs-Élysées and night-time fireworks at the Champ de Mars.

JUNE

Average daytime max: 22°C
Days of rainfall: 8

JULY

Paris in SUMMER

Cinéma en Plein Air

From mid-July to mid-August, free French and international new-release and classic films screen outdoors at Parc de la Villette.

▶ Parc de La Villette, p100

↑ Tour de France

The famous cycling event finishes on the av des Champs-Élysées on the third or fourth Sunday of July.

▶ letour.com

← Paris Plages

From around mid-July to late August, 'Paris Beaches' set up along the Parc Rives de Seine and Bassin de la Villette.

The Seine, p148

Average daytime max: 25°C
Days of rainfall: 8

AUGUST

Average daytime max: 27°C
Days of rainfall: 7

Parisians take summer holidays in July and/or August, when many restaurants and smaller shops shut for several weeks.

Packing Notes

Flat, thick-soled shoes are invaluable, along with a light jumper for cooler evenings.

Check out the full calendar of events

In September, *la rentrée* marks residents' return to work and study after the summer break, with cultural life shifting into top gear.

↙ Journées Européennes du Patrimoine

Step inside otherwise off-limits buildings and monuments during European Heritage Days on the third weekend in September.

▸ journeesdupatrimoine.culture.gouv.fr

→ Fête des Vendanges de Montmartre

Montmartre's grape harvest is celebrated with costumes, concerts, food events and a parade over five days in early October.

▸ fetedesvendangesdemontmartre.com

SEPTEMBER

Average daytime max: 22°C
Days of rainfall: 6

OCTOBER

Paris in AUTUMN

↓ Salon du Chocolat

Five days of chocolate tastings, workshops, demonstrations and children's activities take place at Paris Expo Porte de Versailles.

▸ salon-du-chocolat.com

← Festival d'Automne

The long-running Autumn Festival of arts incorporates painting, music, dance and theatre at venues throughout the city.

▸ festival-automne.com

← Beaujolais Nouveau

From midnight on the third Thursday (ie Wednesday night) in November, the first bottles of Beaujolais Nouveau are opened in Paris wine bars.

Average daytime max: 17°C
Days of rainfall: 8

NOVEMBER

Average daytime max: 11°C
Days of rainfall: 8

All Saints' Day (La Toussaint; 1 November) and Armistice Day/ Remembrance Day (Le Onze Novembre; 11 November) are public holidays.

Packing Notes

By late autumn, the weather is chilly: bring warm clothing and a jacket.

Africolor

Starting in mid-November and running to late December, this five-week African-music festival is primarily held in outer suburbs.

▶ africolor.com

← Illuminations de Noël

Festive lights sparkle along thoroughfares, including the Champs-Élysées, from mid-November to early January, and department stores feature enchanting window displays.

↑ New Year's Eve

The Eiffel Tower and av des Champs-Élysées are the ultimate Parisian locations for welcoming in the New Year.

DECEMBER

Average daytime max: 7°C
Days of rainfall: 10

JANUARY

Paris in WINTER

Le Festival du Merveilleux

The Pavillons de Bercy – Musée des Arts Forains celebrates the festive season with fairground attractions of yesteryear and shows.

▶ arts-forains.com

← Epiphany (Three Kings' Day)

On 6 January, patisseries bake frangipane-filled puff-pastry *galettes des rois* (kings' cakes) concealing a *fève* (trinket), accompanied by a cardboard crown.

↑ Outdoor Ice Skating

Open-air rinks pop up across Paris in picturesque spots such as Galeries Lafayette's panoramic rooftop (venues change annually).

↓ Paris Cocktail Week

In late January, participating cocktail bars and pop-ups create signature cocktails; other events include workshops and masterclasses.

▶ pariscocktailweek.fr

Average daytime max: 6°C
Days of rainfall: 9

FEBRUARY

Average daytime max: 8°C
Days of rainfall: 8

There are public holidays for Christmas (Noël; 25 December) and New Year's Day (Jour de l'An; 1 January).

Packing Notes

A warm jacket, scarf, gloves and boots all help keep winter temperatures at bay.

Easter heralds the arrival of spring. Easter Sunday and Monday (Pâques and Lundi de Pâques; late March/April) are public holidays.

Banlieues Bleues

For four weeks each spring, the Suburban Blues, a jazz, blues and R&B festival, is held at venues in Paris' outer suburbs.

▶ banlieuesbleues.org

↑ Foire du Trône

This huge, ride-filled funfair is held on the Pelouse de Reuilly of the Bois de Vincennes in April and May.

▶ foiredutrone.com

↘ Marathon International de Paris

Starting on the Champs-Élysées and looping through the city, the Paris Marathon is held on a Sunday in early April.

▶ schneiderelectricparismarathon.com

MARCH

Average daytime max: 12°C
Days of rainfall: 8

APRIL

Paris in SPRING

FROM LEFT: ERICKN/SHUTTERSTOCK ©, OSTILL IS FRANCK CAMHI/SHUTTERSTOCK ©, LEONARD ZHUKOVSKY/SHUTTERSTOCK ©, PETR KOVALENKOV/SHUTTERSTOCK ©, NASTINA/SHUTTERSTOCK ©
BACKGROUND: TILIALUCIDA/SHUTTERSTOCK ©

↓ French Open

France's tennis Grand Slam hits up from late May to early June at Stade Roland Garros at the Bois de Boulogne.

▸ rolandgarros.com

← La Nuit Européenne des Musées

On one Saturday, typically in mid-May, key museums across Paris stay open until midnight with free entry for the European Museums Night.

▸ nuitdesmusees.culture.gouv.fr

← Portes Ouvertes des Ateliers d'Artistes de Belleville

Hundreds of artists open their Belleville studio doors over four days in May or early June.

▸ ateliers-artistes-belleville.fr

MAY

Average daytime max: 16°C
Days of rainfall: 8

Average daytime max: 19°C
Days of rainfall: 9

There are public holidays on May Day (Fête du Travail; 1 May), Victory in Europe Day (Victoire 1945; 8 May), Ascension Thursday (L'Ascension; 40th day after Easter) and Whit Monday (Lundi de Pentecôte; seventh Monday after Easter).

Packing Notes

Bring layers for the fickle weather and an umbrella for inevitable showers.

MY PERFECT DAY IN PARIS

By Mary Winston Nicklin
@MaryWNicklin

HISTORY, CHOCOLATE & BOATS

First, coffee. In whatever season, the charms of the Jardin du Luxembourg are hard to beat. Order from one of the kiosks and watch the Paris pageantry unfold. Join a friend at Ambos for a bistro lunch, then head to Patrick Roger's boutique to admire his chocolate sculptures. Gape at the city views from the Panthéon's rooftop terrace (open seasonally), or marvel at the medieval treasures and ancient Roman baths at the Musée de Cluny. Toast the sunset at Quai de la Photo or one of the lively floating bars in the 13eme.

BEST TREASURE HUNTS

Via Turonensis Follow the bronze footpath medallions indicating the Chemin de Saint Jacques pilgrimage route.

Arago Meridian Line Medallions mark the Paris meridian.

Space Invaders Download the app and 'flash' street art to get points.

EQROY/SHUTTERSTOCK ©

JEANLUCICHARD/SHUTTERSTOCK ©

Above left Chocolates by Patrick Roger **Above right** Jardin du Luxembourg (p171)
Far right Jardin-Musée Albert Kahn

By Fabienne Fong Yan
@a.fab.journey

TREATS, GARDENS & NIGHTS OUT

Start with coffee in rue Mouffetard, then head to the Museum of Natural History. Don't leave without visiting the greenhouses. For lunch, make a beeline for Mokonuts, near Bastille. Buy a few cookies from Moko to keep you going while shopping for crafts and fashion in Charonne and Le Marais. Don't forget to take an ice-cream break. Is it aperitif time already? Head to Ground Control, then sit back, relax and enjoy the evening. The night is long...

ELENA DIJOUR/SHUTTERSTOCK ©

↙ BEST SECRET GARDENS

Alpine Garden In Jardin des Plantes.

Musée Bourdelle A sculptural garden.

Jardin-Musée Albert Kahn Scenic with a Japanese heritage.

Arboretum A tree study outside of Paris.

By Danette St. Onge
@globalgastronomiste

PEOPLE, GLITZ & GASTRONOMY

Spend the morning hunting for treasures at a *brocante* (flea market) or *vide-grenier* (boot sale), then pack for a picnic in Parc des Buttes-Chaumont. In the afternoon, hire a boat for a ride down the Canal de l'Ourcq, following this with some people-watching from a cafe terrace. After *apéro* (pre-dinner drink) at L'Avant-Comptoir and dinner at La Table de Colette, glam up for drinks at Prescription Cocktail Club, then head to a jazz club or cabaret, or to La Coupole for dancing till the wee hours.

BEST ASIAN EATS

La Taverne de Zhao X'ian specialities, including tasty momos.

The Hood Modern takes on Southeast Asian classics.

Fondue Chongqing Cook-your-own spicy hotpot.

Sanukiya Low-key Japanese spot specialising in udon and tempura.

7 Things to Know About PARIS

INSIDER TIPS TO HIT THE GROUND RUNNING

1 The French Art of the Bonjour

French people take their *bonjours* seriously – they're not just a hello, they're a sign of respect. Always greet someone with a *bonjour* when you enter a shop, museum, bus, train station, restaurant and any public service space. In the evening, say bonsoir. The safest bet is to use a greeting in every situation.

▶ See Language on p220

2 Paris Water is Safe

Tap water is safe to drink and widely available. If you don't want to pay for bottled water in restaurants, ask for a *carafe d'eau*. Having a reusable bottle is a smart idea as the historic and gorgeous Wallace Fountains offer free tap water all over the city. There are even contemporary fountains serving sparkling water.

3 Double-Check Opening Times

Don't always rely on the opening hours you find online for shops and businesses – call to double-check. In addition, most restaurants close between lunch and dinner unless they are *service continu* (continuous service).

▶ See Opening Hours on p219

4 Keep Your Stuff Secure

Statistically speaking, Paris is a very safe city but pickpocketing is quite common. Like a seasoned Parisian, never have your valuables visible.

▶ See Safe Travel on p214

5 Make Reservations

Whether it's for a museum or a restaurant, it's important that you make reservations in advance. As a COVID-19 pandemic legacy, some museums still prefer that you purchase tickets in advance online for a certain time slot. Restaurant reservations are often easy to make, online or by phone. Keep in mind that popular dining establishments should be booked months in advance.

6 Clothing Considerations

As the cradle of haute couture, Paris is chic and discreet. Trends come and go – for example, sneakers and hip-hop-inspired streetwear are having a moment – but instead of chasing the latest designer looks, the city's denizens generally opt for understated elegance. For example, Parisian women typically invest in a small capsule wardrobe of timeless classics that are suitable for any time or occasion. Don your smarter threads and you'll also stand out less as a tourist. Note that athleisure is frowned upon – unless you happen to be going for a run or to a yoga class. Paris is a walker's city so you'll want to bring sneakers and/or sturdy walking shoes to navigate the cobblestone streets. A favourite local footwear brand is Paris-based Veja, which prides itself on sustainable, ethical operations. A fold-up umbrella is a smart idea for the winter – the Guy de Jean brand is made in France.

7 Transport Tips

Contrary to popular belief, Paris is an incredibly walkable city. The best way to really experience it is on foot. If wheels are more your thing, Mayor Anne Hidalgo has made major changes to inspire more bikes on the road. There are a few bike-rental options from Vélib', operated by the city, and other start-ups. The public transport system is inexpensive and efficient, and taxis and ride-sharing options are plentiful.

▶ See Gettting Around on p210

Read, Listen, Watch & Follow

READ

Pure
(Andrew Miller; 2011) Vivid historical fiction about the origins of the Catacombs ossuary.

An Editor's Burial
(Wes Anderson; 2021) Collection of essays on expatriate life in Paris.

The Hunchback of Notre Dame
(Victor Hugo; 1831) The classic novel that first made the cathedral a national icon.

Americans in Paris
(Adam Gopnik; 2004) Collection of 70 American writers spanning three centuries.

LISTEN

Années sauvages
(Georgio; 2023) This brilliant Parisian rapper pulls lyrical inspiration from his diverse upbringing in the 18e.

The New Paris Podcast
(2023) Author Lindsey Tramuta explores the people and places that are changing the capital.

Louise Farrenc: Ouvertures, Symphonies 1-3
(2023) Laurence Equilbey's Insula Orchestra performs forgotten works by women composers.

Et Alors?
(Adé; 2022) After the breakup of Therapie Taxi, Adélaïde Chabannes de Balsac launched her solo career.

MARC PIASECKI/GETTY IMAGES ©

Éphémère
(Grand Corps Malade, Ben Mazué, Gaël Faye; 2022) Three giants of the French music scene collaborated on this hit EP.

WATCH

Lupin (2021–present; pictured right top) This TV series starring Omar Sy retells the famous story of gentleman thief Arsène Lupin.

Les Misérables (2019) Another side of life in the City of Light by Parisian director Ladj Ly.

Paul Taylor The British-Irish stand-up comedian illuminates language and cultural differences.

Amélie (2001) A whimsical depiction of life in Montmartre.

Call My Agent! (2015–present; pictured right bottom) French celebrities play themselves in this TV series about a fictional Paris talent agency.

FOLLOW

@m_magazine Culture and news from daily newspaper *Le Monde*.

Paris Je T'aime (en.parisinfo.com) Official city website.

Bonjour Paris (bonjourparis.com) The oldest English website about the City of Light.

The Local Paris (thelocal.fr) France's news in English.

@mkrs.family Tells the stories of Paris creatives.

EIFFEL TOWER & WESTERN PARIS

ART | ARCHITECTURE | GARDENS

- Eiffel Tower Outing (p36)
- Don't Leave Paris Without... (p40)
- Garden Follies (p42)
- Museum Hopping (p44)
- Listings (p46)

EIFFEL TOWER & WESTERN PARIS

Trip Builder

TAKE YOUR PICK OF MUST-SEES AND HIDDEN GEMS

Western Paris has some of the lushest parks, the highest concentration of museums in the city, and iconic landmarks such as the Eiffel Tower. The Haussmannian buildings create an elegant backdrop in the sophisticated 16e. Come for the wide array of museums, picture-perfect views, intriguing gardens and excellent dining options.

Trip Notes

Best for Modern museums and classic Paris views.

Transport Metro to Alma-Marceau, Iéna, Trocadéro, Bir-Hakeim or Passy; RER C to Champs de Mars or Pont de l'Alma.

Getting around On foot, bike or bus.

Tip For the best photos of the Eiffel Tower without the crowds, head to rue de la Manutention.

0 1 km
0 0.5 miles
Jardin d'Acclimatation
Marvel at Frank Gehry's architecture housing the Fondation Louis Vuitton (p43).
12 min from metro Les Sablons
Av du Mahatma Gandhi
Stop to smell the roses amid the peacocks in the extraordinary garden at the Parc de Bagatelle (p43).
1 min from Parc de Bagatelle bus stop (line 43)
Bois de Boulogne
Lac Inférieur
Take a swim in Paris' historic art deco Piscine Molitor swimming pool (p47).
10 min from metro Porte d'Auteuil
Bd Suchet
Porte d'Auteuil

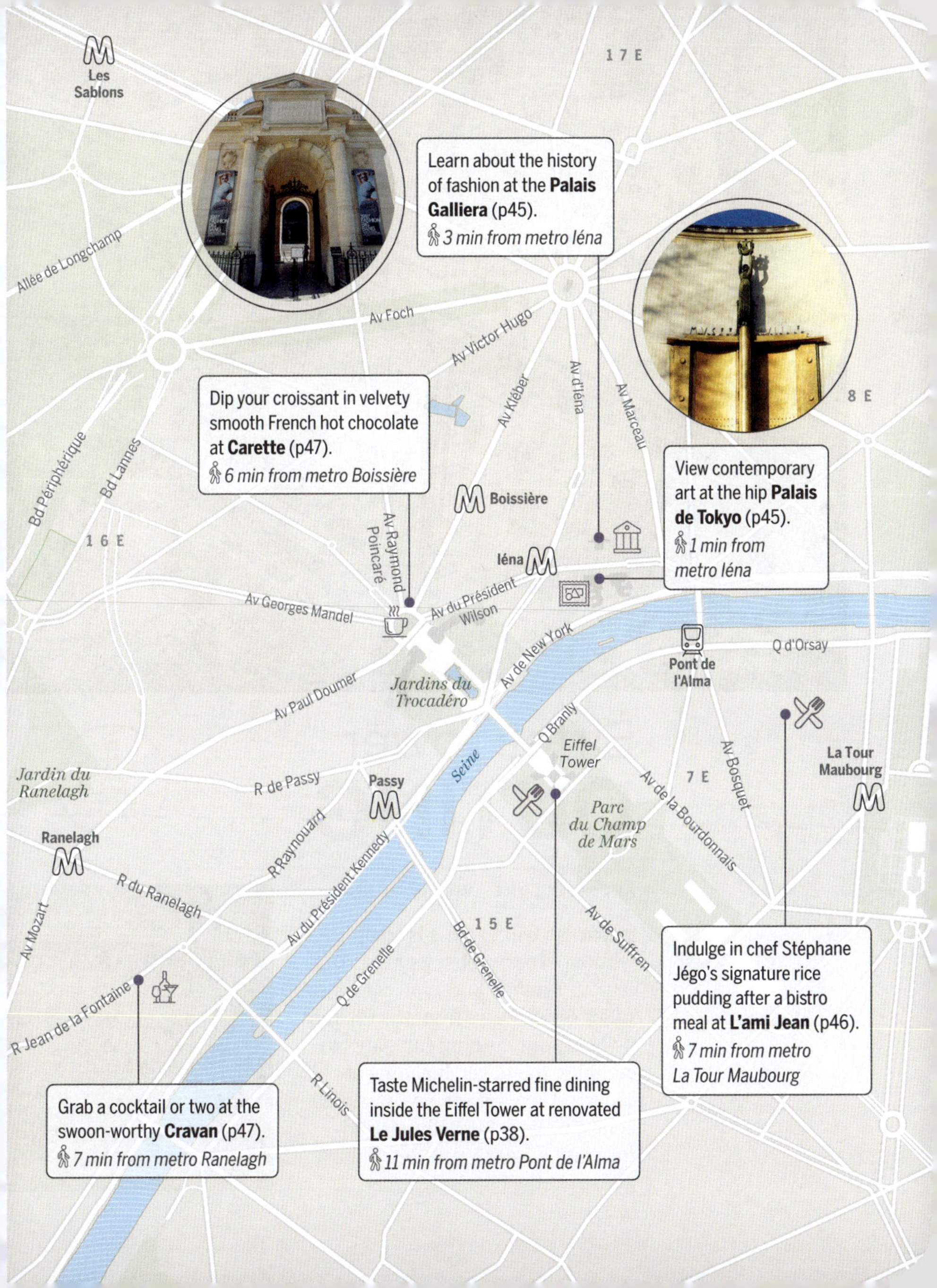

Les Sablons
17 E
Learn about the history of fashion at the **Palais Galliera** (p45).
3 min from metro Iéna
Allée de Longchamp
Av Foch
Av Victor Hugo
Av Kléber
Av d'Iéna
Av Marceau
8 E
Dip your croissant in velvety smooth French hot chocolate at **Carette** (p47).
6 min from metro Boissière
Bd Périphérique
Bd Lannes
Boissière
View contemporary art at the hip **Palais de Tokyo** (p45).
1 min from metro Iéna
16 E
Av Raymond Poincaré
Iéna
Av Georges Mandel
Av du Président Wilson
Av de New York
Q d'Orsay
Pont de l'Alma
Jardins du Trocadéro
Av Paul Doumer
Q Branly
Eiffel Tower
Jardin du Ranelagh
R de Passy
Passy
Seine
7 E
Av Bosquet
La Tour Maubourg
Av de la Bourdonnais
Parc du Champ de Mars
Ranelagh
R Raynouard
R du Ranelagh
Av du Président Kennedy
Av Mozart
15 E
Bd de Grenelle
Av de Suffren
Q de Grenelle
R Jean de la Fontaine
Indulge in chef Stéphane Jégo's signature rice pudding after a bistro meal at **L'ami Jean** (p46).
7 min from metro La Tour Maubourg
R Linois
Taste Michelin-starred fine dining inside the Eiffel Tower at renovated **Le Jules Verne** (p38).
11 min from metro Pont de l'Alma
Grab a cocktail or two at the swoon-worthy **Cravan** (p47).
7 min from metro Ranelagh

01 Eiffel Tower OUTING

ARCHITECTURE | VIEWS | DINING

No trip to Paris is complete without experiencing its most famous symbol. Sure, you can enjoy Eiffel Tower views from the Champ de Mars, but nothing compares to climbing the tower, lunching at Thierry Marx's Madame Brasserie, splurging on a Michelin-starred meal at Le Jules Verne, or clinking glasses at the champagne bar.

JEANLUCICHARD/SHUTTERSTOCK ©

How to

Getting here Metro to Bir-Hakeim or RER C to Champ de Mars – Tour Eiffel.

When to go The Eiffel Tower is open all year from 9.30am to 11.45pm (last ascent to the top, 10.30pm).

Tips Entrance tickets to the tower are available two months in advance on toureiffel.paris/en. Book as soon as you can as they often sell out. You'll need to reserve and pay in advance to dine at one of the tower's restaurants – they book up quickly.

THOMASPT/SHUTTERSTOCK ©

The Iron Lady

The Eiffel Tower is the most iconic symbol of the City of Light. The tower is made up of four sections: the Esplanade, 1st floor, 2nd floor and the Top. Visitors have multiple ticket options to choose their own adventure: take the stairs (647 steps) or lift to the 2nd floor, or choose the pricier options of the stairs and lift, or lift only, to the top floor, where the views are best. It's imperative that you are on time for your reserved ticket time slot, so it is advisable to arrive 15 to 20 minutes early to explore the Esplanade upon arrival and to navigate the queuing system.

Picture Perfect

If you're just after an up-close glimpse of the tower, go to the **Eiffel Tower Carousel**, also known as Carousel XI. It's the only clockwise spinning carousel in the city, with a location from which you can take quick snaps of the tower alone, or with the charming carousel.

FLORIN CNEJEVICI/SHUTTERSTOCK ©

The First Floor

The 1st floor has transparent floors, allowing a bird's eye view of Paris at your feet. You'll also find the tower's largest gift shop on this

Left First floor views **Above left** Second floor (p38) **Above right** Eiffel Tower Carousel

floor, as well as two dining options: **The Buffet**, a cafeteria with grab-and-go options, and **Madame Brasserie**, led by Thierry Marx, the Parisian chef known as much for his social engagement as his culinary wizardry. This all-day dining venue serves a no-reservations breakfast, followed by a lively lunch, afternoon snack time and more upscale dinner. The menu showcases seasonal produce from growers in the Paris region. When you book online for lunch or dinner, you can specify a window table.

The Second Floor

The 2nd floor has the **La Verrière** gift shop, which focuses on reproductions of the tower, as well as two dining options: **The Buffet** (which is the same as the 1st floor Buffet) and Michelin-starred **Le Jules Verne**. Under the helm of chef Frédéric Anton, Le Jules Verne is truly a once-in-a-lifetime dining experience. Diners have access to a private lift that transports them to a chic space created by renowned architect and interior designer

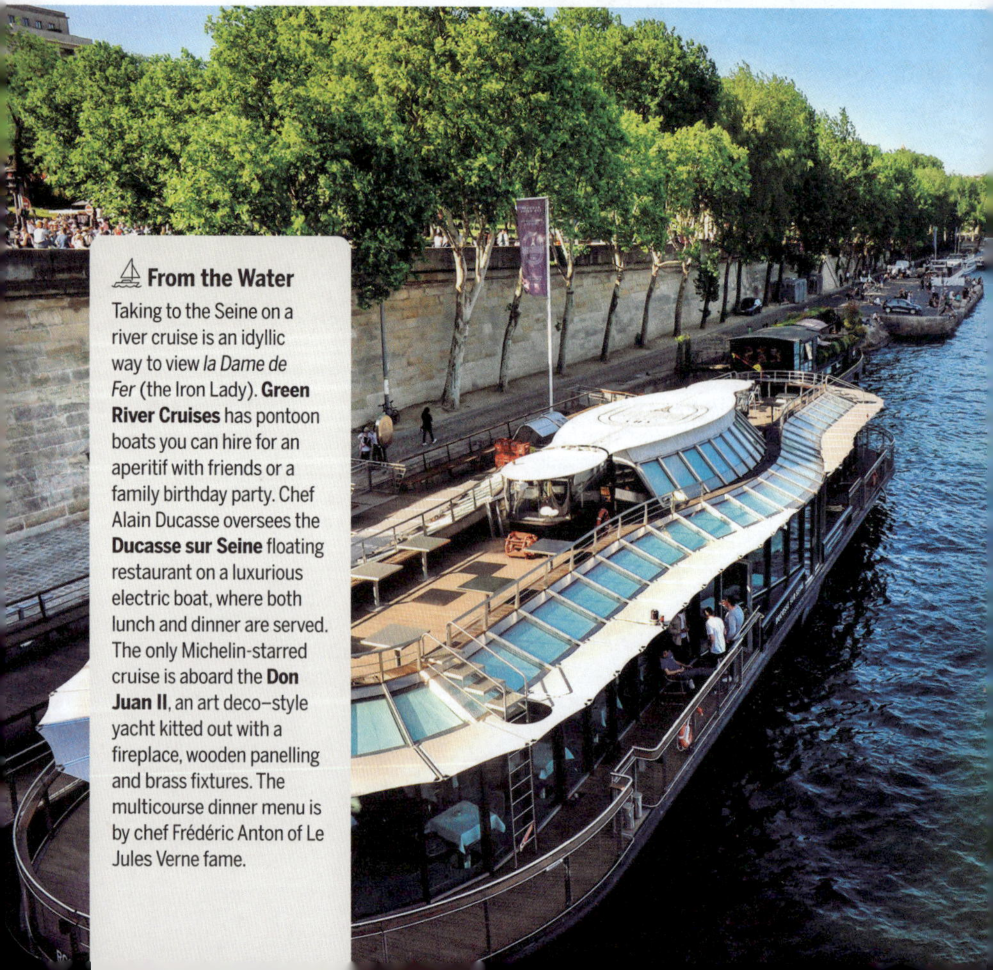

From the Water

Taking to the Seine on a river cruise is an idyllic way to view *la Dame de Fer* (the Iron Lady). **Green River Cruises** has pontoon boats you can hire for an aperitif with friends or a family birthday party. Chef Alain Ducasse oversees the **Ducasse sur Seine** floating restaurant on a luxurious electric boat, where both lunch and dinner are served. The only Michelin-starred cruise is aboard the **Don Juan II**, an art deco–style yacht kitted out with a fireplace, wooden panelling and brass fixtures. The multicourse dinner menu is by chef Frédéric Anton of Le Jules Verne fame.

Far left Ducasse sur Seine
Left Eiffel Tower champagne bar
Below Champs de Mars

Aline Asmar d'Amman, known for her opulent yet contemporary style. The meals are delicious despite the kitchen being unable to cook on open flames, since these aren't allowed in the tower. It is advisable to make reservations at Le Jules Verne months in advance.

The Top

The Top is divided into two smaller floors, one open-air and the other indoor. Beyond breath-taking views, you can also delve deeper into the history of the tower with panoramic maps and a reconstruction of Gustave Eiffel's office. The **champagne bar** serves champagne and fruit juice to help you celebrate reaching the tower's tip.

The Tower for Free

There are great ways to experience the tower up close at no cost. One good option is to pack a picnic with your favourite market finds – try the **Marché Président Wilson** – and head to the **Champs de Mars**, a gorgeous green space at the foot of the Eiffel Tower that once served as a fruit and vegetable garden for Parisians.

DON'T LEAVE
Paris Without...

01 Paris Honey
Urban beekeepers tend hives all over the city, including on the Musée d'Orsay's rooftop. Pick up a pot in the gift shop.

02 Fine Chocolates
Paris has many craft chocolate shops run by the finest cacao artisans. Try Patrick Roger, Jacques Genin or Le Chocolat Alain Ducasse.

03 A Scarf
In her Parisian atelier, stylist Maya Hochman crafts unique pieces from French couture fabrics such as silk, lace and cashmere.

04 Shakespeare & Company Stamped Book
Visit the legendary bookstore and get the inside of your purchase stamped.

05 Metro Tile Ceramics
Local enterprise DÉJÀ-VU makes souvenirs inspired by popular architecture, such as soap dishes that look like Paris Metro tiles.

06 Abstraction Paris Perfume
At this Montmartre atelier, perfumes are aged like wine and packaged in beautiful bottles.

07 Box du Grand Paris

Compose your own box with gourmet specialities made in the Paris region, such as Maison Martin hot sauce.

08 Favourite Artwork

The Musée du Louvre online store has a large catalogue of iconic works available for on-demand printing.

09 Artisanal Soaps

The Atelier Populaire brand is behind a line of handcrafted cosmetics. 'Le Pavé de Paris' is in the shape of the city's famous cobblestones.

10 Paper Delights

Stationery and postcards can be works of art. Lümne notebooks are handmade in Paris.

11 L'Elixir de Paris

Made in Paris from 10 organic ingredients, this non-alcoholic aperitif is packaged in a beautiful glass bottle.

12 Poilâne Treats

From Punitions (its famous butter cookies) to *miches* (a large rustic loaf), Poilâne has delicious fresh treats.

02 Garden FOLLIES

GREENERY | ARCHITECTURE | ART

The Bois de Boulogne is more than a 'green lung of Paris'. In this western wonderland, it's possible to visit the fantastical Frank Gehry–designed Fondation Louis Vuitton to get your art fix in the morning, followed by an afternoon romp through a whimsical garden anchored by an 18th-century chateau born of a bet with Marie-Antoinette.

SERGEI25/SHUTTERSTOCK ©

How to

Getting here Take the metro to Les Sablons, or hop on the Fondation Louis Vuitton's shuttle service, which departs regularly from Charles de Gaulle Etoile station.

When to go The Fondation Louis Vuitton is closed on Tuesdays.

Tip The Fondation Louis Vuitton's popular (and pricey) Le Frank restaurant does not take lunch reservations. Instead of waiting in line, a cheaper option is the food truck (serving pizza and soup) situated outside the exit in the Jardin d'Acclimatation.

FRANCOIS BOIZOT/SHUTTERSTOCK ©

TARAS VERKHOVYNETS/SHUTTERSTOCK ©

Left Parc de Bagatelle **Far left top** Peacock, Parc de Bagatelle **Far left bottom** Tulips, Parc de Bagatelle

A Contemporary Icon Is it a ship? An iceberg? A cloud? The architecture alone makes it worthwhile to visit **Fondation Louis Vuitton**, a Frank Gehry–designed monumental masterpiece with a serious wow factor. A soaring structure covered in 3600 glass panels, the museum offers terraces with sweeping views over the woods and cityscape beyond. And then there's the contemporary art. Since its inauguration in 2014, FLV has staged blockbuster exhibitions that draw culture vultures from all over the world. Concerts are also performed in the auditorium – even Jay-Z has graced the stage. Needless to say, it's crucial to reserve tickets online in advance.

A Royal's Hedonist Playground Less than 2km away, the **Parc de Bagatelle** is an undervisited green oasis designed with grottos, waterfalls and surprising follies. Its jewellery box of a chateau was built by King Louis XIV's younger brother, egged on by Marie Antoinette in a bet. It became a place for romantic rendezvous and wild parties, with the expansive grounds an extension of the palace's pleasures. The Egyptian obelisk and tepees may be long gone, but the pagoda and peacocks remain. Today, Bagatelle is one of the city's four official botanical gardens, and its splendid rose garden, planted with 10,000 bushes, draws rose aficionados from around the world.

Flower Calendar

With dazzling floral displays throughout the year, it's worth making the trip to Parc de Bagatelle in any season. In spring, the rolling lawns bloom with three million bulbs, beginning in February with snowdrops and crocuses, followed by daffodils and tulips. Summer is the time to admire the peonies, irises and roses. The Empress's kiosk offers an enchanting view over the classical rose garden. The autumn colours are enchanting in the 24-hectare park, as are the dahlias. And when the leaves have fallen in the winter, the remarkable trees display interesting silhouettes.

By Amy Kupec Larue, *garden expert, tour guide and permanent jury member of the Bagatelle Rose Commission. @gardenguideparis*

03 Museum HOPPING

VIEWS | ART | CULTURE

Immerse yourself in culture in this museum-packed corner of the 16e. From modern art and architecture to fashion and Asian fine art, the variety of venues is staggering. There's even a newly renovated maritime museum atop the Trocadéro. When you're in need of a pick-me-up, the trendy museum restaurants dish up sublime Eiffel Tower views along with your meal.

ANDERSPHOTO/SHUTTERSTOCK ©

How to

Getting here Take the metro to Trocadéro.

When to go Avoid these museums on Mondays, the weekly day of closure for the Palais Galliera and MAM, and Tuesdays, when the Guimet and Cité de l'architecture are closed.

Tip If you need to relax between museums, head to the the Pavilion, the outdoor space behind the Palais de Tokyo. Chill out on the steps in this art deco jewel and watch the stylish Parisian skaters perform tricks.

FRANCK LEGROS/SHUTTERSTOCK ©

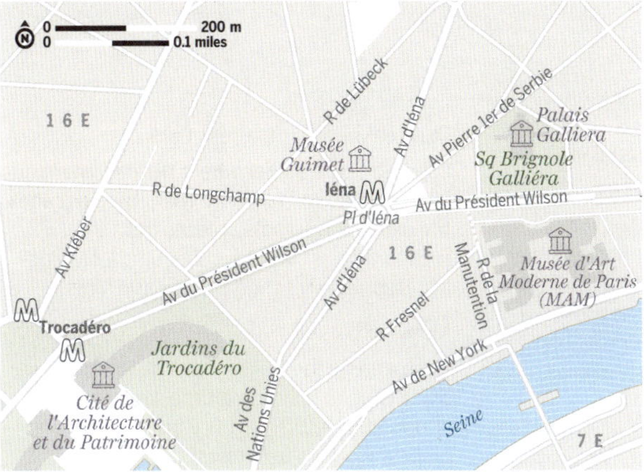

Cité de l'architecture et du patrimoine Housed within the monumental **Palais de Chaillot**, this stellar museum is devoted to French architecture and heritage. The permanent collection is a series of plaster casts taken from the country's finest monuments. As you wander the sun-lit galleries, you'll catch glimpses of the Eiffel Tower framed through the windows.

Musée Guimet Peruse a remarkable collection of Asian arts spanning an entire continent and more than 5000 years. Highlights include 1st-century CE Gandhura Buddhas from Afghanistan and Pakistan, and the finest grouping of Khmer art outside Cambodia. Don't miss the nearby secret garden with the Panthéon Bouddhique.

Palais Galliera This Italian Renaissance–style palace is one of the few museums in the world dedicated solely to fashion and its history. The blockbuster temporary exhibits draw the crowds, but the permanent collection is exciting, too. The 200,000 pieces encompass garments, accessories, drawings and photographs.

Musée d'Art Moderne de Paris (MAM) Owned by the City of Paris, this museum offers free entry to the permanent collection. Not to be missed is Raoul Dufy's *La Fée Electricité*, a monumental mural that takes up an entire room. MAM shares a building with the **Palais de Tokyo**, Europe's largest contemporary art space, which hosts edgy and provocative temporary exhibitions. Even if contemporary art isn't your thing, the Palais de Tokyo's cool bookshop is worth a stop.

Far left top Palais Galliera **Far left bottom** Sculpture, Palais de Chaillot

Dining Options

Forget what you know about museum restaurants. In Paris, they're fashionable, full of flavour and, in this part of town, privy to glorious Eiffel Tower views. **Girafe** is housed in the Cité de l'architecture, with a separate hangout called the **Suite Girafe** suspended on the 9th floor in the former curator's apartment. Vegetables are the focus at **Forest**, a popular restaurant by chef Julien Sebbag inside the MAM. In the Palais de Tokyo, **Bambini** is a trendy trattoria serving Italian comfort food. And the **Monsieur Bleu** has been drawing celebrities for the glam art deco interiors and terrace vistas since 2013.

Listings

BEST OF THE REST

Other Noteworthy Museums

Musée Marmottan Monet

Housed in a former hunting lodge, it has the world's largest collection of Monet paintings as a result of a generous donation from the artist's only heir. Additionally, the museum exhibits its comprehensive Impressionist collection, which includes masterpieces from Pissarro, Manet and Renoir.

Musée Baccarat

This crystal-glass museum, set in a mansion decorated by Philippe Starck, displays major Baccarat heritage pieces. There's also a Baccarat shop and a restaurant in an impressive setting, beneath shining chandeliers, aptly named the Cristal Room.

Musée du quai Branly – Jacques Chirac

This museum and research centre, dedicated to showcasing and studying indigenous art and cultures found around the world, was completed by President Jacques Chirac. Located near the Eiffel Tower, it's a great place at which to seek out greenery as the museum is covered in a plant wall and surrounded by a hectare of trees and plants.

Maison de Balzac

The charming home of Honoré de Balzac now serves as a free museum dedicated to the Parisian writer and his works. On entering, you'll find a lovely garden and a tearoom with offerings from the famed Rose Bakery.

Musée de la Contrefaçon

This small and wonderfully odd museum, dedicated to counterfeit goods, exhibits more than 350 seized items from customs or court settlements besides their authentic originals.

Musée Yves Saint Laurent Paris

Located in the atelier where the designer and his team worked for more than three decades, the exhibitions display pieces from the museum's vast archive collection, including accessories, sketches, photos and films.

Musée d'Ennery

Overseen by the Guimet, this museum inside an av Foch mansion is a time capsule that shows off the 19th-century bourgeoisie's fascination for the Far East.

Gourmet Dining

Bellefeuille €€€

The Saint James Paris, the city's only chateau hotel, has one of the loveliest garden terraces in town, and at its Michelin-starred restaurant, chef Julien Dumas sources ingredients from local producers.

L'ami Jean €€€

Located near the Eiffel Tower, this loud but inviting bistro serves up generous portions of bistro classics with a Basque touch. You cannot leave without trying chef Stéphane Jégo's signature *riz au lait* (rice pudding).

IRENA IRIS SZEWCZYK/SHUTTERSTOCK ©

Maison de Balzac

Substance €€€

Michelin-starred chef Matthias Marc was a contestant on *Top Chef* France and his inventive cooking draws discerning foodies to the 16e. Let yourself be wowed by the multicourse tasting menu.

Comice €€€

Beyond this Michelin-starred establishment's sublime contemporary cuisine and artisanal wine list, it's the warm hospitality from a husband-and-wife team that has secured a loyal following.

Brach €€€

This trendy, Philippe Starck–designed hotel attracts the cool crowd for its Sunday brunch, a grand spread of homemade breads, sweets, seafood, and Italian, Greek and Lebanese specialities. There are ample veg options, too.

Unwind

Hotel Molitor

After an €80-million investment, the historic, art deco Piscine Molitor swimming pool complex was reborn as a luxury hotel in 2014. The stunning pools remain the star and can be accessed by hotel guests, club members and those who splurge on a spa treatment.

Jardin d'Acclimation

This charming amusement park with a petting zoo, roller coasters, trampolines and pony rides was inaugurated in 1860 by Napoléon III and Empress Eugénie.

Jardin des Serres d'Auteuil

Next to the Roland Garros tennis stadium, these greenhouses were first opened in 1898 with a large collection of tropical plants.

Le Chalet des Îles

This cosy and calm restaurant is located on an island on Lac Inférieur, the smaller of two lakes in the Bois de Boulogne. A free water shuttle that regularly runs throughout the day will help you cross to the island and back. The food and drinks are pricey but great.

Jardin des Serres d'Auteuil

Île aux Cygnes

Paris' little-known third island was built in 1827 to protect the river port. Traversed by a tree-lined walkway, the artificial island is home to a one-quarter-scale Statue of Liberty replica.

Cocktails, Crudités & Chocolate

Marché Président Wilson

The largest open-air market in Paris pops up every Wednesday and Saturday. You'll find myriad stalls with the best of French terroir. It's a great place to shop, and the quintessential place to watch how locals interact with each other and food. Best to go before lunch.

Carette €€

Tourists and locals alike flock to this spot on the Place du Trocadéro for hot chocolate, sweets and savoury canapé sandwiches. It's people-watching central.

Cravan €€

On a quiet street, Cravan is a captivating cocktail bar in a tasteful cafe setting with mirror-filled walls. Its small plates are perfect for *apéro* but it also serves snacks and coffee during the day. Come early to secure a table.

CHAMPS-ÉLYSÉES & GRANDS BOULEVARDS

FASHION | CULTURE | NIGHTLIFE

- **The Charms of the Champs** (p52)
- **Ghost Hunting at the Opéra** (p56)
- **Drinks in a Palace** (p58)
- **Trendsetting Shopping** (p60)
- **Listings** (p62)

CHAMPS-ÉLYSÉES & GRANDS BOULEVARDS
Trip Builder

TAKE YOUR PICK OF MUST-SEES AND HIDDEN GEMS

Grandiose in layout, this area is graced with majestic boulevards in elegant symmetry. Shopping is a prime attraction, with historic department stores sharing turf with luxury flagships and atmospheric covered passageways. An entertainment hub since the Belle Époque, it's also home to theatres and the Palais Garnier opera house.

Trip Notes

Best for High-end shops, fine dining and nights out.

Transport Metro line 1 stops along the Champs-Élysées; the Grands Boulevards are served by lines 8 and 9.

Getting around Explore on foot or find Vélib' stations throughout both areas.

Tip For views without queues and admission charges, head to the Galeries Lafayette Haussmann rooftop terrace.

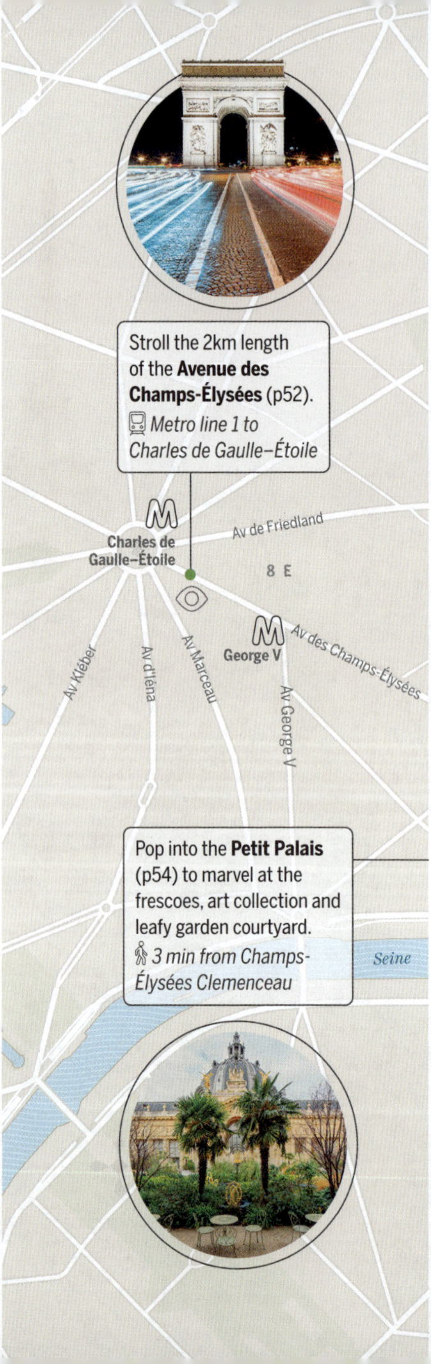
Stroll the 2km length of the Avenue des Champs-Élysées (p52).
Metro line 1 to Charles de Gaulle–Étoile
Charles de Gaulle–Étoile
Av de Friedland
8 E
George V
Av des Champs-Élysées
Av Kléber
Av d'Iéna
Av Marceau
Av George V
Pop into the Petit Palais (p54) to marvel at the frescoes, art collection and leafy garden courtyard.
3 min from Champs-Élysées Clemenceau
Seine

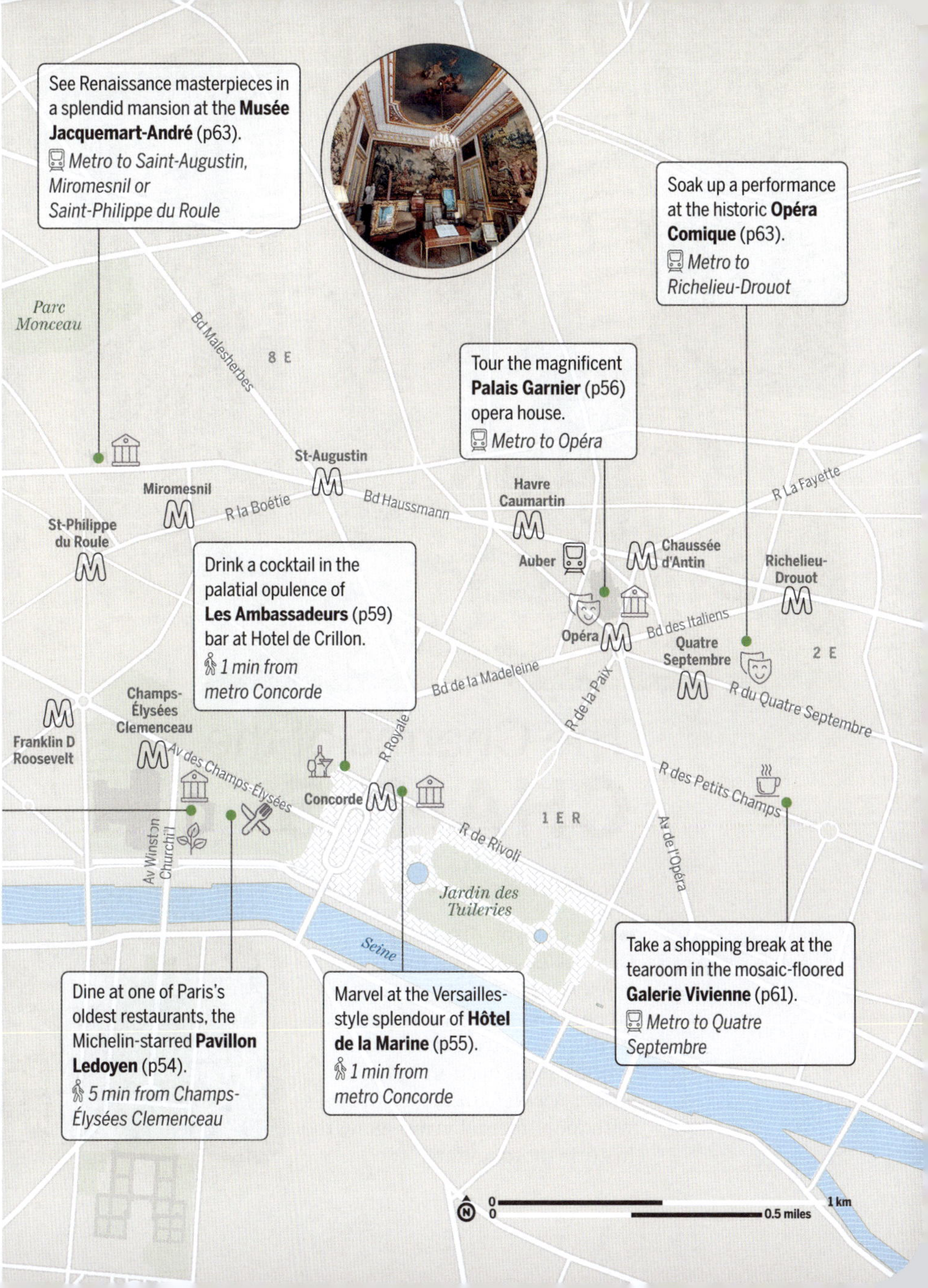

See Renaissance masterpieces in a splendid mansion at the Musée Jacquemart-André (p63).
Metro to Saint-Augustin, Miromesnil or Saint-Philippe du Roule
Soak up a performance at the historic Opéra Comique (p63).
Metro to Richelieu-Drouot
Tour the magnificent Palais Garnier (p56) opera house.
Metro to Opéra
Drink a cocktail in the palatial opulence of Les Ambassadeurs (p59) bar at Hotel de Crillon.
1 min from metro Concorde
Dine at one of Paris's oldest restaurants, the Michelin-starred Pavillon Ledoyen (p54).
5 min from Champs-Élysées Clemenceau
Marvel at the Versailles-style splendour of Hôtel de la Marine (p55).
1 min from metro Concorde
Take a shopping break at the tearoom in the mosaic-floored Galerie Vivienne (p61).
Metro to Quatre Septembre
Parc Monceau
8 E
Bd Malesherbes
St-Augustin
Miromesnil
R la Boétie
Bd Haussmann
St-Philippe du Roule
Havre Caumartin
R La Fayette
Auber
Chaussée d'Antin
Richelieu-Drouot
Opéra
Bd des Italiens
Quatre Septembre
2 E
Bd de la Madeleine
R de la Paix
R du Quatre Septembre
Champs-Élysées Clemenceau
Franklin D Roosevelt
Av des Champs-Élysées
R Royale
Concorde
R des Petits Champs
1 E R
R de Rivoli
Av Winston Churchill
Av de l'Opéra
Jardin des Tuileries
Seine
0
1 km
0
0.5 miles
N

04 The Charms of the CHAMPS

ARCHITECTURE | POMP | FLÂNERIE

Lest you dismiss the Champs-Élysées as a tourist trap, consider the city's staggering recent investment to restore its cachet. A stroll along the 'world's most beautiful avenue' showcases the grandeur of Paris with monumental vistas along the historic thoroughfare.

BENNY MARTY/SHUTTERSTOCK ©

How to

Getting here Metro line 1, 2 or 6 to Charles de Gaulle–Étoile.

When to go The avenue is most dazzling in winter, with elaborate holiday lights in the trees and window displays drawing crowds.

Pedestrians The Champs-Élysées is pedestrian-only the first Sunday of each month, a great time to stroll its length without the usual traffic chaos.

Tip Seek serenity in the hidden garden oasis of the Jardin de la Nouvelle France.

YU XICHAO/SHUTTERSTOCK ©

A City Symbol

You can't visit Paris without walking the 2km-long Champs-Élysées. Taking its name from the Elysian Fields ('heaven' in Greek mythology), it's a major urban artery connecting the Arc de Triomphe and the Place de la Concorde. It's the famous stage for the Bastille Day parade, New Year's Eve fireworks and the finale of the Tour de France, yet as a commercial hub, with mass-market chains occupying retail space next to high-fashion flagships, the avenue had lost its place in the hearts of Parisians. To restore its authenticity, the city embarked on a vast renovation program prior to the 2024 Olympic Games. Key to the makeover? Pedestrianised zones and greenery galore.

JACKY D/SHUTTERSTOCK ©

The Davioud Bench

Named for the architect who designed it in the 1860s, Paris' double-seated public bench is a beloved urban emblem. More than 100 have been restored as part of the 'Réenchanter les Champs-Élysées' project. Footpaths were also repaired, with the granite stones transported by river barge to lower the carbon footprint.

Left Tour bus on the Champs-Élysées **Above left** Champs-Élysées **Above right** Arc de Triomphe

Climb the Arc de Triomphe

Start your day at Napoléon's arch. The mighty monument was commissioned in 1806 but not finished until 1836, long after Napoléon's fall from power. At ground level, you can admire the sculpted friezes and the **Tomb of the Unknown Soldier**, commemorating lives lost in WWI. Inside there are interesting museum exhibits, but the highlight is the **viewing platform**. From the top of the 50m-high arch, the urban landscape of Haussmann's Paris unfurls in all its majesty. Twelve avenues radiate out from Étoile like spokes in a wheel. The Arc de Triomphe is slap bang in the middle of the historic axis extending west from place de la Concorde to the soaring skyscrapers of La Défense.

Architectural Stunners

Both the **Grand Palais** and **Petit Palais** were constructed for the 1900 Exposition Universelle (World Fair). Capped with an art nouveau glass roof, the Grand Palais stages

Gourmet Pavilions

Starting in the 19th century, the Champs-Élysées became a destination for dining. The **Pavillon Ledoyen**, where Napoleon reportedly met Joséphine, is today the beating heart of chef Yannick Alléno's gourmet empire. The elegant two-storey structure is home to three Michelin-starred restaurants, including a sushi counter. Nearby, **Pavillon Élysée** was constructed for the 1900 Exposition Universelle. Today it's an events space with a glass-walled rotunda and domed turret. **Le Laurent,** on neighbouring av Gabriel, was once a hunting lodge, then a revolution-era *guinguette* (dance hall), before its reincarnation as a refined restaurant that's a favourite of French politicians.

ANDERSPHOTO/SHUTTERSTOCK ©

Far left Pavillon Ledoyen Left Grand Palais Below Hôtel de la Marine

some of the city's biggest shows in its exhibition spaces, newly renovated for the Olympics. Equally gorgeous, the Petit Palais houses the city's fine arts museum, with a free permanent collection. The interiors are sublime – all marble, mosaics and fresco-painted ceilings – but wait until you see the serene courtyard garden. Grab lunch from the cafe and take a seat surrounded by palm trees.

Place de la Concorde

Dating from the late 18th century, the city's largest public square was the site of grisly executions by guillotine during the French Revolution. One side is open to the Seine, while the other is flanked by opulent palaces designed by architect Ange-Jacques Gabriel, of Palace of Versailles fame. In fact, the **Hôtel de la Marine** monument offers Versailles-style grandeur right in the heart of Paris. Presiding over it all is the pink granite **Luxor Obelisk** that was a diplomatic gift from Egyptian ruler Muhammad Ali in 1831. The best place to gawk at the city's oldest monument is from the elevated end of the **Jardin des Tuileries** – the ultimate vantage point for ogling the Champs-Élysées in all its glory.

FAR LEFT: JANE TREGELLES/ALAMY STOCK PHOTO ©, LEFT: FRANCK LEGROS/SHUTTERSTOCK ©

05 Ghost Hunting at THE OPÉRA

MYSTERY I ARCHITECTURE I LITERATURE

The Palais Garnier, aka the Opéra, is one of the most opulent buildings of the 19th century. Being accessible only to society's richest, it was easy for those who had never been there to concoct fantasies. The discovery of a skeleton in the Opéra sparked Gaston Leroux' imagination, and his 1909 novel, *The Phantom of the Opera*, revealed the ghost whose mystery has remained in the building since.

POSZTOS/SHUTTERSTOCK ©

How to

Getting here Take the metro to Pyramides or Opéra, or the train to Auber.

When to go The Palais Garnier is open year-round, but can be especially magical in winter.

Tours Self-guided tours allow easy access to the building's public areas and exhibitions. Guided tours can be more educational. Visits to the auditorium may be restricted or impossible for technical or artistic reasons.

Tickets For tours, operadeparis.fr/en/visits/palais-garnier; for plays, operadeparis.fr/en/programme-and-tickets.

KIKO PHOTOS/SHUTTERSTOCK ©

CATARINA BELOVA/SHUTTERSTOCK ©

The Making of a Ghost For his bestselling novel, Leroux took inspiration from real-life events and legends. The Salle Le Peleter, previously home to the Paris Opera, was destroyed by fire in 1873. The story goes that a pianist's face was disfigured in the tragedy, and he hid beneath the newly commissioned Palais Garnier to grieve for his ballerina fiancée who had died. This rumour grew into myth with the discovery in the building's foundations of a skeleton (now identified as that of a Paris Commune revolutionary).

A number of other mysterious, inexplicable accidents inspired Leroux' work. Erik, the fictional ghost, haunted Box 5, where he could easily plot mischief, such as dropping the enormous chandelier onto the audience. Such a horrific event actually happened; a chandelier counterweight fell and killed a woman in the audience in 1896.

A Mysterious Underground Lake The novel has Erik living in a secret lake below the Palais Garnier, and there is actually a water tank below the building. While digging the foundations, the architect Charles Garnier ran into surprisingly high groundwater levels. Workers tried to pump the water out, but that didn't work. In the end, Garnier decided to control the water instead and he created a double-layered basement, filled with water, to protect the structure from moisture. Today, this cistern, closed to the public, is used by Paris firefighters for training exercises.

Above left Palais Garnier **Far left top** Palais Garnier interior **Far left bottom** Palais Garnier rooftop detail

Voices from the Past

The ghost of the Opéra may be fictional, but voices from the past can still be heard. In 1907, time capsules were sealed and 'buried' in the caves of the Palais Garnier. They contained gramophone records of the most famous singers of the time, left by Alfred Clark, who ran the Gramophone Company's offices in Paris. The time capsules were apparently not to be opened for a century. In 2008, they were extracted, listened to and digitised. They are now kept in the archives of the French National Library.

06 Drinks in a PALACE

LUXURY | COCKTAILS | NIGHTLIFE

Need a dose of Parisian glamour? France's 'palace hotels' are in a class of their own, recognised for their *excellence à la française* in every respect, from dreamy design to concierge service worthy of a curtain call. Only a dozen have earned this coveted distinction in Paris. An evening cocktail is a way to experience an exceptional setting at a fraction of the price of an overnight stay.

PATRICK KOVARIK/AFP VIA GETTY IMAGES ©

How to

Getting here Metro line 1, 8 or 12 to Concorde (Hotel de Crillon, Le Meurice); line 9 or 13 to Miromesnil (Le Bristol).

When to go The three bars are open daily and don't require reservations. After 10pm from Tuesday to Saturday, Le Bar du Bristol hosts 'Bristol After Dark' soirees with a DJ-spun soundtrack.

What to wear A chic outfit; sportswear or shorts aren't recommended.

How much A single cocktail will set you back around €30.

PETR KOVALENKOV/SHUTTERSTOCK ©

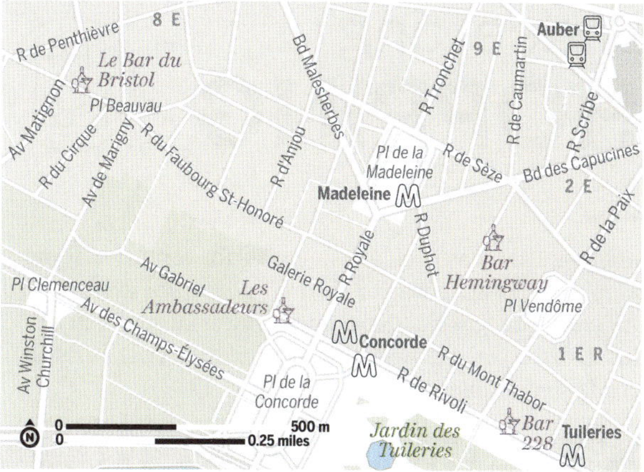

Far left top Les Ambassadeurs at Hôtel de Crillon **Far left bottom** Le Bristol hotel

Les Ambassadeurs at Hôtel de Crillon Marble walls, crystal chandeliers, ceiling frescos...the setting alone is worth a trip to the Crillon. Formerly a restaurant for Le Tout Paris in the 19th century, Les Ambassadeurs reopened as a bar in 2017 and it's been luring the *beau monde* ever since. Visionary mixologists experiment with themed cocktail menus – one was illustrated as a board game in which you rolled the dice to pick your poison. Bonus: there's live music from Tuesday to Saturday.

Bar 228 at Le Meurice Salvador Dalí brought his pet ocelot, Spain's King Alfonso XIII held court while in exile and Coco Chanel staged fashion shows – Le Meurice has been stealing hearts since 1835. History also oozes from the wood-panelled walls at the bijou Bar 228. Sit at the bar, with its Carrara marble counter designed by Philippe Starck, or sink into a leather armchair and order up a signature 'Meurice Millennium' with Cointreau and champagne.

Le Bar du Bristol The luxury Le Bristol hotel on the rue du Faubourg-Saint-Honoré is home to Socrate, a resident Birman cat that can be found riding the historic lift or napping on Louis Vuitton luggage. Le Bristol isn't just a favourite of felines, though. Celebrity guests appreciate the warm service from a team that's worked here for decades. Le Bar du Bristol is a chic watering hole designed like a cabinet of curiosities.

Suze & Chartreuse

When it comes to original spirits, France offers an encyclopedia of references. To name a few: Chartreuse liqueur is made by monks, Suze is flavoured from the gentian plant and Bénédictine is crafted from a secret recipe of 27 different herbal ingredients.

Many of today's most interesting cocktails are concocted from such old-school spirits. Colin Field, the long-time head bartender at the **Bar Hemingway**, makes his signature 'Serendipity' with Calvados, the apple brandy from Normandy.

Arrive early! A line forms before the 6pm opening of the storied watering hole at the Ritz Paris, which Ernest Hemingway claimed to have 'liberated' in 1944.

07 Trendsetting SHOPPING

HISTORY | SHOPPING | FASHION

When it comes to shopping, Paris has been a tastemaker for centuries. From 1799, its covered passages were an innovative way to *'faire les boutiques'* even in inclement weather. Later, the *grands magasins* (department stores) ushered in a fashionable new wave. In this district, you can walk through the history of Parisian shopping trends, picking up a few covetable items along the way.

KIEV.VICTOR/SHUTTERSTOCK ©

How to

Getting here Take the metro to Grands Boulevards.

When to go The French sales *(soldes)* take place twice a year on dates mandated by the government. Discounts happen in increments, with the biggest bargains to be found towards the end of the sales.

Tip Put on a pair of comfortable walking shoes for a fun day of shopping and exploring. For excellent style-spotting, visit during Paris Fashion Week. Dates can be found at fhcm.paris/en.

DAVE Z/SHUTTERSTOCK ©

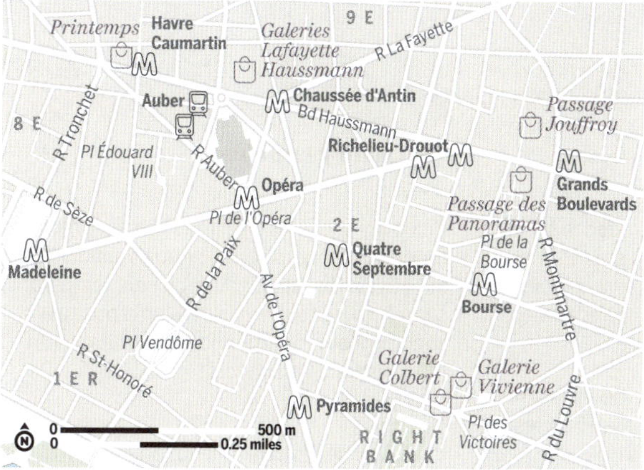

Explore the World's First Shopping Malls For a taste of 19th-century shopping, wander through the labyrinthine network of glass-roofed shopping arcades, each with its own character. The oldest is the **Passage des Panoramas**, dating from 1799, and its shops sell collectable stamps, antique books and prints. The graceful **Galerie Vivienne**, built in 1823, has elaborate mosaic floors and a glass cupola, plus a tea salon and independent boutiques. There's also **Passage Jouffroy** and the elegant **Galerie Colbert**.

Shop like it's 1912 at the Grands Magasins Channel the Belle Époque with a stop at a pair of department stores. Both **Printemps** and **Galeries Lafayette Haussmann** show off striking historical details and art nouveau glass domes. During the festive season, Parisians and visitors alike flock to the windows to check out the Christmas decor. In addition to up-and-coming design labels, you'll find departments focusing on secondhand and vintage fashion.

Today's Luxury Destination As the capital of couture, **rue Saint-Honoré** is firmly connected with the Parisian pastimes of *flânerie* (leisurely strolling) and *lèche-vitrines* (window shopping; literally 'window licking'). Here you'll find all the big names in French fashion: Hermès, Dior, Louis Vuitton, Balmain and more. Coco Chanel got her start in 1918 with a showroom at 31 rue Cambon. The nearby **place Vendôme**, home to the Ritz Paris, is another luxury shopping mecca.

Far left top Galerie Vivienne **Far left bottom** Galeries Lafayette Haussmann

The First Caviste

Situated inside Galerie Vivienne, **Legrand Filles et Fils** is an iconic wine shop and restaurant that got its start in 1880 as a gourmet grocer. In the post-WWII years, Lucien Legrand invented the profession of *caviste* (wine merchant), travelling to vineyards in the French countryside and selecting wines directly from winegrowers. This was revolutionary at the time, with most Paris wine sold in bulk from barrels at Bercy until the 1970s. Take a seat at the *comptoir* (counter) and taste wines by the glass, or reserve a table for lunch.

Listings

BEST OF THE REST

Quick Bites

Bouillon Chartier €

A distinguished institution, founded in 1896, in a lovely and airy art nouveau space. The traditionally dressed waiters serve classic, retro-priced brasserie fare at shared tables.

Lafayette Gourmet €

The ultimate gourmet grocery, the department store's food hall is brimming with delicacies from some of the top purveyors in France. There's a wine bar and counter service.

Le Shack €€

Tucked away in a cobblestone passageway near the Palais Garnier, Le Shack is a cool hybrid concept housed in a former publishing house. Along with a restaurant and bar, there are co-working spaces, recording studios and a meditation room.

Unique Boutiques

Librairie Artcurial

The bookshop of the Artcurial auction house, inside an elegant 19th-century mansion, carries a wide selection of books on contemporary art, photography, design and architecture, including English-language tomes.

Laulhère

A venerable maker of traditional berets since 1840, offering classic and contemporary styles in in its main boutique in a courtyard on rue du Faubourg St-Honoré.

Hôtel de la Marine Boutique

This museum concept shop carries items made in France exclusively for the Hôtel de la Marine, including elegant earrings inspired by the building's monumental glass roof.

Luxury Lunches

Onor €€€

Celebrity chef Thierry Marx is an advocate for disadvantaged youth through solidarity initiatives. His latest haute-cuisine restaurant serves divine food while making a positive social impact; he employs 20% of the team from his training schools.

Prunier €€€

In 2022, chef Yannick Alléno took over the historic seafood house on av Victor Hugo with sublime results. Dine on caviar and *crustaces* (shellfish) surrounded by art deco splendour.

Nonos et Comestibles €€€

Chef Paul Pairet, who's amassed a following for his Shanghai restaurants, returned to France with a meat-focused brasserie at the Hôtel de Crillon. Some dishes are served tableside from a chic carving trolley.

La Scène €€€

It's a smart scene at Stéphanie Le Quellec's Michelin-starred restaurant, which is designed like a curtained theatre. Her mission? To democratise haute cuisine.

Prunier

Restaurant Alan Geaam €€€

Self-taught Lebanese chef Alan Geaam has a mini empire of Parisian restaurants, including the Faurn pizzeria and Qasti Shawarma and Grill. Reserve his eponymous eatery in the 16e for a Michelin-starred meal.

Pastries, Sweets & Teatime

L'Éclair de Génie €

Chef Christophe Adam's sleek shops (in rue Montmartre and Lafayette Gourmet food hall) sell the most beautiful and luscious handcrafted éclairs, in creative, seasonal flavours such as basil mint and lemon yuzu.

À la Mère de Famille €

The oldest sweet shop in Paris, dating from 1761, is a tiny jewel packed with chocolates, regional French candies, cakes and more.

Mariage Frères Étoile €€

An elegant tearoom with an old-world ambience and antique decor serving pastries, jelly and savoury dishes made with the brand's gourmet teas, plus refined brunches.

Cédric Grolet Opéra €€

Lines form around the block for this famous *pâtissier's* trompe l'oeil creations that steal the show on Instagram. Almost too pretty to eat, his signatures have an uncanny resemblance to real fruits.

Operas, Films & Art

Grand Rex

A vast and stunning 1930s art deco cinema, today it still screens films, but is also a concert venue and nightclub. Self-guided tours in English are available.

Musée Jacquemart-André

A museum housing an extensive art collection, with a focus on Italian Renaissance masterpieces, in a lavish bd Haussmann mansion once home to a wealthy 19th-century couple.

À la Mère de Famille

Opéra Comique

See an opera in the intimate and ornate neo-baroque theatre where Bizet's *Carmen* premiered in 1875. All performances have English subtitles.

Distinguished Drinks & Nightlife

Harry's New York Bar

A cosy, wood-panelled hangout founded in 1911. Legend has it that Gershwin composed 'An American in Paris' in the piano bar.

Crazy Horse

Founded in the 1950s as a 'cowboy saloon', this famous cabaret offers glittering spectacles with dancers wearing wigs and not much else.

Silencio

Eclectic club owned by David Lynch, with a program of concerts, DJs and films. It's members-only until midnight, then open to the public.

Folies Bergère

Dating from 1869, this historic music hall is where Josephine Baker performed La Revue Nègre wearing her famous banana skirt. Today, shows span musicals, concerts and comedy.

L'Olympia

This famous music hall was born at the end of the 19th century, hosting big names such as Édith Piaf and Jimi Hendrix over the years.

HOTEL REGINA

THE LOUVRE & LES HALLES

HISTORY | ART | SHOPPING

- **Love at the Louvre** (p68)
- **Coffee at the Palais Royal** (p72)
- **Food Shopping in Montorgueil** (p74)
- **Listings** (p76)

THE LOUVRE & LES HALLES

Trip Builder

TAKE YOUR PICK OF MUST-SEES AND HIDDEN GEMS

Old meets new in this historic centre, home of the world's largest art museum, former royal palaces and the city's oldest commercial streets. Royals, politicians, entrepreneurs and artists have left their mark on the neighbourhood and its architecture. Come to be immersed in history and the Parisian way of life.

Trip Notes

Best for Marvelling at art and architecture, exploring quiet galleries, drinking coffee at a terrace, shopping for fresh food and sampling the best pastries.

Transport Around central Châtelet-Les Halles station.

Getting around Explore on foot so you don't miss any architectural detail or shop.

Tip Mind your personal belongings.

Eat ramen in rue Sainte-Anne's **Japanese quarter** (p76) while enjoying Haussmannian architecture.
5 min from Palais Royal

Stroll from the place de la Concorde through the Jardin des Tuileries (pictured below) to the **Louvre** (p68).
5 min from metro Palais Royal–Musée du Louvre

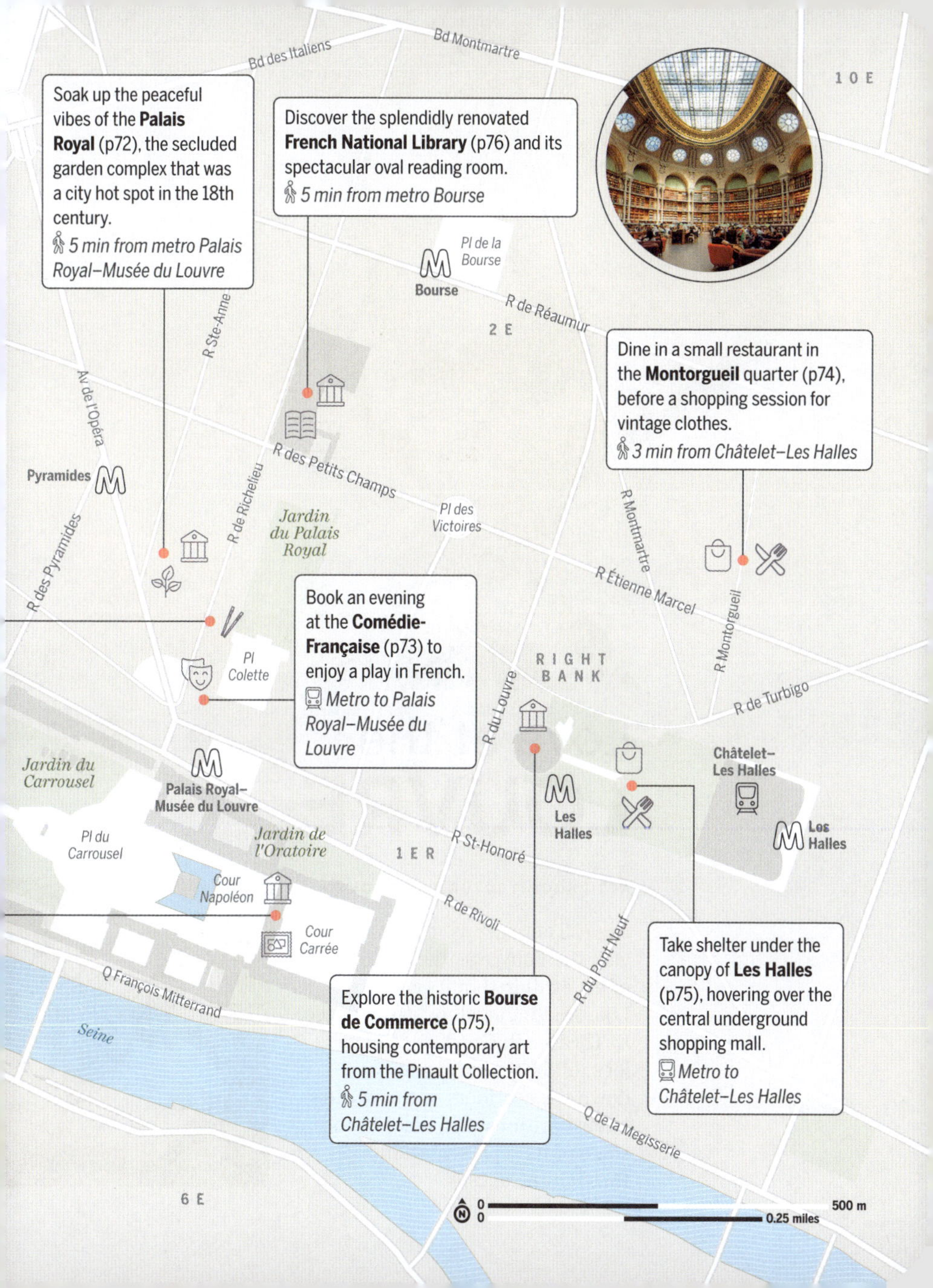

Soak up the peaceful vibes of the **Palais Royal** (p72), the secluded garden complex that was a city hot spot in the 18th century.
5 min from metro Palais Royal–Musée du Louvre

Discover the splendidly renovated **French National Library** (p76) and its spectacular oval reading room.
5 min from metro Bourse

Dine in a small restaurant in the **Montorgueil** quarter (p74), before a shopping session for vintage clothes.
3 min from Châtelet–Les Halles

Book an evening at the **Comédie-Française** (p73) to enjoy a play in French.
Metro to Palais Royal–Musée du Louvre

Explore the historic **Bourse de Commerce** (p75), housing contemporary art from the Pinault Collection.
5 min from Châtelet–Les Halles

Take shelter under the canopy of **Les Halles** (p75), hovering over the central underground shopping mall.
Metro to Châtelet–Les Halles

08 Love at the LOUVRE

ART | ARCHITECTURE | HISTORY

There are as many ways to visit the Louvre as there are works of art exhibited in its galleries. Like Ariadne's ball of string gifted to Theseus in Greek mythology, let's follow the thread of 'love' down the corridors of the world's largest art museum, discovering some of its representations through the ages.

How to

Getting here Take the metro to Palais Royal-Musée du Louvre.

When to go Start with the paintings section, preferably in the morning, as it's the most popular and tends to fill up by 11am.

Online booking Buy tickets on ticketlouvre.fr.

How much A full-price ticket is €17, but the museum is free of charge for anyone under 18 and for residents of the European Economic Area (EEA) up to the age of 26. For other visitors, entry on the first Sunday of each month is free.

Mythical Figures of Love

Who else could begin our love journey other than the *Venus de Milo*? Dating from around 150 BCE, she was identified as a 'Venus', the Roman counterpart of Greek goddess Aphrodite and an antique representation of love and female beauty, because of her nudity and curves. Excavated and made famous in the 19th century, she remains one of the world's most notable Venuses, along with Botticelli's painting *The Birth of Venus* (which hangs in Florence's Uffizi Gallery).

Now walk to room 403 in the Denon wing. *Psyche Revived by Cupid's Kiss* is much admired for the delicateness in the choice of the scene, composition and textures. Its sculptor, Antonio Canova, represented the climax of Psyche and Cupid's story in this ode to love.

Louvre Explore

The Louvre has rich online resources to help you prepare for, or extend, your visit, and to admire its masterpieces on screen. Browse the 'Explore' tab of the museum's website to dive into major courtyards, rooms and galleries. Find it at louvre.fr/en/explore.

Left *Raherka et Meresankh* (p170)
Above left *Psyche Revived by Cupid's Kiss*
Above right *Venus de Milo*

The lovers are reunited after overcoming all obstacles, including travelling to hell and back. Impressed, Zeus allows their union and that's how Psyche, born mortal, enters the divine pantheon as the goddess of the soul.

Marital, Courtly & Sacred Love

Skip the *Seated Scribe* in the Department of Egyptian Antiquities and focus on *Raherka et Meresankh* in room 635 – a warm gesture by the woman expresses her feelings towards her husband. The modelled couple is believed to have lived under the 4th or 5th Egyptian Dynasty, between 2600 and 2400 BCE.

Let's travel a few millennia ahead, to room 504 in the Richelieu wing. Have a look at *L'offrande du Coeur* (Offering of the Heart), a 12th-century tapestry representing courtly love. This refers to courtship between two unmarried people in medieval times. It mainly consisted of poetry and chivalrous gestures.

Indoor Garden

Enter the Louvre and discover the **Cour Marly** and **Cour Puget**, two immense courtyards with tiered architecture, hosting two centuries of French sculpture. Are we inside or outside? Both courtyards used to be open before architects IM Pei and Michel Macary started the renovation of the museum in 1983. But how to exhibit sculptures intended for the outdoors, without them suffering any damage? The idea of a glass-covered space was born, bathing the marble masterpieces in natural light. Walk among the statues and olive trees, enjoy the vistas and soak in the morning light.

HERITAGE IMAGES/GETTY IMAGES ©

Far left Cour Puget Left *Le Verrou*
Below *L'offrande du Coeur*

FAR LEFT: NIKOLPETR/SHUTTERSTOCK ©, LEFT: HERITAGE IMAGES/GETTY IMAGES ©

It is worth noting that, eventually, the outcome of such wooing was always supposed to be based on mutual consent.

Going through European religious art and Renaissance masterpieces, you will come across many painted representations of the Madonna and Child, who are central figures in Christian imagery. This scene of sacred love created a lasting impression of maternity, which influenced people's perception of femininity through the centuries.

A Controversy

Walk to room 929 in the Sully wing and look for a painting that hangs in complete contrast to the religious artworks: *Le Verrou* (The Bolt), by Jean-Honoré Fragonard. It is famous for its erotic tension, expressed by the lascivious movement of the characters, the undone bed and a reference to original sin in the discreet apple. However, the interpretation of the scene is controversial: the woman seems to be pushing the man's face away, and his decided posture makes him look like he could be forcing himself on her. In the context of the emerging ideas of freedom in 18th-century France, it is unclear whether the woman in this piece is consenting or being forced.

09 COFFEE at the Palais Royal

ART I HISTORY I HAVEN

Tucked between the Louvre and the Palais Garnier, the Jardin du Palais Royal can't be seen from the main avenues and is considered a local haven. Enter from hidden passages beneath the 18th-century galleries and breathe in the tranquillity of this peaceful park – fronted by a former royal palace – that is also a major landmark for contemporary art.

LIONEL BONAVENTURE/AFP VIA GETTY IMAGES ©

How to

Getting here Take the metro to Palais Royal-Musée du Louvre or Pyramides.

When to go The park is a popular lunch spot for people who work in the neighbourhood, so avoid lunchtime if you want to easily find somewhere to sit.

Takeaway Several cafes have seating under the galleries, but Parisians often bring their own coffee or lunch to the park – there are plenty of takeaway food and drinking options nearby.

MISTERVLAD/SHUTTERSTOCK ©

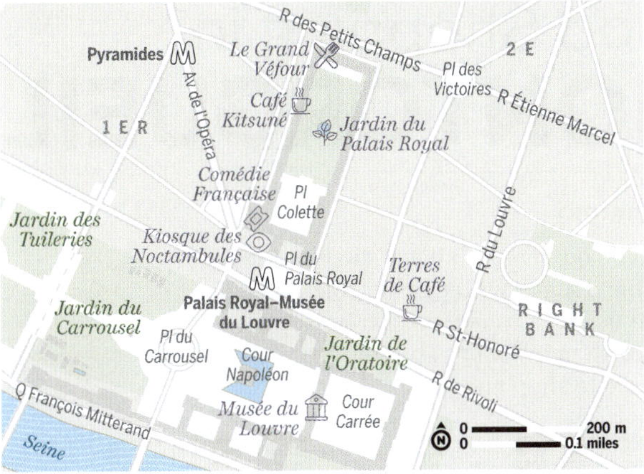

Far left top Le Grand Véfour **Far left bottom** Jardin du Palais Royal

From Royal Palace to Cradle of the Arts At the end of the 18th century, Duke Philipe d'Orléans transformed the Palais Royal into a popular square with commercial galleries, residences and the city's first restaurants. Soon it became a location for cabarets, brothels and gambling houses, as the police were not allowed into the square. This festive period ended in the 1830s, leaving the galleries as we know them today. **Le Grand Véfour**, the only original institution under the arcades, is a historic cafe where Victor Hugo used to come for lunch.

A Historical Cultural Residence Over time, authors and artists took up residence in the Palais Royal, among them Jean-Honoré Fragonard, Stefan Zweig and Colette. The proximity of many giants of the art world – **Comédie-Française**, the **Louvre** and the **French National Library** – made it an inspirational place to be. In 1959, the building also welcomed the headquarters of the French Ministry of Culture.

A Playground for Modern Art You'll see Daniel Buren's zebra-striped **columns**, Pol Bury's **spherical fountain** and, a bit further south on place Colette, Jean-Michel Othoniel's colourful **Kiosque des Noctambules** (Kiosk of the Night Owls). Buy takeaway coffee from **Terres de Café** on rue Saint-Honoré or **Café Kitsuné** on the Palais Royal, and take a seat on one of the gardens' green chairs. Notice the poetry on some – 'Les Confidents' celebrates the moments spent daydreaming in Paris' public gardens, coffee in hand.

Instagram the Invisible

Daniel Buren's 260 black-and-white-striped columns, regularly climbed on by tourists and passers-by, are perfect for Instagram photos. They were controversial when first erected in 1985 because of the clash between historic heritage and modern art, but they are now very much part of the site. The installation is actually named *Les Deux Plateaux* (The Two Levels), in reference to the artist's geometrical work: two invisible plateaus can be visualised through the alignment of some of the columns' tops. Walk around to find the right angle at which to see them!

10 Food Shopping in MONTORGUEIL

FOOD TOUR | SHOPPING | HISTORY

Paris' largest market stood here for almost nine centuries. Fascinated by its teeming life, French writer Emile Zola called Les Halles 'the Belly of Paris'. It is now a trendy pedestrianised area extending to Montorgueil, with many shops still selling fresh food produce. It's the perfect place to shop and eat.

PETR KOVALENKOV/SHUTTERSTOCK ©

How to

Getting here Take the metro to Sentier, Châtelet or Les Halles.

When to go For a relaxed market experience, come between 9am and noon. In the afternoon, the place becomes crowded with shoppers, terrace lovers and passers-by.

Tip Explore the area on foot, starting from the top of rue Montorgueil or Les Halles' central hub. Sweet tooths: there's a high concentration of pastry shops in this area – browse first before making your final selection.

HERE NOW/SHUTTERSTOCK ©

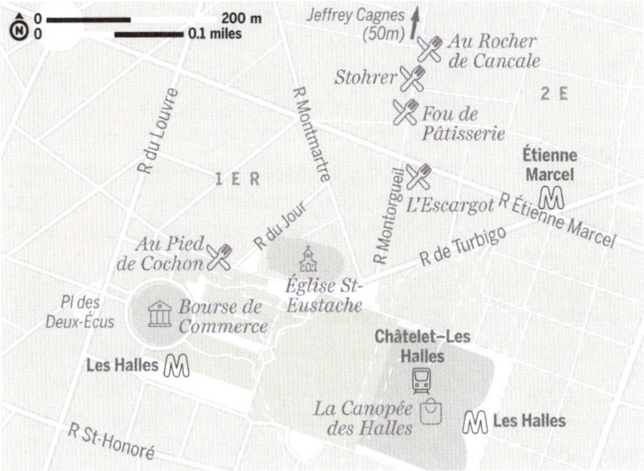

Gourmet History When walking along rue Montorgueil, pay attention to all the vintage shop signs. Always a busy commercial spot, the area became popular for fresh seafood in the 17th century. **Au Rocher de Cancale** (No 78) continues the tradition by serving oysters à la carte. **Stohrer** (No 51), the oldest bakery in Paris, is another historic institution. Try its famous *Puits d'Amour* (Wells of Love) for a taste of traditional French pastry. If you're curious about French buttered snails, look for the giant golden snail hanging above No 38. **L'Escargot** still serves three dozen snails for a costly €80. Pastry fans shouldn't miss **Jeffrey Cagnes**' elegant shop and the **Fou de Pâtisserie**, showcasing a range of treats from the city's top *pâtissiers*.

The Saint-Eustache Market Where rue Montorgueil meets Les Halles, a food market takes place every Thursday and Sunday morning. Beyond it, look for rue du Jour, which leads behind the atmospheric Saint-Eustache church up to **Au Pied de Cochon**, one of the rare Paris restaurants still open round the clock! Then continue either to **Les Halles** shopping mall, under its modern canopy roof, or the **Bourse de Commerce**, once the grain and commodities exchange and now home to the Pinault Collection of contemporary art. Its top-floor restaurant, the **Halle aux Grains**, was conceived by the Bras family as a homage to the building's heritage.

Far left top Au Rocher de Cancale
Far left bottom Stohrer pastries

In Search of the Best Deli

What amazes me is the ever-changing atmosphere in Montorgueil: at 9am, all you see are early-bird vendors, and barely anyone else. One hour later, it's completely different. It's a great place to relax at a cafe terrace and a definite must for food shopping! There are five bakeries and two cheese shops in this street alone. Some of my favourite things to do include discovering new cheese from all regions of France at La Fermette, tasting Durum's pitta bread and looking through the windows of every cake shop in search of my cake of the day.

By Tasnime Mounavaraly, *a curious foodie and Parisian pastry lover. @curioseaty*

Listings

BEST OF THE REST

Literature, Arts & Photography

French National Library – Site Richelieu

The historic site of the National Library is an architectural jewel. Following a 10-year renovation, the museum and majestic Salle Ovale reading room are open to the public.

Musée des Arts Décoratifs (MAD)

Located in two wings of the Louvre, the MAD aims to keep the French art of living and design alive through permanent collections and exhibitions on contemporary design themes.

Gaîté Lyrique

This cultural institution and performance venue showcases post-internet culture art: digital art, 3D and video games. It regularly hosts playful workshops and interactive events.

59 Rivoli

Formerly an artist squat, this is now a contemporary art gallery hosting parties, concerts and exhibitions. The building features a huge face sculpted into the facade, contrasting with the classical architecture of rue de Rivoli.

Japanese Quarter Stops

Kodawari Tsukiji €€

The authentic experience of a traditional Japanese fish market, decor included, except that it's in the heart of Paris. Beware the hustle and bustle while you enjoy its ramen.

Pâtisserie Tomo €€

This small tearoom tucked behind the Palais Royal is famous for its *dorayaki* (Japanese pancake) and homemade red-bean paste. Sit at the counter with a cup of green tea imported directly from Japan.

Junkudo

One of the largest Japanese stationery and bookshops in Paris. Shop for limited editions, secondhand manga, traditional Japanese paper and origami tutorial books.

French Tables

La Fresque €

A typical French restaurant with agreeable staff. The mural inside is a reminder of what life used to be like when the area was the largest market in town, known as 'the Belly of Paris'. Good value for money.

Le Chardonnay €

The team behind neighbourhood institution Les Crus de Bourgogne also runs this bistro a few doors down. Classic French dishes, such as croque-monsieur with truffle, are cooked to perfection.

Le Verre Luisant €

A friendly restaurant with an open terrace near Châtelet, specialising in free-range chicken and traditional French food. Open all afternoon and excellent value for money.

Frenchie €€€

Chef Grégory Marchand took up residence on rue du Nil in 2009 and he's transformed the place into a foodie district. Along with the Michelin-starred original, he operates a slew of other popular eateries.

Lively Bars & Cosy Tea Rooms

La Cantine des Pieds Nickelés €

There's no friendlier and more convivial place than this local canteen. It's been around for ages and serves fresh, homemade food along with a good selection of wines.

Sunset/Sunside Jazz Club

One of the most appreciated jazz clubs in the centre of Paris. With a rich and diverse program, there's a concert – or concerts – almost every night.

Yam'tcha Boutique €€

A quiet, sophisticated tearoom that is an offshoot of the Michelin-starred Yam'tcha restaurant. Through the open kitchen, see the traditional baskets in which the bao buns are steamed.

Experimental Cocktail Club €€

This drinking den launched the craft-cocktail revolution in Paris when it opened in 2007, as well as spawning an entire group of bars, restaurants and hotels in the city – and beyond.

Local Vegetarian Dining

Mûre €

A restaurant serving only seasonal dishes, with vegetables coming from its own farm 30km from Paris. Avoid lunch hour (1pm to 2pm). You must try the honey madeleines.

Tekés €€

This vegetarian hot spot from Assaf Granit, the Israeli chef behind Shabour, is a fun and lively scene serving inventive cocktails and cuisine.

Bakeries & Pastry Shops

Bo&Mie €

A creative twist on the most iconic French breakfast and dessert items, with subtle flavours and textures. Try the strawberry cruffin (a mix between croissant and muffin) and the hazelnut and praline flan.

Cloud Cakes €

A small vegan cafe with a large selection of pretty, tasty cakes, plus good coffee and vegan croissants. The tiny terrace is enjoyable in the afternoon sun.

FRANCK LEGROS/SHUTTERSTOCK ©

La Samaritaine

The French Bastards €

An entrepreneurial trio set out to innovate the city's bakery scene when they opened their first boulangerie in the Oberkampf area in 2019. Now they've got four eco-responsible bakeries, including one near Montorgueil.

Crafts & DIY

Mokuba

A haberdashery where you will find all sorts of ribbons, drawing on the textile tradition of the Sentier area. Conveniently located near Montorgueil.

Rickshaw

A vintage shop where you can find all types of Indian-style furniture items and antiques: knobs and hooks, unusual home accessories and iron-cast letters of the alphabet. Worth paying a visit just for its unique atmosphere.

Luxury Shopping

La Samaritaine

After a 16-year closure, the legendary department store reopened in 2021 after a painstaking renovation by its owner, the luxury powerhouse LVMH. Beyond being a one-stop shopping destination, it has 12 eating and drinking venues.

MONTMARTRE & NORTHERN PARIS

HISTORY I CULTURE I NIGHTLIFE

Experience Montmartre & Northern Paris online

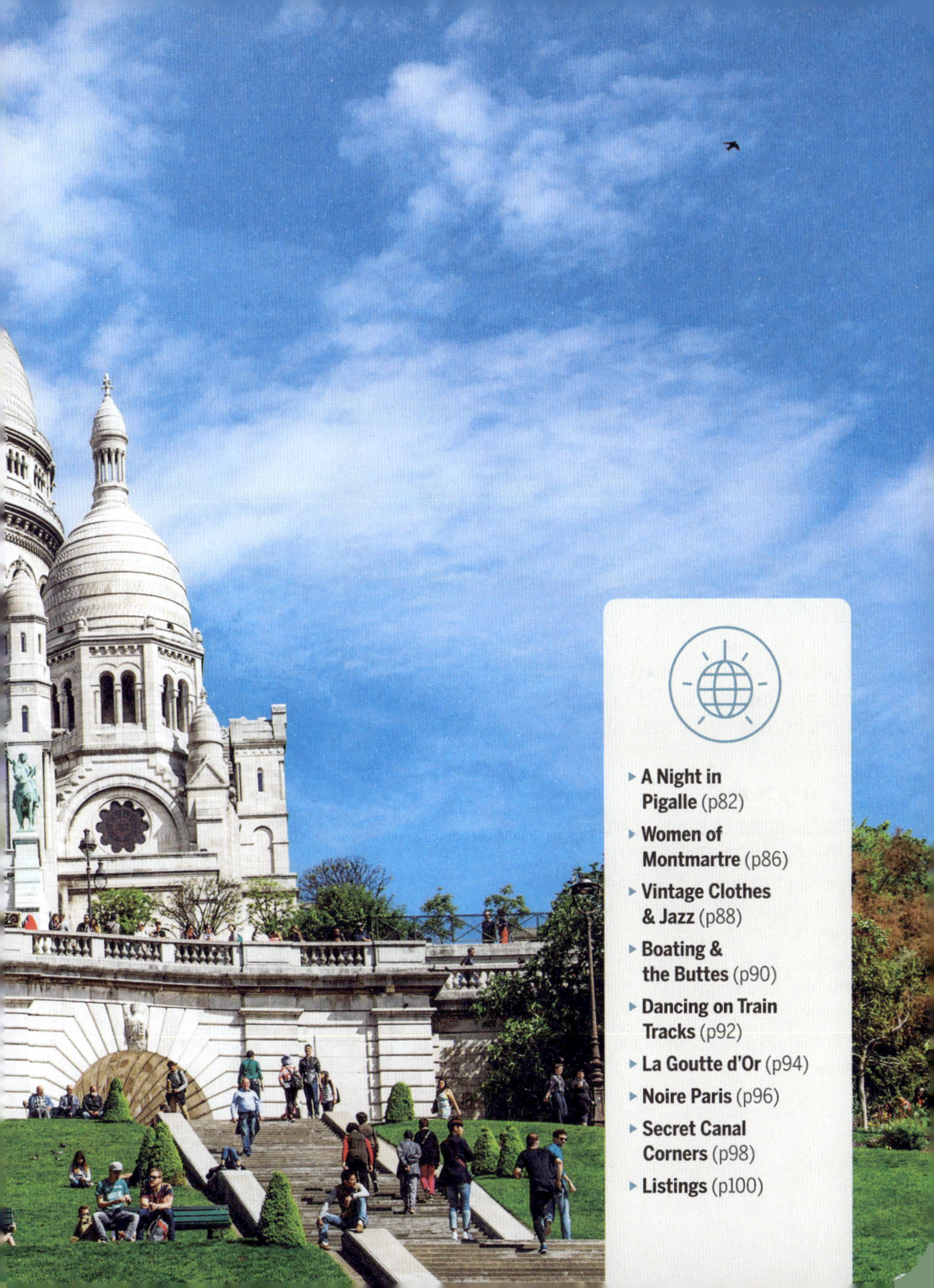

- A Night in Pigalle (p82)
- Women of Montmartre (p86)
- Vintage Clothes & Jazz (p88)
- Boating & the Buttes (p90)
- Dancing on Train Tracks (p92)
- La Goutte d'Or (p94)
- Noire Paris (p96)
- Secret Canal Corners (p98)
- Listings (p100)

MONT-MARTRE & NORTHERN PARIS

Trip Builder

TAKE YOUR PICK OF MUST-SEES AND HIDDEN GEMS

Quirky and bohemian Montmartre manages to retain its village feel and artistic sensibilities despite its popularity with visitors. Other parts of northern Paris are relatively off the tourist track and offer tranquil parks, hip cultural centres, live music and vibrant nightlife.

Trip Notes

Best for Charming streets, traditional cabaret and hip nightlife.

Transport Metro lines 12, 2 and 4 for Montmartre; line 2 for Pigalle; line 5 for parks and canals.

Getting around Hilly Montmartre, with steep slopes and stairs, is best explored on foot.

Tip The area around Barbès and Gare du Nord can be dodgy.

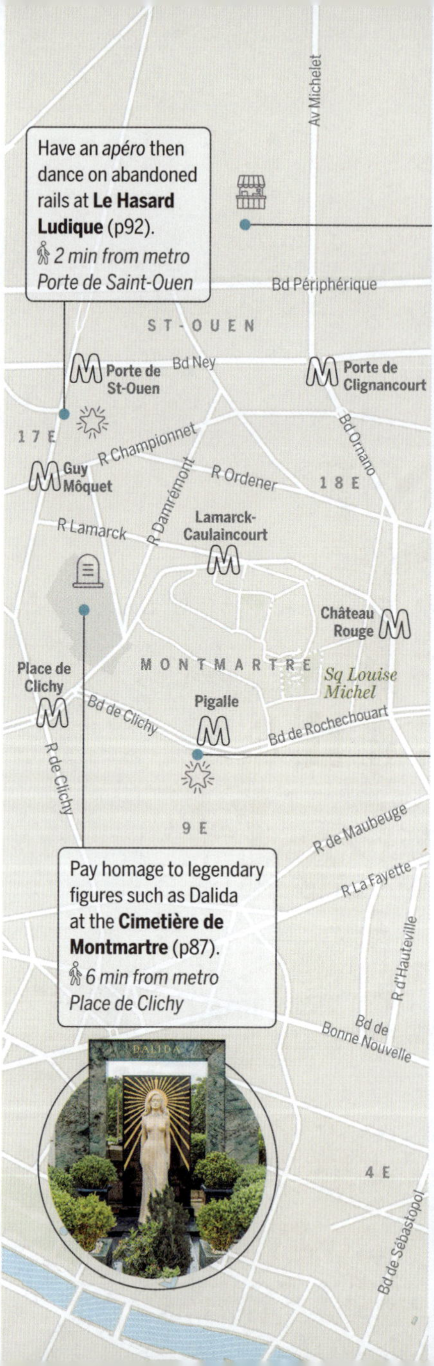

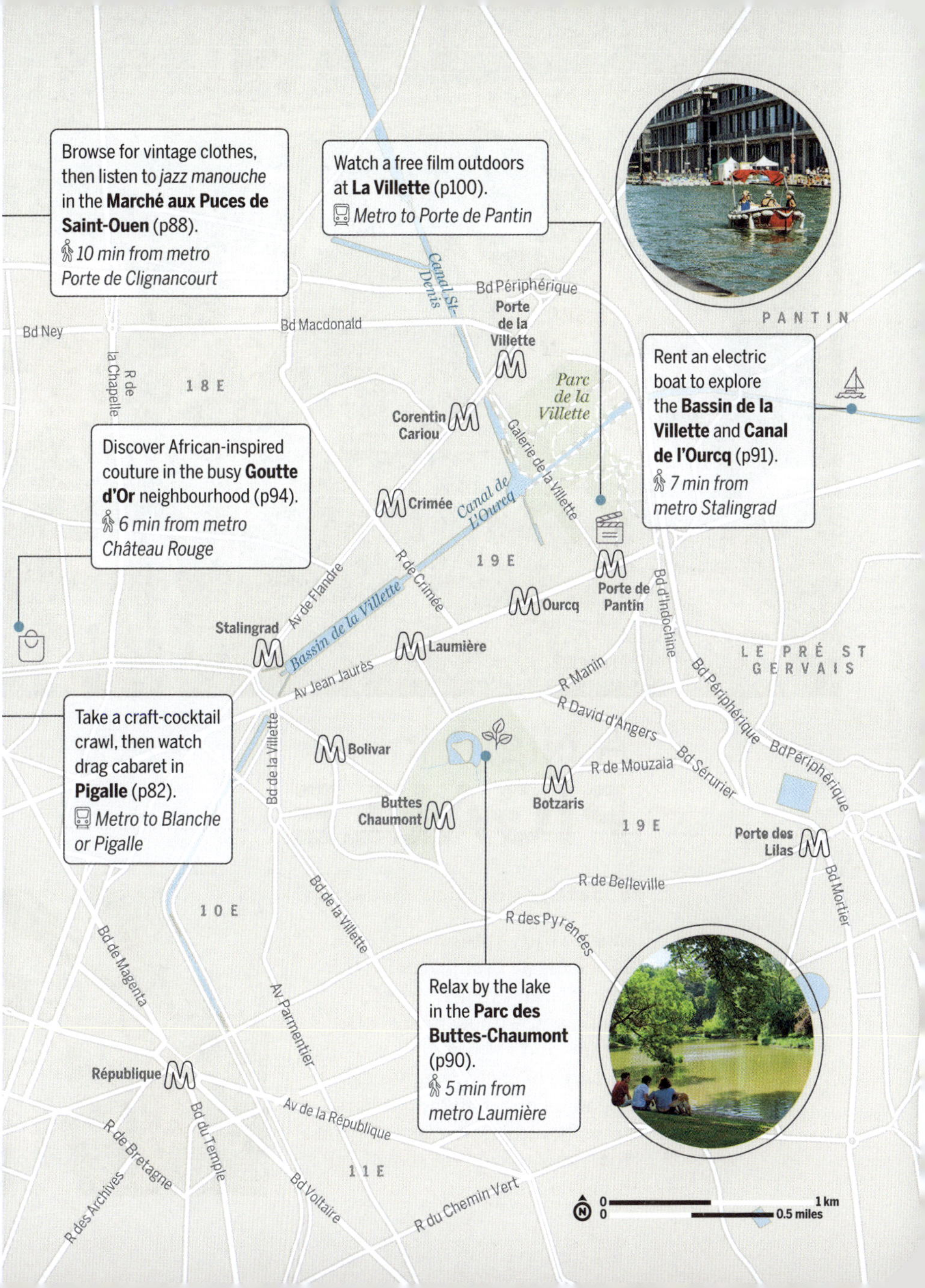

Browse for vintage clothes, then listen to *jazz manouche* in the **Marché aux Puces de Saint-Ouen** (p88).
10 min from metro Porte de Clignancourt
Watch a free film outdoors at **La Villette** (p100).
Metro to Porte de Pantin
Rent an electric boat to explore the **Bassin de la Villette** and **Canal de l'Ourcq** (p91).
7 min from metro Stalingrad
Discover African-inspired couture in the busy **Goutte d'Or** neighbourhood (p94).
6 min from metro Château Rouge
Take a craft-cocktail crawl, then watch drag cabaret in **Pigalle** (p82).
Metro to Blanche or Pigalle
Relax by the lake in the **Parc des Buttes-Chaumont** (p90).
5 min from metro Laumière
Canal St-Denis
Bd Périphérique
Porte de la Villette
PANTIN
Bd Ney
Bd Macdonald
R de la Chapelle
18E
Parc de la Villette
Corentin Cariou
Galerie de la Villette
Crimée
Canal de L'Ourcq
19E
Porte de Pantin
Bd d'Indochine
R de Crimée
Av de Flandre
Ourcq
Stalingrad
Bassin de la Villette
Laumière
LE PRÉ ST GERVAIS
Av Jean Jaurès
R Manin
Bd Périphérique
R David d'Angers
Bd de la Villette
Bolivar
Bd Sérurier
Bd Périphérique
R de Mouzaia
Buttes Chaumont
Botzaris
19E
Porte des Lilas
Bd Mortier
R de Belleville
10E
Bd de la Villette
R des Pyrénées
Bd de Magenta
Av Parmentier
République
Bd du Temple
Av de la République
R de Bretagne
11E
Bd Voltaire
R du Chemin Vert
R des Archives
0 1 km
0 0.5 miles

11

A Night in PIGALLE

COCKTAILS I CABARET I NIGHTLIFE

Gritty-yet-trendy Pigalle is one of the best places in town for an expertly crafted drink, and with so many bars, venues and clubs within walking distance of each other, it's easy to spend an entire night out here, transitioning from evening drinks to a raucous cabaret show to all-night dancing.

How to

Getting here and around Metro line 2 to Blanche; lines 2 or 12 to Pigalle. From either station, everything is within a 10-minute walk.

When to go Many of these bars are tiny, with limited seating, and get packed on weekends. For a greater chance of snagging a spot, try going either early evening or late at night.

Tip English-language songs are performed at Chez Michou, but Madame Arthur is strictly French-only.

A Craft-Cocktail Crawl

Composer Georges Bizet allegedly once lived in the opulent 19th-century mansion that's now **Le Carmen**, a plush, ultra-hip bar. Perfect for early evening cocktails, it specialises in a dizzying array of house-infused gins. Later it morphs into a trendy, all-night club, but it's tough to get past the highly selective bouncers unless you look the part (as in, part of Paris Fashion Week).

In a one-time Belle Époque brothel turned luxury boutique hotel, the elegant yet relaxed **Maison Souquet** lounge bar features red velvet settees and shelves of leather-bound books. The bartenders mix up artisanal cocktails named after famous courtesans.

Steeped in retro charm, **Lulu White Drinking Club** is a cosy little New Orleans–style

18th-century Cabaret Central

Though only Chez Michou and Madame Arthur remain today, nearly half of rue des Martyrs' buildings were cabarets or *guinguettes* (open-air dance halls) in the 1780s. This was because Montmartre was outside Paris and not subject to its taxes, so wine was much cheaper there.

Left Madame Arthur (p85) **Above left** Chez Michou (p85) **Above right** Dirty Dick (p84)

bar offering excellent speciality cocktails, absinthe with all the antique accoutrements, and a regular roster of live jazz and blues bands.

Despite its awful name, **Dirty Dick** is one of Pigalle's best cocktail spots. In a compact, dimly lit space, it's a true tiki bar with tropical decor, Hawaiian shirts and modern interpretations of exotic cocktail classics, such as the flaming Zombie.

A Bite to Eat

Break up the bacchanalia with a food fest. Lively Pigalle is packed with good restaurants. Awarded a Michelin 'Bib Gourmand' for value, **Le Pantruche** serves revisited bistro classics in a retro-cool atmosphere – think wall mirrors and a zinc counter. A selection of tartines, croques and rillettes will sate the appetite at **Buvette**, an all-day dining destination. If you're hankering for authentic Mexico tacos, **El Nopal** is just the ticket.

More Cocktails & Cabaret

With just the right combination of vintage grit and retro glamour, **Sister Midnight** is the perfect place to celebrate Pigalle's racy past. A regular rotation of drag queens parade through on a near-weekly basis to put on crazy-fun cabaret shows. Even on non-cabaret nights, this spot is worth a stop for some of Paris' best cocktails. Try the 'Suicide' for a spicy surprise! The drinks are so good, you'll forget your dinner plans. Luckily, it has an excellent ploughman's plate with English cheeses, pickled eggs and veg from Emperor Norton, snack suppliers to many bars and cafes around town.

Recommended by Forest Collins, Paris cocktail expert and France Academy Chair for The World's 50 Best Bars. @52martinis

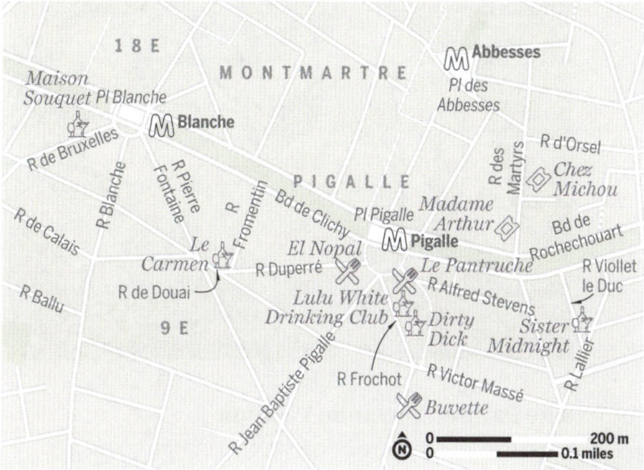

Far left Sister Midnight **Below** *Divan Japonais* by Toulouse-Lautrec

See a Drag Cabaret

In an intimate 1930s space in rue des Martyrs, **Chez Michou** cabaret was launched in 1956 by local celebrity Michou. Known as 'The Blue Prince of Montmartre' for his habit of always dressing head-to-toe in blue, Michou departed on his last 'voyage', as he called it, in 2020, but the show goes on. The long-running cabaret features *transformiste* performers who lip-sync as Cher, Lady Gaga, Bette Midler and Celine Dion, as well as French pop stars. It's a formula that might feel familiar today, but this venue was one of the first of its kind in Paris. Before the show, dinner is served by the performers themselves.

Just across the street, at the historic Divan du Monde (formerly the Divan Japonais cabaret painted by Toulouse-Lautrec), **Madame Arthur** is a younger and more modern show. Featuring a rotating cast of talented performers, the troupe tackles a new musical theme or artist each week, such as Abba, Queen, Disney or Beyoncé, performing Frenchified versions of the songs. Unlike most drag cabarets, the performers here actually sing, accompanied by live piano or accordion music in the traditional French fashion. The bar makes great cocktails and once the cabaret show ends at midnight, the venue turns into an all-night dance club, with DJs primarily spinning vintage French hits.

Women of Montmartre

GET TO KNOW THESE UNDER-RECOGNISED MONTMARTROISES

Montmartre is well known as the old stomping ground of countless famous men, among them Picasso, Van Gogh, Debussy and Truffaut. But there are also many women whose achievements have faded into the background. Their stories provide fascinating insights into historic, artist-adored Montmartre, best appreciated on a self-guided walking tour.

Left *Reclining Nude* by Suzanne Valadon **Middle** La Goulue **Right** Dalida

SEPIA TIMES/UNIVERSAL IMAGES GROUP VIA GETTY IMAGES ©

The Painter: Suzanne Valadon

Raised in Montmartre by her mother, an impoverished laundress, Valadon started out as a trapeze artist, but a fall put an end to circus work. She turned to modelling for the many artists who lived on the hill, posing for painters such as Toulouse-Lautrec, Modigliani and Renoir. But she was far more than just an artist's muse. A talented artist in her own right, she was encouraged by her friend Edgar Degas. In 1894, she became one of the first women admitted to the Société Nationale des Beaux-Arts, a stunning achievement for a woman from a working-class background with no formal training. Her frank and unromanticised nudes were years ahead of their time. Although she achieved international recognition during her lifetime, she has been mostly forgotten outside of Montmartre – and excluded from the history of French art – in the subsequent years. Valadon lived in Montmartre's oldest building at 12 rue Cortot for more than 25 years. It's now the **Musée de Montmartre**, with her atelier as it was in 1912. Another haunt was the **Moulin de la Galette**, a dance hall before it became a restaurant, where she slid down the bannisters wearing only a mask.

The Dancer: La Goulue

Like Valadon, Louise Weber grew up poor as the daughter of a laundrywoman and also modelled for Renoir before finding her own renown. One of the **Moulin Rouge's** early stars in the 1890s, the boisterous redhead was immortalised in many posters by Toulouse-Lautrec. She earned her nickname, La Goulue (The Glutton), through her healthy

HI-STORY/ALAMY STOCK PHOTO ©

PIERRE VAUTHEY/GETTY IMAGES ©

appetite and cheeky habit of emptying customers' wine glasses as she danced past their tables. Credited with developing the high-energy can-can from an earlier dance called the *chahut*, her fame and fortune were such that she was also known as 'The Queen of Montmartre'. After leaving the Moulin Rouge in 1895 for an unsuccessful turn as a lion tamer, she fell into oblivion and spent her last days in poverty. In 2021, Montmartre's Jardin Burq park was renamed in her honour.

The Singer: Dalida

Dalida sang in 10 languages, toured the world numerous times, and was one of the first singers to be awarded a diamond disc for selling more than 10 million albums.

The glamorous chanteuse known as Dalida was born Iolanda Gigliotti to Italian parents in Cairo in 1933. In the 1950s, she moved to Paris and quickly became a sensation, first as a pop star and later as a disco diva. She sang in 10 languages, toured the world numerous times, and was one of the first singers to be awarded a diamond disc for selling more than 10 million albums. A superstar in France, Europe and the Middle East, she received a lukewarm reception – and remains relatively unknown – in the anglophone world. In 1962, she bought a mansion in Montmartre in rue d'Orchampt and lived there for more than 20 years. Although she was spectacularly successful in her career, her private life was repeatedly marked by tragedy, and in 1987 she took her own life. She is buried in **Cimetière de Montmartre** and a bronze bust can be found in the small **place Dalida**.

The Writer: Colette

Though Colette is widely recognised as one of France's greatest writers, her early struggles are less known. Her husband Willy published her wildly popular debut novels in his name; when she left him in 1906, he kept all royalties and she turned to performing in music halls to survive. Her 1907 act at the Moulin Rouge with Missy de Morny caused such a scandal that the police threatened to shut down the cabaret. After Willy's death in the 1930s, Colette went to court to have his name removed from the Claudine books and her authorship restored.

12 Vintage Clothes & JAZZ

SHOPPING I FASHION I JAZZ

The sprawling Marché aux Puces de Saint-Ouen flea market – a labyrinth of stands selling everything under the *soleil* – can easily overwhelm. But if you know where to go, rare treasures are to be found, especially if vintage clothing is your thing. Spend a morning browsing the stalls, then have lunch while listening to some live *jazz manouche*.

OLIVEROUGE 3/SHUTTERSTOCK ©

How to

Getting here Metro line 4 to Porte de Clignancourt.

When to go The weekend is the best time to visit, since many shops and stands in the market are only open on Saturdays and Sundays.

Tip Stay alert and keep an eye on your valuables – the market is a prime area for pickpockets. Note that the vendors around and beneath the overpass are not part of the official market.

ELENA DIJOUR/SHUTTERSTOCK ©

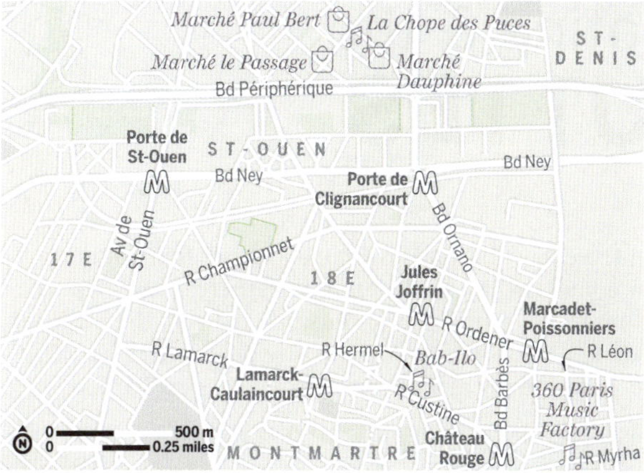

Browse the Shops & Stalls Hit the market early for the best finds; most places open between 10am and 10.30am. On the 1st floor of the **Marché Dauphine**, **Falbalas** is one of the market's biggest and best-stocked vintage-clothing shops, carrying anything from 18th-century outfits to funky '70s duds, plus every period accessory you could imagine. The owners, Françoise and Erwan, also sell their own line of vintage and antique reproduction shoes. **Chez Sarah**, in the **Marché Le Passage**, sells vintage apparel from 1900 through to the 1990s, as well as a wide selection of vintage haberdashery. **Les Merveilles de Babellou** has a shop in **Marché Paul Bert** at stand 12. Both specialise in vintage French haute couture, from Chanel, Dior and Yves Saint-Laurent to Paco Rabanne. Also in the Marché Paul Bert, at stands 112 and 114, **de Laurentis** focuses on vintage avant-garde fashion from designers such as Martin Margiela and Comme des Garçons.

Get into the Swing Once you've combed the racks, head to **La Chope des Puces** for some *jazz manouche* (also known as gypsy jazz, gypsy swing or hot club jazz) and hearty, traditional French fare. The legendary Django Reinhardt, the originator of the style, played here, along with other greats. The low-key, convivial bistro features live performances every Saturday and Sunday from 12.30pm to 7pm. On the upper floors of the building, there's also a musical-instrument shop, a luthier workshop, a *jazz manouche* school and a recording studio.

Far left top Marché Dauphine **Far left bottom** Vintage brooches

More Live Music in Northern Paris

I feel privileged to be a jazz singer walking the same streets as Brassens, Piaf and Aznavour. In the evenings, I head to **Bab-Ilo,** tucked away on rue du Baigneur. The best of the Paris jazz scene flock to this intimate spot, one of Paris' last genuine jazz clubs, welcoming musicians from emerging artists to Grammy winners.

For more eclectic concerts, I love the **360 Paris Music Factory** in the heart of the Goutte d'Or, the area's African quarter. The place hums with creative activity and a superb world-music program. There's a bar and restaurant, and Sunday brunches have the added joy of a live, local jazz band.

By Liv Monaghan, *singer, songwriter and vintage-clothing seller living in Montmartre. @livmonaghanmusic*

13 Boating & the BUTTES

PARKS | CANAL | PICNIC

It's a fantastical sight: a craggy butte rises from a swan-dotted pond, its rocky pinnacle crowned by a faux Greek temple. From the ethereal Parc des Buttes-Chaumont, a 10-minute walk brings you to the open vistas of the artificial lake known as the Bassin de la Villette, where you can hire an electric boat. This duo of unexpected delights is seemingly a world away from classical Paris.

HEMIS/ALAMY STOCK PHOTO ©

How to

Getting here Metro line 7B to Buttes Chaumont or Botzaris.

When to go When the weather's nice on the weekends, sunseekers flock to Parc des Buttes-Chaumont and it can get uncomfortably crowded.

Tip Book your boat with Marin d'Eau Douce online. Add on a pre-packed *apéro* hamper or bring your own. During Paris Plages in the summer, you can plunge into the dedicated swimming pools set up in the Bassin de la Villette.

DANIEL_GAUTHIER/SHUTTERSTOCK ©

Picnic in the Quirkiest Park Once a gypsum quarry and rubbish dump, the **Parc des Buttes-Chaumont** is one of the city's largest green spaces and a favourite with Parisians. It was given its present form by Baron Haussmann for the opening of the 1867 Exposition Universelle. The hilly topography reveals grottoes, waterfalls and pathways lined with concrete hand railings sculpted to look like wood. Lording over it all is the **Temple de la Sibylle**, perched atop the butte. Locals practise Tai Chi, take the kids to puppet shows and dance at the **Rosa Bonheur** *guinguette* (dance hall). The rolling lawns are perfect for a picnic – pick up supplies on the nearby market street, **av Secrétan**.

Cruise the Canal From a kiosk on the **quai de la Seine**, Marin d'Eau Douce hires easy-to-manoeuvre electric boats (no licence required) for exploring the **Bassin de la Villette** and **Canal de l'Ourcq** at your own pace. It even rents out *pétanque* sets so you can dock for a game on the banks. The canal bridges open at regular intervals to allow boat traffic to pass. There's nothing better than sharing an *apéro* with friends while cruising the waterway, listening to music and watching the local life on the quays. Just be sure to keep an eye on the clock – you'll need to return the boat at the designated time.

Far left top Canal de l'Ourcq **Far left bottom** Parc des Buttes-Chaumont

Trendy Pantin

Navigate your boat northeast to the *banlieue* (suburb) of Pantin, nicknamed 'the Brooklyn of Paris'. From the water, you can glimpse the suburb's rich industrial heritage in buildings such as the **Magasins Généraux**, where hipsters hang out at the **Dock B** restaurant. There's been a metamorphosis over recent decades, as businesses such as Hermès, BNP and Chanel have moved in, alongside artists and *bobos* (bohemian bourgeois). Keep an eye out for the street art visible from the canal – the mural of actress Marion Cotillard was painted from a Harcourt portrait. Plan a return trip to see the **Galerie Thaddeus Ropac**, inside a former ironworks factory.

14 Dancing on Train TRACKS

LOCAL LIFE I FOOD I CULTURE

If you're hungry for a taste of modern Paris, head to Le Hasard Ludique, a vibrant, multifunctional cultural space, concert venue, nightclub and bar-restaurant set in a former 19th-century train station along the Petite Ceinture. Located just northeast of Montmartre, near the Porte de Saint-Ouen, it's a side of the city well off the tourist track.

EETU AHANEN/LE HASARD LUDIQUE ©

How to

Getting here Metro line 13 to Porte de Saint-Ouen (two-minute walk) or Guy Môquet (four minute walk). The closest Vélib' station is on rue Jacques Kellner.

When to go Best in summer, when the bar moves outdoors and there are activities and events on the rails.

Tip Most of Le Hasard Ludique's programming is French-only. For health and safety reasons, only certain portions of the Petite Ceinture are open to the public.

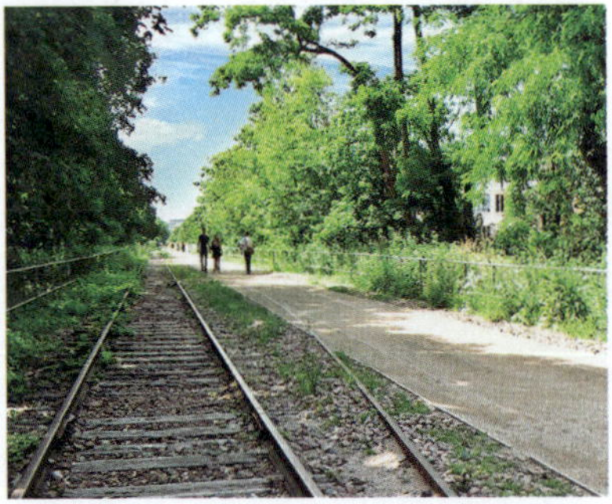

DELPIXEL/SHUTTERSTOCK ©

Left REcyclerie **Far left top** Le Hasard Ludique **Far left bottom** Petite Ceinture

Daytime Offerings By day, **Le Hasard Ludique** offers creative workshops, fitness and wellness classes and family-friendly programs, as well as a variety of regular events ranging from art fairs, pop-up shops and by-the-kilo secondhand clothing sales to *pétanque* matches and markets featuring organic fruit and veg from local producers.

Bites & Tipples The casual on-site eatery, **La Cantine de Léon**, offers coffee, tea, juices and lunch deals during the day. In the evenings, creative fusion tapas, with plenty of veggie and vegan options, are perfect for an *apéro* or low-key dinner. Sunday brunch includes unlimited coffee and tea.

There's seating and tables indoors and outdoors on the Victorian railway platform, which is covered in colourful graffiti, and even along the abandoned tracks themselves, now reclaimed by greenery.

The bar sells draught and bottled beer, with a focus on local craft brews, plus organic and natural wines, and cocktails ranging from classic to creative.

After Dark Things get livelier in the evenings, with tango balls, drag bingo and a diverse schedule ranging from funk, rap and soul to electro-pop, indie, folk and Latin music. There are frequent club nights and DJ sets, as well as quirky 'danceoké' nights at which attendees copy the moves in their favourite music videos.

What's the Petite Ceinture?

The 3 (Little Ring) is a former railway line surrounding Paris, built in 1852 to connect the city's main train stations. Mostly disused since 1934, it's gradually been taken over by plants and wildlife, and has become a sort of open-air, street-art gallery. Unknown even to many Parisians, it's great for peaceful strolls, but access is permitted only at certain points and only to some portions of the tracks that have been converted to parks. In the 18e, the access points are located at the **Hasard Ludique** and the **REcyclerie**, both installed in former Petite Ceinture stations.

15 La Goutte D'OR

STROLLING | FASHION | AFRICAN CULTURE

Though many Parisians can be guarded at first, they soon warm up. In the 18e, in contrast, you're likely to be immediately received with open arms. This popular neighbourhood, known as La Goutte d'Or or Chateau Rouge, has a strong African presence and is notable for the warm welcome that's integral to African culture.

HEMIS/ALAMY STOCK PHOTO ©

How to

Getting here Metro to Barbès-Rochechouart or Château Rouge. If you come by car, be prepared for traffic and very little parking.

When to go Visiting in the afternoon is best as most shops in the area don't open before noon.

Tip The Institut des Cultures d'Islam offers tours and art exhibits.

Information The Little Africa Paris Village concept store at 6bis rue des Gardes has maps and tour information.

AFROMEALS/SHUTTERSTOCK ©

JACQUELINE NGO MPII/LONELY PLANET ©

Left Window display, La Goutte d'Or **Far left top** La Goutte d'Or neighbourhood **Far left bottom** Jollof rice

Fabrics, Fashion & Inspiration Whether you decide to explore La Goutte d'Or on your own or on a walking tour, one of the first things you'll learn is that le sac Barbès originated here. This iconic bag was created by the founder of the Tati discount store, a neighbourhood institution before it closed in 2020. The sturdy plastic bag was popularised by luxury brands, including Louis Vuitton and Balenciaga, which were inspired to create their own €1500 versions. La Goutte d'Or has also inspired the fashion world with African fabrics. Today a new generation of designers of African descent have set themselves up in this creative hub. Rue de Léon and rue de Doudeville are full of shops offering patterns, ready-to-wear clothing and custom-made services. A popular stop is **La Bonne Couture** boutique on rue des Gardes, a street that's been nicknamed 'rue de la Mode', while perhaps the most famous is the boutique of **Maison Château Rouge**, a popular lifestyle brand named for the neighbourhood metro station.

Traditional Food After wandering La Goutte d'Or looking for that special head-turning outfit, you might start to feel hungry. Good news: there's a great choice of restaurants with authentic, generous portions of African-inspired food – specifically North Africa (Morocco, Tunisia and Algeria), West Africa (Senegal and Mali) and Central Africa (Nigeria and Cameroon). If you want to try your hand at cooking a traditional dish, such as *thieboudienne, mafé,* couscous, jollof rice or *ndolé,* head to rue Dejean and Marché Barbès to pick up ingredients.

A Neighbourhood Primer

La Goutte d'Or (the Drop of Gold) takes its name from the golden colour of the wine that was produced here up until the 19th century. The district was only incorporated into the city of Paris in 1860. Before then, it wasn't subject to its taxes, so it attracted a working-class population, mostly immigrants. Today it's a dynamic, cosmopolitan place with a youthful vibe. Tati may be closed but two other institutions remain: the **Le Louxor** cinema, a historic monument first inaugurated in 1921, and the multi-level **Brasserie Barbès**, complete with a rooftop overlooking Sacré-Coeur.

By Jacqueline Ngo Mpii
Born in Cameroon and raised in France, Jacqueline is the founder and CEO of Little Africa, a multimedia and cultural agency. @littleafricaparis

GASTON PARIS/GETTY IMAGES ©

Noire Paris

AN INTRODUCTION TO THE CITY'S AFRICAN CULTURE

Every country that has a history of colonisation and slavery will have a history intertwined with immigration, and cities influenced by the people who left their countries, but carried their precious culture with them. Paris is one of those cities.

Paris projects such a strong, and often clichéd, image around the world – of romance, rudeness and women draped in Chanel – that it has been difficult for travellers to imagine there's a significant black population living in the city. From the souvenir shops in Montmartre to the tourist office by Palais Garnier, visitors are only presented a one-dimensional history. When some travellers arrive at Charles De Gaulle Airport and take the train to the city centre, they're probably not even aware that the train crosses the Seine-Saint-Denis, a state-region that contains the largest African population in France.

When talking about black Paris, there are different segments because there are many different communities of African descent. The community the world knows most about is the African American community in Paris from the 1920s to the 1960s. Most people have heard about Josephine Baker, James Baldwin and Richard Wright and how they found a haven in Paris; a place where their colour wasn't a barrier. This part of black Paris is well documented in books, documentaries and narrations by tour companies. Many people, however, don't know about the large communities from the former French colonies in Africa (primarily Senegal, Ivory Coast, Cameroon and Mali) and the Caribbean people (primarily from Guadalupe, Martinique and French Guiana) who have made Paris their home for generations. From the Latin Quarter – well known for the Sorbonne University, an institution that welcomed prominent black figures such as Paulette Nardal, Leopold Sedar Senghor and Aimé Césaire – to the neighbourhoods of La Goutte d'Or and

Left Josephine Baker **Middle** Tomb of Félix Eboué **Right** Musée national de l'histoire de l'immigration (p125)

TATIANA DIUVBANOVA/SHUTTERSTOCK ©

HEMIS/ALAMY STOCK PHOTO ©

Château d'Eau, which are the beating hearts of the African presence in Paris, there is a lot to see and explore.

One of the easiest ways to recognise the black French presence is to pay attention to street and metro names: place Félix Eboué (metro Daumesnil), named after the first person of African descent to become governor of a *département* in France and to be buried at the Pantheon; rue Dahomey (11e); rue Congo (12e); rue Soudan (15e); rue Timbuktu (18e); and rue Chevalier de Saint-George (8e).

While debates around immigration increase in Europe, some people still deny what streets, buildings, cuisines and faces boldly show: Paris is multicultural and influenced by African culture.

Then there are museums such as the Quai Branly (p46), a garden of classical African art that made history by returning stolen artefacts to their countries of origin. Above all, visit Musée national de l'histoire de l'immigration (p125). Built for the last international colonial exhibition of France in 1931, the building is massive, with an allegorical facade that displays the economic contributions of the former French colonies. Inside, visitors can learn stories of all types of immigrants' contributions, ranging from food and art to music.

While debates around all kinds of immigration increase in Europe, some people still deny what plaques, bridges, streets, buildings, cuisines and faces boldly show: Paris is multicultural and influenced by African culture. Like gold miners overlooking a lode of gold, those missing this part of the story (which needs to be told) are missing a vibrant part of Paris.

Further Reading

To keep exploring black Paris read *La France Noire* and *Le Paris Noir,* both by historian Pascal Blanchard, who specialises in colonialism. In these two books, he covers black history in France over the last three centuries, including how Paris became the meeting point for black communities from the USA, the Caribbean and Africa. He also talks about how the contributions of black communities have shaped the country's political, artistic, cultural and economic landscape.

16 Secret Canal CORNERS

AUTHENTIC | BOBO | WALKING

Shaded by chestnut trees and crisscrossed by iron footbridges, tranquil Canal Saint Martin is a favourite hipster hangout. The cool crowd pack the canalside cafes, shop at trendy boutiques and enjoy aperitifs along the towpaths. Over two centuries, the canal has witnessed a vast transformation. Traces of industrial heritage provide a glimpse of canal life before it was in vogue.

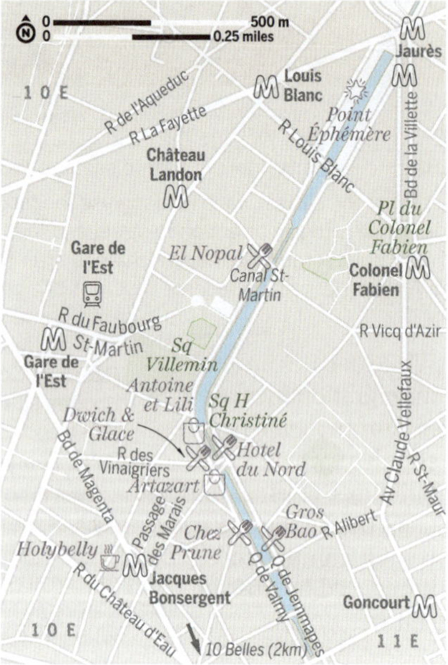

How to

Getting here Metro line 5 to Jacques Bonsergent.

When to go The canalside roads are closed to traffic every Sunday and public holiday from 10am to 6pm (8pm in summer). The city is advancing a project to pedestrianise the area permanently.

Tours Canal cruises take boats through the locks. Sign up for a guided tour with Ça se visite!, an organisation that champions urban discovery in a sustainable, authentic and participative way.

An Urban Artery Napoleon commissioned the canal system to provide drinking water and to ease boat traffic on the Seine. Inaugurated in 1825, the 4.5km-long Canal Saint Martin was designed with locks and pivoting swing bridges that still exist today. Barges carried merchandise to Paris, and the surrounding neighbourhood teemed with industry. By the 1960s, this traffic had declined and businesses vacated. The canal was nearly paved over for a highway, but local residents rallied to save it. Soon, artists, designers and students discovered its charms, leading to gentrification by the *bourgeois-bohêmes* ('bobos').

The first wave of cool addresses, such as **Chez Prune**, **Artazart** and the brightly hued **Antoine et Lili** boutique, are fixtures on the scene today. Housed inside a former merchandise depot, **Point Éphémère** opened in 2004 as a culture and concert venue. These early trendsetters were followed

VIENNASLIDE/ALAMY STOCK PHOTO ©

by the likes of **El Nopal**, **10 Belles** and **Holybelly**. Nowadays, street-food options run the gamut from vegetarian sandwiches at **Dwich & Glace** to pork buns at **Gros Bao**.

Vestiges do remain of the quarter's working-class roots, best discovered on a guided walking tour. Authenticity abounds in alleyways and original buildings that are a favourite movie set for filmmakers. François Truffaut shot scenes of *The Last Metro* in the **Passage des Marais**, while the **Hotel du Nord**, now a popular restaurant, was the setting for a book and 1938 film depicting its hardscrabble residents.

Hidden in Plain Sight

A few minutes' walk from the canal, the **Couvent des Récollets de Paris**, a former Franciscan friary, narrowly escaped demolition before it was listed as a historic monument. Now it's home to the vibrant **Café A** and two architectural associations. Ring the buzzer at 5 rue Legouvé to explore **Les Douches la Galerie**, a photography gallery inside an old public bathhouse. Across the canal, **Hôpital Saint-Louis** was built by Henri IV and the buildings are reminiscent of the place des Vosges. The public garden is a peaceful haven.

Above Point Éphémère

Listings

BEST OF THE REST

Memorable Meals

Pétrelle €€€

At the foot of Montmartre, this romantic, candlelit hideout, decorated in retro, flea-market style, offers a seasonal tasting menu that changes weekly (a two-course menu is available at lunchtime).

Le Pavillon du Lac €€

A relaxed, airy restaurant in Parc des Buttes-Chaumont serving refined, modern Mediterranean cuisine. In spring and summer, there's also terrace seating and an outdoor bar.

Café de Luce €€

After working for some of the top chefs in France, Amandine Chaignot opened this cafe in 2021, channelling the bistros of yesteryear with dishes like *oeufs* (eggs) mayo, frog legs and beef tartare.

Bouillon Pigalle €

A sprawling, bustling restaurant serving traditional French classics and wines at jaw-droppingly reasonable prices. The menu changes often but is always simple and hearty.

La Mascotte €€€

A favourite with locals, this elegant 1900s brasserie is known particularly for its seafood, including oysters, *bigorneaux* (periwinkles), *bulots* (whelks) and *amandes* (cockles).

Brewpubs & Chic Cocktails

Paname Brewing Company €

Craft brewery on the Canal de l'Ourcq offering house draught beers and hearty pub fare. When the weather's nice, snag a table on the floating terrace out front.

Le Très Particulier €€

Hidden behind a tall gate on a quiet residential street, the ultra-stylish cocktail bar in this luxury boutique hotel has *Twin Peaks* vibes, craft cocktails, weekend DJs and idyllic garden seating.

Pavillon Puebla €

Stylish hangout in the Parc des Buttes-Chaumont. In summer, the spacious terrace nestled among the trees features *apéro* cocktails and Mediterranean bites. In winter, it has an après-ski vibe and mulled wine.

Museums, Sites & Cultural Centres

Halle Saint-Pierre

This unusual museum in a former 19th-century market hall puts on *art brut* (outsider art) exhibitions and has a tranquil tearoom/cafe, as well as an interesting bookshop.

La Villette

Vast arts and culture complex in a sprawling park, presenting concerts, contemporary-art exhibitions and installations, dance performances, and free, open-air film screenings in the summer.

Musée de la Vie romantique

At the end of a cobbled lane in the Nouvelle Athènes quarter, this tranquil villa was once the setting for popular salons and today houses a museum dedicated to Romantic-era artists.

Sacré-Cœur

This towering, white basilica atop Montmartre hill draws visitors from around the globe. It's worth a climb to the top of the dome for the sweeping views.

Craft Coffee Shops

Le Pavillon des Canaux €

Charming canal-side coffee shop on several floors of an old house furnished with antique decor. Enjoy coffee or tea in the bedroom or curled up on colourful cushions in the bath.

Ten Belles €

The first location for the popular coffee roaster and sandwich shop opened in 2012 near the Canal Saint Martin. Sip your coffee on the terrace, or order takeaway to enjoy next to the canal.

Café Lomi €

A craft coffee shop and roastery in a rustic, industrial space. Besides coffee and cakes, it offers light breakfast and lunch.

Unique Boutiques

Macon & Lesquoy

The art of embroidery is celebrated in brooches, badges and original creations at this boutique near the Canal Saint Martin.

Flash Vintage

Compact, funky vintage-clothing boutique that's worth a dig-through for some well-priced finds, with a focus on '70s and '80s apparel and accessories for men and women.

Nightclubs & Cabarets

Bus Palladium

Legendary Pigalle nightclub and rock-concert venue where Mick Jagger and Salvador Dalí were regulars. These days, events include concerts, DJs and rock karaoke nights backed by a live band.

Chez Ma Cousine

Convivial wood-lined restaurant and cabaret in the heart of Montmartre village offering dinner and a show, with classic French fare and traditional *chanson* to match.

Au Lapin Agile

Au Lapin Agile

Storied cabaret where Picasso used to hang out, preserving the art form as it was in the 19th century – traditional French songs accompanied by piano and accordion.

La Maroquinerie

Housed in a former leather workshop, this concert hall has been an important venue for the indie music scene for decades. There's also a restaurant.

Chocolate & Cheese

Kozak

This tiny shop is one of the best places in Paris to find artisan bean-to-bar chocolates from around the world. In the summer, it morphs into an ice-cream shop.

Fromagerie Chez Virginie

With two locations, in rue Damrémont and rue Caulaincourt, this lovely, established cheese shop is one of only a few in Paris that age cheeses in their own cellars.

La Laiterie de Paris

Pierre Coulon, the first cheesemaker in Paris, sources milk from small dairies in Normandy and Brittany to create a delicious selection of cheeses, often accented with fresh herbs and spices.

LE MARAIS, MÉNILMONTANT & BELLEVILLE

HISTORY | SOCIETY | POP CULTURE

Experience Le Marais, Ménilmontant & Belleville online

- Royal Intrigue in Le Marais (p106)
- Jewish Culture in the Pletzl (p110)
- Sunset in Belleville (p112)
- The 100 Nationalities of Belleville (p114)
- Gravestones & Greenery (p116)
- Listings (p118)

LE MARAIS, MÉNIL-MONTANT & BELLEVILLE

Trip Builder

TAKE YOUR PICK OF MUST-SEES AND HIDDEN GEMS

A study in contrasts, these neighbourhoods offer very different experiences. Le Marais, now heavily gentrified, was home to dukes and princesses, while Belleville and Ménilmontant have kept their working-class legacy and still resonate with popular songs. Seeing these distinct quarters helps visitors to understand the city today.

Trip Notes

Best for Shopping in Le Marais, Chinese food in Belleville.

Transport Take the metro to Hôtel de Ville or Saint-Paul (for Le Marais), Belleville or Jourdain (for Belleville), or Gambetta (for Ménilmontant).

Getting around Because of narrow streets, it's preferable to walk rather than drive.

Tip Plan to spend several hours in the vast Père Lachaise cemetery.

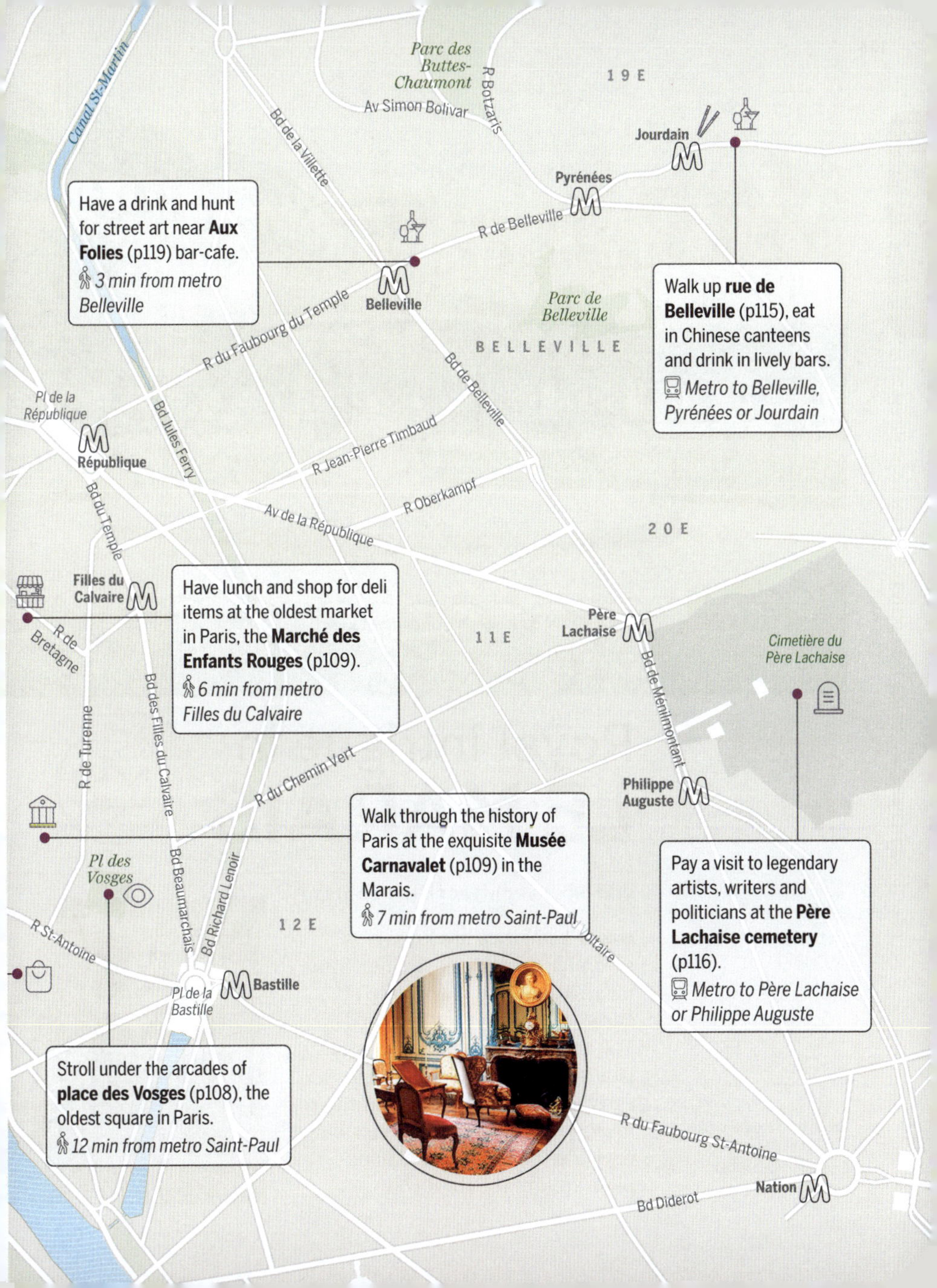

Have a drink and hunt for street art near **Aux Folies** (p119) bar-cafe.

3 min from metro Belleville

Walk up **rue de Belleville** (p115), eat in Chinese canteens and drink in lively bars.

Metro to Belleville, Pyrénées or Jourdain

Have lunch and shop for deli items at the oldest market in Paris, the **Marché des Enfants Rouges** (p109).

6 min from metro Filles du Calvaire

Walk through the history of Paris at the exquisite **Musée Carnavalet** (p109) in the Marais.

7 min from metro Saint-Paul

Pay a visit to legendary artists, writers and politicians at the **Père Lachaise cemetery** (p116).

Metro to Père Lachaise or Philippe Auguste

Stroll under the arcades of **place des Vosges** (p108), the oldest square in Paris.

12 min from metro Saint-Paul

17

Royal Intrigue in LE MARAIS

HISTORY | ARCHITECTURE | SOCIETY

Le Marais has known several historical and architectural incarnations and is now one of Paris' trendiest neighbourhoods. The area was home to influential ladies (and royal mistresses) as early as the 17th century and their *hôtels particuliers* (mansions) were once the theatre of scandalous plots around the royal court.

Above left place des Vosges (p108) **Above right** Hôtel Lamoignon (p109) **Right** Passage Saint-Paul

MISTERVLAD/SHUTTERSTOCK ©

How to

Getting here Take the metro to Saint-Paul, Pont Marie or Bastille.

When to go Every Sunday from 10am to 6pm (7.30pm in summer), most of Le Marais becomes a pedestrian-only zone.

Narrow streets Traffic isn't great, especially on weekends when the area can get very crowded.

Bookings If you're visiting museums or historic buildings, call to book in advance if possible.

PACK-SHOT/SHUTTERSTOCK ©

The Affair of the Poisons

In 1666, a scandalous murder rocked the court of Louis XIV. It started with Madame de Brinvilliers at her husband's mansion, Hôtel d'Aubray, in Le Marais. In order to live a luxurious life with her penniless lover, she poisoned her own father and brothers. She was later found out, tortured and beheaded. However, her trial revealed a more intricate network of poisoners, with ramifications throughout the nobility. La Reynie, chief of the royal police, led a thorough investigation, which resulted in the execution of 36 people almost 15 years later.

PACK-SHOT/SHUTTERSTOCK ©

Le Marais & its Secret Passages

Explore the dozen antique shops around the concealed **Village Saint-Paul** near Madame de Brinvilliers' mansion. Don't miss **Passage**

At the Heart of Parisian History

Le Marais is one of the only neighbourhoods in Paris where you can still travel through 1000 years of history if you know where to look. Head back to the 12th century at the ruins of Philippe-Auguste's wall in rue des Archives.

By Bohémond Josseran de Kerros, a historian, tour guide and former stonemason who was born and raised in Paris. @Interkultur_fr

Saint-Paul, which makes its way inside the church through a side door. Then cross over to **Hôtel de Sully**. At the back of its gardens, look for the passageway to the arcades of place des Vosges.

Built under the reign of Henri IV in 1605, **place des Vosges** is one of Le Marais' most emblematic landmarks and Paris' oldest square. In the 17th century, the greatest minds flocked to luxury apartments at place des Vosges to exchange ideas. Key Enlightenment principles were discussed and there was a wealth of intrigue at these literary salons convened by noble women of the time.

A Society of Powerful Women

A bit further north, not far from the hidden Arnaud Beltrame square, Françoise Scarron, known as Madame de Maintenon, used to host her own circle. Louis XIV's mistress, Madame de Montespan, was her best friend and a regular. Ironically, a decade later, it

Queen of the Literary Circles

At 36 rue des Tournelles, just behind place des Vosges, **Ninon de Lenclos** hosted her own literary circle every day. Her '5-to-9' became extremely popular, and she rapidly became the symbol of the educated, aristocratic libertines of the 17th and 18th centuries. She was independent and ravishing, and won hearts. Ninon led her life freely and opened her salon to the greatest politicians, artists and writers of the time, including La Fontaine, Perrault, Lully, Madame de Sévigné, Racine and even Philippe d'Orléans, who became regent of France.

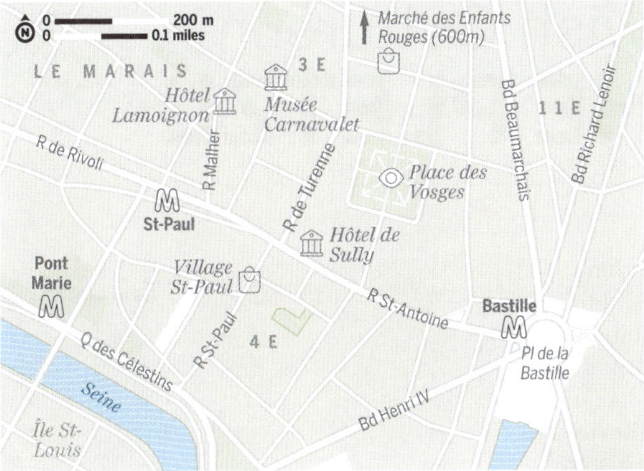

Far left Portrait of Ninon de Lenclos
Below Courtyard, Musée Carnavalet

was Madame Scarron who became the king's mistress, even marrying him in secret.

Another grand *salonnière* was Madame de Scudéry, who held popular meetings on rue de Beauce, a very narrow street tucked behind the oldest market in Paris, the **Marché des Enfants Rouges**. A hidden garden is named in her honour. On the way there, you'll pass **Hôtel Lamoignon**, another renowned salon attended by Madame de Sévigné, among others.

A Museum Must

A renowned woman of letters, Madame de Sévigné lived in the Hôtel Carnavalet from 1677 until 1696. The mansion was transformed into a museum devoted to the history of Paris in 1880. Over the years, the **Musée Carnavalet** – expanded to include a nearby mansion – became a popular destination in the Marais. A dramatic transformation was unveiled in 2021 after a costly restoration that lasted more than four years. The vaulted cellars were excavated and now showcase some of the Neolithic canoes discovered at a Seine archeological site in 1991. In the summer season, **Fabula** restaurant sets up in the garden courtyard.

18 Jewish Culture in THE PLETZL

HISTORY | FOOD | CULTURE

Jewish communities have existed in Paris since the Middle Ages. In the 19th century, they founded the 'Pletzl' in Le Marais – the 'small place' in Yiddish, as opposed to the larger place des Vosges. Rue des Rosiers was the main street of the historic Pletzl quarter, and some of its shops and restaurants still testify to the neighbourhood's Jewish heritage.

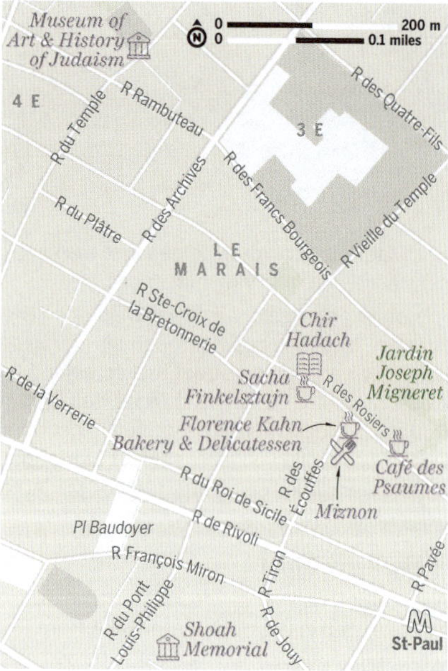

How to

Getting here Take the metro to Saint-Paul or Pont Marie.

When to go Every Sunday from 10am to 6pm (7.30pm in summer), most of Le Marais becomes a pedestrian-only zone. The Museum of Art & History of Judaism (mahJ) is closed on Mondays.

Tip The narrow streets aren't easy for traffic, especially on weekends when the area can get very crowded with shoppers. The mahJ offers Jewish-themed walking tours of Le Marais in the summer.

Pastries & Pastrami In rue des Rosiers, stop at **Sacha Finkelsztajn's** little yellow shop for cheesecake, strudel, poppy-seed rolls or the famous pastrami sandwich. Across the street, the **Chir Haddach** bookshop often has entertaining pieces in the window. **Café des Psaumes** is a place of discussion and exchange for both religious and non-religious Jewish people. Nearby, on the rue des Ecouffes, **Miznon** is a hot spot for Israeli street food. The **Florence Kahn Bakery & Delicatessen**, adorned with a stunning blue mosaic, is also popular.

Museum of Art & History of Judaism The **mahJ's** setting is reason enough to visit: the Hôtel de Saint-Aignan is a 17th-century mansion with a statue of Captain Dreyfus in the cobblestone courtyard. This important cultural venue has more than 12,000 works illustrating the history of Judaism in France. Highlights include a 3rd-century oil lamp found in the Charente, and the the king's 1790 proclamation of emancipation of Jews in France.

ZOONAR GMBH/ALAMY STOCK PHOTO ©

An Art Nouveau Synagogue

The **Agoudas Hakehilos Synagogue** on rue Pavée is the only religious building designed by Parisian architect Hector Guimard. A significant figure in the art nouveau movement, he is mostly known for his traditional 19th-century entrances to metro stations, only two of which have survived. He originally built the synagogue for his wife, who was Jewish. The facade's undulating and vertical lines show the influence of the art nouveau movement inspired by nature. It is one of six synagogues in the neighbourhood, with another located just behind place des Vosges.

War Traces & Stories The area holds strong memories of the tragic events of WWII: **rue des Écouffes**, one of the poorest streets at the time, was the most raided in 1942. At **17 rue des Rosiers**, there's a hidden synagogue, where a miracle took place during the Vel d'Hiv raid – though authorities knew about the place and that people were hiding inside, they overlooked it, sparing dozens of lives. On rue Geoffroy l'Asnier, the **Shoah Memorial** is Europe's largest research and information centre on the Jewish genocide.

Above Café des Psaumes

19 Sunset in BELLEVILLE

GARDENS I HISTORY I STREET ART

The steep streets and hills of Belleville, with its cafe terraces and family-run restaurants, make it an atmospheric neighbourhood to explore, away from the most-visited landmarks. To experience a more relaxed side of Paris, head to the 20e and Parc de Belleville for a sunset picnic, or to simply wander its staircased alleys and winding streets.

DAVID BLEEKER PHOTOGRAPHY/ALAMY STOCK PHOTO ©

How to

Getting here Take the metro to Couronnes (lower) or Pyrénées (upper).

When to go In spring and summer for the greenery, but more generally on clear, sunny days to watch the sunset from the top of the hill.

Opening hours From 8am Monday to Friday and 9am Saturday and Sunday; closing hours vary depending on the time of year and season.

Hilly area The Parc de Belleville is the highest park in Paris from top to bottom.

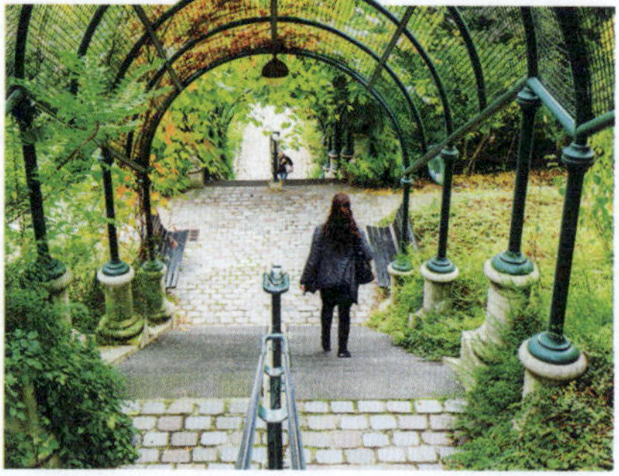

CHRISTIAN MUELLER/SHUTTERSTOCK ©

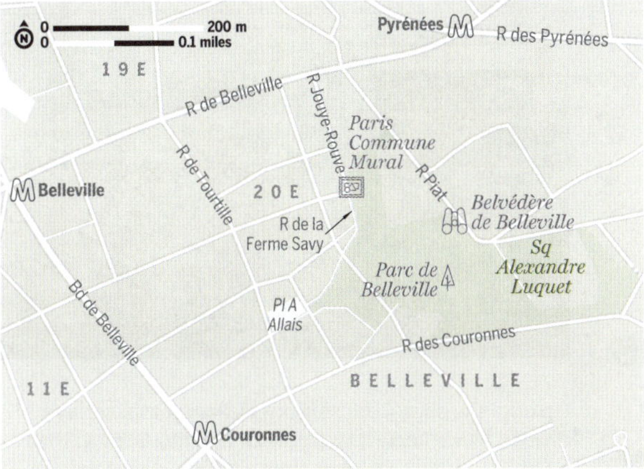

Far left top & far left bottom Parc de Belleville

On Top of the City's Highest Hills The highest point above sea level in Paris is not Montmartre; it's actually the top of the Parc de Belleville. Until the 19th century, Belleville was mainly farmland and vineyards. It's hard to believe now, but farm animals used to graze on the slopes of Belleville. There was once a cattle farm just below metro Belleville – discreet signs of it are still visible on rue de la Présentation.

Sunset Belleville Boulevard It's a totally different atmosphere here now, and **Parc de Belleville** is the perfect place to exercise, either by going up its steps or taking a slow walk under the shadow of the levelled trees, until you meet the waterfall. Children will love the boat-like climbing playground – adults may regret not being allowed onto it! Don't miss the **Belvédère de Belleville** on rue Piat, decorated with many street-art murals. It's the most beautiful view of Paris, according to locals. Your sunset awaits...

The Paris Commune Mural This is worth mentioning, since you're already there: look for the human-size mural commemorating the Paris Commune on the lower exterior walls of the park on rue de la Ferme Savy. The 72-day revolt culminated in bloodshed on the streets of Belleville – a tragic but iconic event that has left its mark on the local rebellious spirit.

A Refuge for All

Belleville people like to believe that Belleville is not Paris, and never has been. The area is marked with a long history of working-class people and immigration, which has shaped its landscape, economic life and spirit. What I like the most about Belleville is the way it has stayed popular and, to some extent, a refuge for all. From the Belleville Chinese community to to the heritage of the Paris Commune to the spirit of Belleville found in songs and music, don't ever forget: Belleville is Belleville!

By Donatien Schramm, a long-time Belleville resident and tour guide.

The 100 Nationalities of Belleville

HILLTOP NEIGHBOURHOOD HARBOURING A MELTING-POT POPULATION

It is said that there are 100 different nationalities living in Belleville. Arriving at Belleville metro station, it's obvious that the energy of the neighbourhood is quite different from some other areas in Paris. But how did the area become so diverse?

FRÉDÉRIC SOLTAN/GETTY IMAGES ©

Left, Middle & Right Belleville neighbourhood

Up until the early 20th century, Belleville was not as diverse as we know it today. Most families living in the neighbourhood then were from working-class families born and raised in and around Paris. The great works of Haussmann had chased some poorer families out of more central locations and the proximity of the main industries had attracted workers from further away. All in all, cheap housing had made Belleville a place of choice for industry workers.

It was those same circumstances that attracted a new foreign population in the 1920s. After WWI, mostly Polish, Turkish-Armenian, Belgian and Italian migrants came to live in Belleville. Then the 1930s marked the development of 'Yiddish Belleville' and its shoe-making industry with the arrival of the Ashkenazi Jews from Eastern Europe. At that time, both Belleville and Le Marais were Jewish quarters. Belleville still bears traces of this heritage through several synagogues close to the perimeter of Parc de Belleville. They are now shared with the Sephardi Jews, who arrived later in the 1960s, mainly from Tunisia.

The Making of an Immigration Quarter

The 1950s to '60s marked a turning point in Belleville's history of immigration. The combination of low rent, a need for a bigger labour force in the aftermath of WWII and the end of the Algerian War in 1962 led to important waves of immigration from North African countries. Very present in the commercial landscape, and benefitting from a strong linked network, those communities became so visible that, until the 1980s, the neighbourhood was mostly considered Arabic.

LEMBI/SHUTTERSTOCK ©

PAUL MAGUIRE/SHUTTERSTOCK ©

Despite the way some Bellevillois felt at the time, it's interesting to note that this didn't push away the descendants of other communities. In fact, what happened in Belleville is often what happens in areas where there are large migrant communities: when the second or third generation becomes more well-off, they leave the cheaper areas that had welcomed their parents. Other populations in need of cheap housing then come and inhabit the area.

Walking up rue de Belleville is like diving into a melting pot: Chinese shopkeepers, Kabil pizzerias, Mediterranean restaurants and Parisian cafes coexist in a bustling atmosphere.

The Rise of Chinese Belleville

History repeats itself. In the 1980s, people of Chinese origin came to Belleville, along with communities from African countries and the West Indies, attracted by cheap accommodation, though the area had fallen into disrepair. The Chinese impact on Belleville is obvious today. Relying on a strong community infrastructure, including shops, restaurants, game circles, cultural groups and activities and health networks, they created an appeal for the rest of the community, which in turn encouraged people to stay put when immigrants previously would have stayed only temporarily.

More recently, in the 1990s, people from Pakistan and the former country of Yugoslavia arrived in Belleville. Walking up rue de Belleville is like diving into a melting pot: Chinese shopkeepers, Kabil pizzerias, Mediterranean restaurants and Parisian cafes coexist in a bustling, multilingual atmosphere.

From Quarries to Gardens

Tucked away behind Belleville, the **Mouzaïa** district is almost impossibly picturesque, its small cobblestone lanes lined by charming houses draped in flowers and greenery. This neighbourhood used to be called Amérique. However, it had nothing to do with the USA, although legend has it that the limestone extracted from its quarries used to be shipped to the other side of the Atlantic. The name is likely to have come from the fact that the place was far away and not easily accessible to workers. The former quarries were exploited from the Middle Ages to the 1860s.

20 Gravestones & GREENERY

ART I HISTORY I NATURE

Originally designed like an English garden by neoclassical architect Alexandre Brongniart, Père Lachaise cemetery is not only the largest graveyard in Paris but also one of the most important reserves of biodiversity in the city, with more than 3000 trees and 500 animal species.

STOCKBYM/GETTY IMAGES ©

How to

Getting here Take the metro to Philippe Auguste (line 2), Père Lachaise (lines 2, 3) or Gambetta (line 3).

When to go The cemetery is open daily from around 8am to 6pm (hours change seasonally). Autumn is particularly beautiful with the changing foliage.

Main entrance Get off at metro Philippe Auguste to start your visit from the main avenue of the cemetery.

Take a map Maps of the cemetery are often available at the entrance, or can be found online.

HUANG ZHENG/SHUTTERSTOCK ©

PREMIER PHOTO/SHUTTERSTOCK ©

Left Monument at Theodore Géricault's grave **Far left top** Père Lachaise cemetery **Far left bottom** Jim Morrison's grave

Mindful of Nature When Napoléon Bonaparte declared the right of every citizen to be properly buried in 1804, he started the Père Lachaise cemetery project. Influenced by the Romantic movement, it was designed with curved alleys, a layered structure and an abundance of nature – so abundant that some tombs are being swallowed by giant roots today!

The Oldest is the Most Romantic An area of maple trees partly covers the oldest, 'Romantic' section, where many Romantic artists rest, including Chopin and Géricault. However, they're accompanied by older remains – the neo-Gothic tomb of cursed medieval lovers Héloïse and Abélard – and younger ones such as Jim Morrison's. Look for symbolic trees as you go: on the main avenue leading to Bartolomé's impressive memorial to his wife are green oaks – a symbol of longevity. Walk left, itowards 19th-century novelist Honoré de Balzac's sepulchre, and you'll pass under yew trees, which symbolise immortality. In spring, you'll see wildflowers, butterflies and red squirrels, which love yew trees. There's even a family of foxes living here.

Famous Residents Many celebrities are buried at Père Lachaise. Millions of visitors come each year to pay their respects to Sarah Bernhardt, Édith Piaf and Marcel Proust, among others. Some graves have become venerable shrines. Oscar Wilde's stone tomb, for example, became so damaged by lipstick 'kisses' left by visitors that a protective glass barrier had to be erected.

Fake Skeletons or Real Ghosts?

Like many graveyards, the Père Lachaise cemetery has its share of myths and supernatural stories. However, one tomb is related to a real ghost story. Look for a grave ornate with skulls, carrying the name Etienne-Gaspard Robertson. An abbot, but also a painter, illustrator, physicist and keen balloonist, he became an influential developer of phantasmogaria – an ingenious art show that used lanterns to create ghostly apparitions. His shows, in which he used magic lanterns to project skeletons and demons onto walls, was extremely popular in the Tivoli Gardens (now Saint-Lazare).

Listings

BEST OF THE REST

Belleville's Chinatown

Chez Alex Wenzhou €

A highly recommended restaurant, with a warm welcome, specialising in dishes from Wenzhou, a city near Shanghai. Try fried buns, sautéed aubergines and the *xiao long bao* (soup dumplings).

Guo Xin €

A family-run restaurant with some of the best, fresh homemade dumplings in Paris. Fillings vary from minced pork with vegetables, celery and beef, egg and shrimp, or simply vegetables only.

Chez Trois €

For lovers of spicy soups, this Chinese restaurant serves dishes from the north of Beijing and is generous with chilli. Conveniently located around the corner from Aux Folies.

Best Tofu €

A shop serving traditional silky tofu. Opt for takeaway as the shop is always full of locals lining up to get their daily tofu fix.

Global Flavours

Boubalé €€€

Chef Assaf Granit expands his culinary empire with a Marais hot spot inside the new Grand Mazarin hotel. Meaning 'my little darling' in Yiddish, Boubalé serves Eastern European Ashkenazi cuisine.

Bang Bang €€

Palate-tickling taste combinations are the name of the game at this tucked-away Belleville eatery. Chefs from Colombia and Denmark infuse the shared plates with more than a soupcon of spice.

Green Spaces

Jardin des Rosiers – Joseph Migneret

A hidden haven off rue des Rosiers, with bird houses and vines in a sign of the historical Jewish presence. Its name commemorates a school director who tried to hide Jewish children during WWII to keep them safe.

Gardens of the National Archives

Few people know that these gardens – among the most beautiful in Paris – are free to enter, although located within the National Archive Museum.

Pierre Emmanuel Natural Garden

A tiny garden dedicated to wildflowers, which could be seen across the city when Paris was less urbanised. The garden adjoins the southern tip of Père Lachaise cemetery.

Cake Shops & Tearooms

Le Loir dans la Théière €€

A very popular cake shop with a large selection of pies and fruit tarts. Go for its extraordinary lemon tart: the meringue layer will be at least four times as high as the curd!

Une Glace à Paris €€

Founded by two pastry chefs with a passion for ice cream, this excellent ice-cream parlour is also a creative shop where ice cream is constantly reinvented into cakes.

Bontemps La Pâtisserie €€

An elegant, flowery tearoom with an almost countryside feel. The ingredients are inventive and the combination of flavours is bold. Try the *sablé* biscuits (shortbreads) and seasonal tarts.

Cocktails & Lively Bars

Sherry Butt €€

Cocktail connoisseurs will enjoy this trendy, dimly lit cocktail bar in Le Marais. Often crowded in the evening.

La Bellevilloise €

A very popular venue for concerts, dancing, drinks and Sunday jazz brunches, as well as exhibitions, conferences and even balls.

Le Perchoir Ménilmontant €€

Great for sunny after-work drinks, this party rooftop was a first of its kind in the area. It's now appreciated by locals too and, although spacious, it fills up fast on beautiful days.

La Sardine €

Located on a small village-like square, this pleasant bar is perfect for people-watching and 'reinventing the world', as the French say, through passionate conversation.

Aux Folies €

A young Édith Piaf sang here when it was a cabaret. The bar-cafe has held onto its local popularity.

Art & Photography

Musée de la Chasse et de la Nature

This eclectic museum offers a chance to consider nature, animals and our relationship to them. Located in an immense restored mansion in Le Marais.

Musée Cognacq-Jay

Inside the Hôtel Donon, this bijou museum displays a treasure trove of artwork and *objets d'art* collected by Ernest Cognacq and his wife Louise Jay.

Maison Européenne de la Photographie (MEP)

An exhibition venue, with a library and auditorium, dedicated to photography. It's one of the largest specialised libraries in Europe.

Jardin des Rosiers – Joseph Migneret

Crafts & Shopping

Village Saint-Paul

A hidden labyrinth of alleys and small courtyards. These jewellers, craft shops and small restaurants keep the shopkeeping tradition of Le Marais alive.

Papier Tigre

A creative stationery brand that doesn't just make simple notebooks, but also 'stationery tools' for thinkers and artists. Its collection is renewed every season.

LGBTIQ+ Venues

Tata Burger €

A fun restaurant with very suggestive burgers served by more than extroverted waiters, and that's all good!

Le Freedj

A small gay bar/nightclub, recommended for a younger crowd, though anyone is welcome. Two levels of good music with a highly festive atmosphere.

Duplex Bar

Highly recommended for a chilled evening, with an arty touch as paintings are often exhibited on the walls. A welcoming and friendly place.

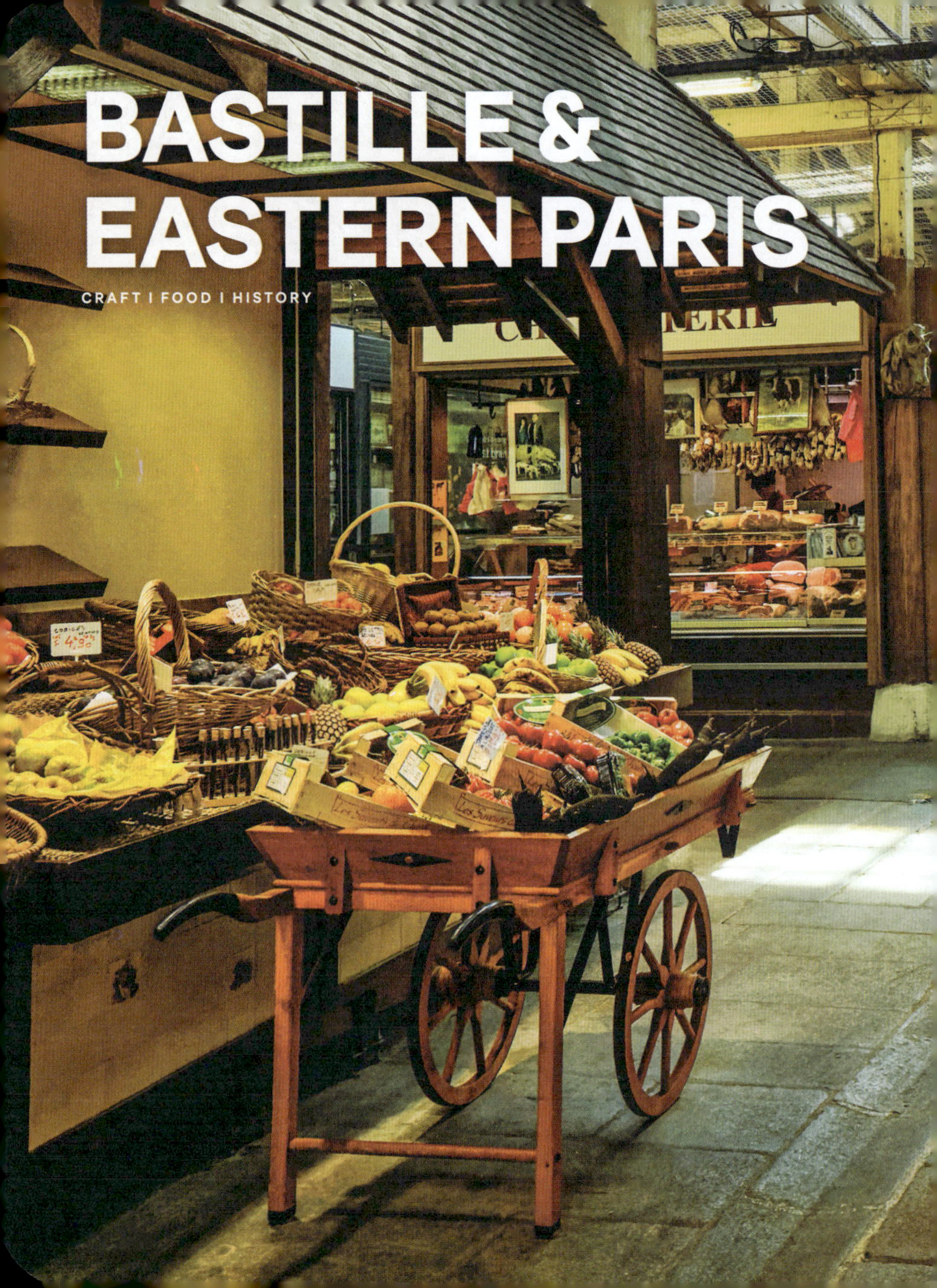

BASTILLE & EASTERN PARIS

CRAFT | FOOD | HISTORY

- **Green Line Rambles** (p124)
- **The Urban Farms of Paris** (p126)
- **Saint-Antoine's Artisans** (p128)
- **A Brief Guide to Cheese** (p130)
- **Market Finds at Aligre** (p132)
- **Listings** (p134)

BASTILLE & EASTERN PARIS

Trip Builder

TAKE YOUR PICK OF MUST-SEES AND HIDDEN GEMS

With a strong heritage of artisanship, the 11e and 12e arrondissements around Bastille have retained their popular and village-like atmosphere, welcoming artists and new shopkeepers alike. Local communities are very active, bringing a lively feel to the district's charming restaurants, bars and workshop yards.

Trip Notes

Best for Nightlife and convivial dinners, secret courtyards and soothing strolls in urban gardens.

Transport Metro Bastille or Charonne.

Getting around Walking is best so you don't miss any alley or courtyards you'd like to pop into.

Tip Head to bars and cafes north of place de la Bastille – around Parmentier – for a more relaxed local vibe.

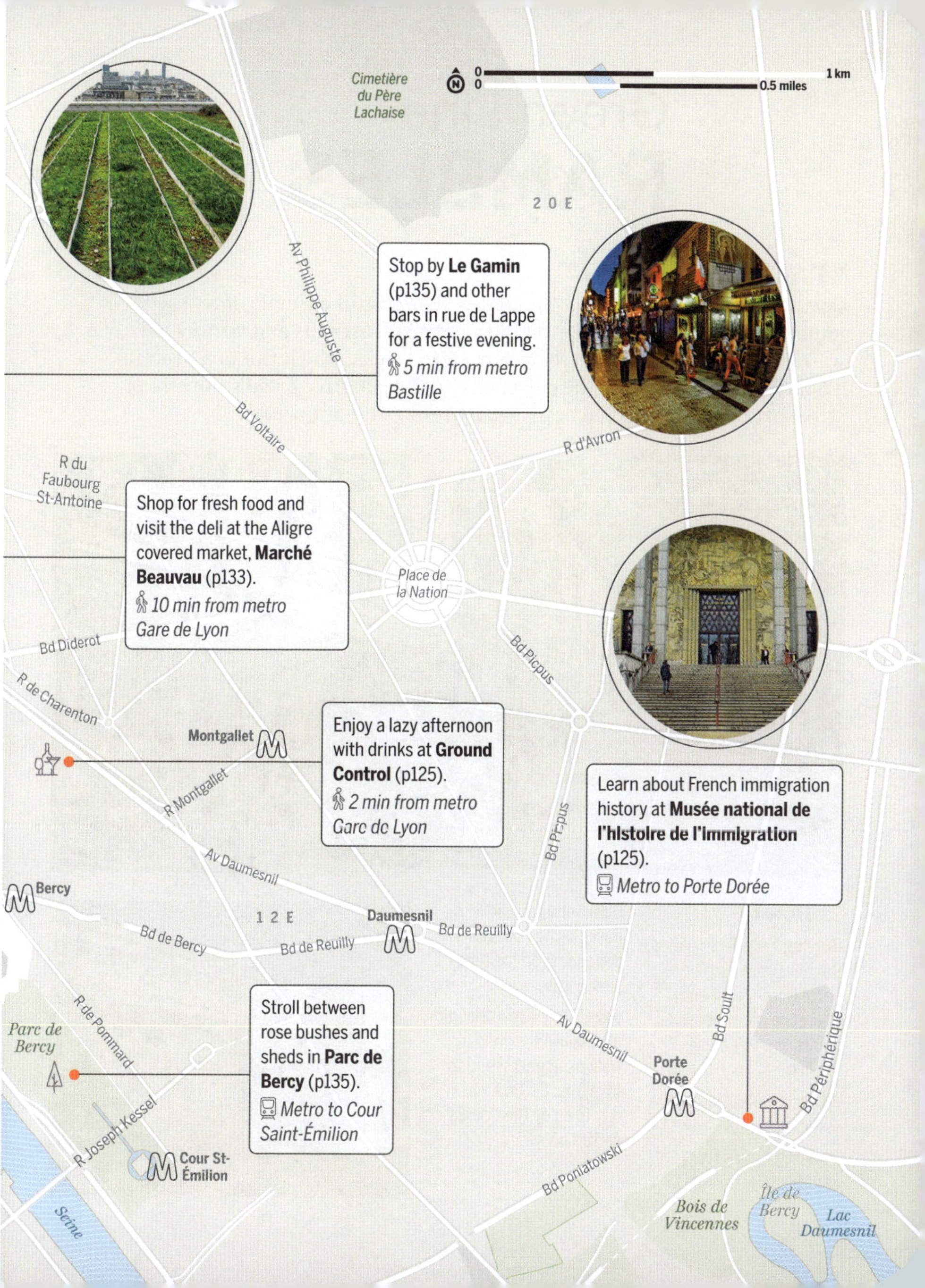

Cimetière du Père Lachaise
0 1 km
0 0.5 miles
20E
Av Philippe Auguste
Stop by **Le Gamin** (p135) and other bars in rue de Lappe for a festive evening.
5 min from metro Bastille
Bd Voltaire
R d'Avron
R du Faubourg St-Antoine
Shop for fresh food and visit the deli at the Aligre covered market, **Marché Beauvau** (p133).
10 min from metro Gare de Lyon
Place de la Nation
Bd Diderot
R de Charenton
Bd Picpus
Montgallet
Enjoy a lazy afternoon with drinks at **Ground Control** (p125).
2 min from metro Gare de Lyon
R Montgallet
Learn about French immigration history at **Musée national de l'histoire de l'immigration** (p125).
Metro to Porte Dorée
Av Daumesnil
Bd Picpus
Bercy
12E
Daumesnil
Bd de Bercy
Bd de Reuilly
Bd de Reuilly
R de Pommard
Stroll between rose bushes and sheds in **Parc de Bercy** (p135).
Metro to Cour Saint-Émilion
Parc de Bercy
Av Daumesnil
Bd Soult
Porte Dorée
Bd Périphérique
R Joseph Kessel
Cour St-Émilion
Bd Poniatowski
Seine
Bois de Vincennes
Île de Bercy
Lac Daumesnil

21 Green Line RAMBLES

WALK I GARDENS I STREET ART

The Coulée verte René-Dumont is a successful example of regenerated industrial infrastructure from the 19th century. Parisians and visitors alike can walk – and partly cycle – these ancient train tracks, which run in a peaceful 4.5km green stretch from the city centre to the suburbs. Artist's workshops, street-art murals and collaborative gardens dot the promenade.

BRUNO DE HOGUES/GETTY IMAGES ©

How to

Getting here From metro Bastille (west end) or Porte Dorée (east end). There are many possible points of entry along the line.

When to go Spring and summer.

Opening hours From 8am Monday to Friday, 9am Saturday and Sunday: closing hours vary depending on the time of year and season.

Jogging space Although it's mainly designed for walkers, joggers tend to take over. Go on a weekday to enjoy the Coulée verte slowly.

HEMIS/ALAMY STOCK PHOTO ©

The **Coulée verte** was created on an old train line. Opened in 1993, it was the world's first elevated park walkway.

Viaduc des Arts The gardens were initially a 19th-century viaduct and you'll be above the ground for the stretch between the Bastille and the **Jardin de Reuilly**. The arches beneath have been converted into a series of workshops, known as the **Viaduc des Arts**, so don't hesitate to head down – and up again – to discover trendy designers and artists, including glass-blowers.

Train Memories The section between the Jardin de Reuilly and **Square Charles Péguy** is where you can see some traces of the gardens' heritage as a train line. Slightly off allée Vivaldi, notice the building with turquoise shutters – it's an old train station. After a couple of tunnels decorated with commissioned street art, look for an old green-and-white building with a hexagonal roof – this old water tower was where steam trains used to stop to replenish their water supply.

The Circular Ring Other abandoned tracks were transformed into gardens, and the circular ring is still being regenerated by the City of Paris. It's easy to miss, but the Coulée verte hits another promenade at the former junction of both lines. The southernmost branch leads to the **Musée national de l'histoire de l'immigration**, and the other heads to the **Bois de Vincennes**, where you can row boats on Lac Daumesnil.

Far left top Viaduc des Arts **Far left bottom** Ground Control

A Food Court in a Former Rail Depot

Don't miss **Ground Control** if you're passionate about revamped industrial places. Located in a former rail depot belonging to the French national railway services, this is an immense space behind Gare de Lyon that now hosts food stalls, art exhibitions, pop-up shops, cultural events and DJs. Ground Control supports actions to avert the climate crisis, with a focus on the local, ethical and sustainable. Head there for drinks early in the evening if you want to find a seat, before the place get crowded and you need to line up to get a hot cone of crispy French fries.

The Urban Farms of Paris

EXPLORE A BUMPER CROP OF CITY SITES

In one of Europe's most densely populated cities, urban agriculture is having a moment. Unused spaces such as rooftops and car parks are blooming with greenery. These organic farms showcase the benefits of local food production, while combatting the effects of global warming. They're also a treat for the traveller.

Left & Right Nature Urbaine **Middle** BienElevées saffron cultivation

FREDERIC REGLAIN/ALAMY STOCK PHOTO ©

Crocus Up Top

The **Opéra Bastille** doesn't draw selfie-takers like the older Palais Garnier, in all its gilded glory, does. Built in the 1980s, the modern opera house overlooks the bustling place de la Bastille, which played a leading role during the French Revolution. But if only the photographers knew about the Opéra's rooftop farm. From this lofty perch, the panoramas are postcard-perfect, and the crop itself is an unexpected miracle for the milieu.

It's here that saffron is cultivated by **BienElevées**, a startup launched by four sisters. Requiring no irrigation, the *Crocus sativus* is surprisingly well adapted for urban cultivation. Sign up for a workshop (bienelevees.com) and you can taste a saffron infusion while learning about the plant's cultivation, culinary uses, medicinal properties and spicy legends. You can even help harvest the fragile flowers in October and November. The saffron is sold in pretty metal boxes in the e-boutique, alongside other gourmet products. It's also purchased directly by Paris chefs such as the *pâtissier* at the Lucas Carlton restaurant, who incorporates it into his award-winning desserts.

BienElevée operates a total of six Paris saffron farms, including on the rooftops of a Monoprix supermarket in the 13e and a school near Raspail.

A Green Movement

Saffron isn't the only crop germinating in Paris. With the support of the city government, farms are flourishing in unused spaces all over the capital. Microgreens are grown in parking garages (Wesh Grow uses hydroponics), craft brewers plant hops on public walls and a farm called

HEMIS/ALAMY STOCK PHOTO ©

FREDERIC REGLAIN/ALAMY STOCK PHOTO ©

La Ferme du Rail has sprouted in an old car junkyard next to the Petite Ceinture train tracks in the 19e. Many of these farms host fun activities and events open to the public.

The benefits are myriad: shortening food-supply chains, fostering biodiversity, fighting climate change by absorbing CO_2, reducing the city's so-called 'heat islands' and improving the energy efficiency of buildings. But perhaps most important of all is the community and educational component. The goal is not to feed the city in its entirety, since an immense surface area is required to grow food for such a big population, but to help build green consciousness and environmental awareness.

> From the Opéra Bastille's lofty rooftop farm, the panoramas are postcard-perfect, and the crop itself is an unexpected miracle for the milieu.

The World's Largest Urban Rooftop Farm

Situated on top of Paris Expo's Pavillon 6 at the Porte de Versailles, **Nature Urbaine** (NU) produces hundreds of kilos of fruits, vegetables and aromatic herbs in 14,000 sq metres of gardens. You can find its produce on the menu at the on-site **Le Perchoir** restaurant, which is an outpost of the trendy rooftop bars popular among Parisians. The produce is also sold locally to the grocery store, street market and neighbouring restaurants and hotels. Take a tour of the sprawling space, or sign up for a yoga class amid the greenery.

If you want to seek out other urban farms and gardens, search online for Parisculteurs, the City of Paris program that supports these green initiatives.

City Forests

From new cycling lanes to increased vegetation, Paris is undergoing a green revolution. Central to sustainability efforts is the often overlooked tree, with ambitious planting schemes in the works to mitigate the effects of climate change. The first such 'urban forest' is arising at **place de la Catalogne**, a square in the 14e that's undergoing a dramatic transformation from the concrete uniformity often criticised by residents. Announced in 2022, the 'Plan Arbre' will see some 170,000 new plants in six years – which corresponds to the expected number of births in Paris in the same period.

22 Saint-Antoine's ARTISANS

WALKING TOUR I ARTISANSHIP I ARCHITECTURE

Since the 15th century, the residents of the Saint-Antoine district have had a tradition of artisanship. First it was woodworkers and furniture makers, then boilermakers and people working with earthenware. In narrow alleys and courtyards, the artisans perfected their art. Today, many workshops remain and are gradually being invested in again by modern makers and artists.

JEROME LABOUYRIE/SHUTTERSTOCK ©

The Bastille Victors' Hometown

Mainly inhabited by working-class populations, the district of Saint-Antoine has long been the hearth of civil unrest. Each time a revolt is sparked, barricades spring from the ground in the neighbourhood. When the Bastille fell in 1789, almost 70% of the rebels were workers from Saint-Antoine.

Trip Notes

Getting here Take the metro to Bastille (lines 1, 5, 8); finish at Ledru-Rollin (line 8).

When to go Many of the old workshops are closed on weekends, so pick your day wisely or you may find doors closed!

Be discreet You will be visiting private alleys, some residential and some with actual workshops, so try to keep your photos and Instagram poses unobtrusive.

01 Originally an industrial site founded by an ironmonger, **Cour Damoye** then hosted many rag pickers and scrap dealers whose workshops were on the ground floor.

02 Abundantly green, **Passage Lhomme** (pictured far left) still hosts some old artisans' workshops, such as a comic book and toy shop.

03 Look for the many engravings and sculptures, symbols of the neighbourhood's industrial past, on **Passage de la Main d'Or**.

04 In picturesque **Passage du Chantier**, you will suddenly be immersed in the Bastille's surviving legacy of furniture makers.

05 Also known as 'Musketeers' yard', the red doors of the paved **Cour du Bel Air** are almost entirely covered in vines.

A Brief Guide to **CHEESE**

01 Saint-Nectaire
Originally made by women, a soft cow's milk cheese from the volcanic Auvergne region. Has a slight hazelnut taste.

02 Maroilles
Quite a strong-smelling cheese from the north of France, made from cow's milk. Tastes of spices and hazelnut – the smell can be stronger than the taste!

03 Crottin de Chavignol
A goat's cheese from the Loire valley. It becomes more crumbly as it ages.

04 Saint-Félicien
A creamy cow's milk cheese from the Rhône-Alpes region. Cousin of St-Marcellin, a smaller town in the same area.

05 Mont d'Or
Produced 700m above sea level in Haut-Doubs. Strapped into a spruce box, it's served cold or warm with white wine.

06 Tomme de Savoie
A cheese with an ancient history made from cow's milk in the French Alps region. Tomme from other regions exists.

07 Mimolette
Orange-paste cheese from the north made from cow's milk, originally inspired by Edam

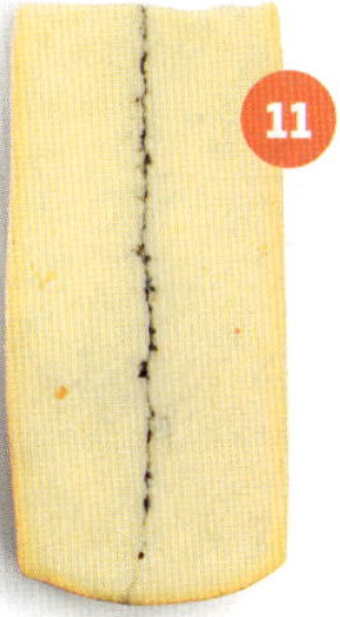

cheese. More salty and crumbly as it matures.

08 Roquefort
A blue cheese made from sheep's milk. Perfect with nuts, or spread on a fresh baguette. Stronger alternative: Bleu de Bresse.

09 Munster
A strong-smelling cow's milk cheese made in the Vosges mountains. Some eat it with cumin seeds.

10 Comté
From the Jura mountains, made from unpasteurised cow's milk. Delicious on a cheese board or melted, its taste is described as 'fruity'.

11 Morbier
Soft cow's milk cheese from the Jura mountains Sometimes used as an alternative to *raclette.*

12 Reblochon
A soft and creamy cow's milk cheese from Savoie. Famous in France for its use in the winter dish *tartiflette.*

13 Brillat-Savarin
A triple cream cow's milk cheese produced in Burgundy. Named after an 18th-century French gourmet.

23 Market Finds at ALIGRE

FOOD TOUR I DRINKS I CULTURE

Marché d'Aligre is referred to as the 'soul of the district'. Almost every morning, food vendors open their stalls at the covered Marché Beauvau, and there are three other sections here too: a more popular one outside in rue d'Aligre, an organic food area, and sellers of antiques and everything else on the semicircular square.

NOPPASIN WONGCHUM/SHUTTERSTOCK ©

How to

Getting here Take the metro to Ledru-Rollin, Gare de Lyon or Bastille.

When to go Marché d'Aligre is open 7.30am to 1.30pm Tuesday to Friday, and 7.30am to 2.30pm Saturday and Sunday.

French food souvenirs Besides delicious fresh produce, there are many tasty French food souvenir options, such as olive oil, cheese, mustard and spices, on offer in the market.

JOAO PAULO V TINOCO/SHUTTERSTOCK ©

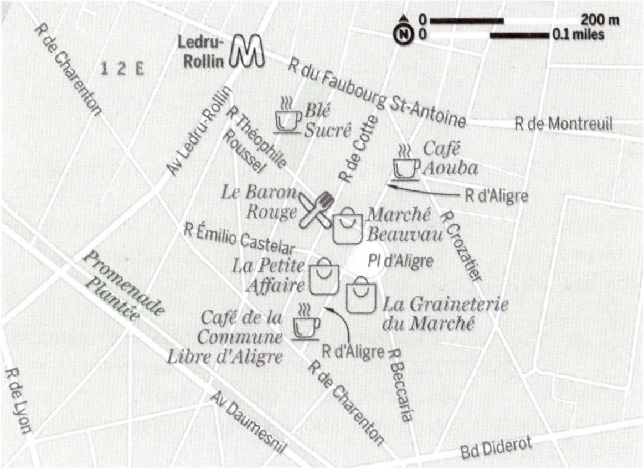

Far left top Fresh produce, Marché d'Aligre **Far left bottom** Wooden masks, Marché d'Aligre

A Long History Dating from the 1600s, Aligre is one of the Paris' oldest markets. Originally it supplied the area's artisan population, including the immigrant carpenters who worked on Louis XIV's decorative furniture at the Chateau de Versailles. Over time, it became a neighbourhood fixture, and still exudes a working-class spirit.

People-Watching with Croissants From 7.30am onwards, Aligre draws foodies wanting to taste and feel the local vibe of Faubourg St-Antoine. Start with a croissant from **Blé sucré**, a terrific bakery on nearby rue Antoine Vollon. Sit at a terrace for an early coffee and some people-watching around place d'Aligre, or stand at the bar at **Café Aouba**. Finally, walk into the orange-tiled **Marché Beauvau**. Classified as a historic monument, the building is home to venues such as **Early Bird Artisanal Coffee Roasters**.

Flea Market Shopping Already noon? Slurp some oysters at **Le Baron Rouge**, where glasses of wine are poured directly from wooden casks, then browse the secondhand items in the *puces*, or flea market, area of Aligre, where vintage treasure might be found amid the antiques, African masks and jewels. This *puces* tradition dates back to a royal edict allowing the poor to sell wares in areas outside the city; Aligre was not part of Paris at the time. Don't miss a shop called **La Graineterie du Marché**, an old-fashioned *épicerie* (grocery store) brimming with spices, condiments and other goodies.

Alternative Aligre

Aligre is not just an area, it's a whole community. Beyond giving the impression of a village, the super-local **Commune Libre d'Aligre** (Free Aligre Commune) association organises cultural and solidarity initiatives in the quarter. Named after the Paris Commune, it has a community cafe in rue d'Aligre, but opening times are unreliable. In the same street, other shops such as **La Petite Affaire** – a small supermarket known for encouraging the sale of close-to-best-before-date products at much lower prices – continue with a mindset of solidarity that's characteristic of the Aligre area, with its strong working-class heritage.

Listings

BEST OF THE REST

Cakes, Brunch & Coffee

Passager €

A cafe with a sweet selection of pancakes, ideal for relaxed brunches, with tartines and bagels, too. Located back-to-back with traditional paved alleyways.

Aujourd'hui Demain €€

A vegan restaurant with excellent cakes and vegan brunches. It's also a vegan concept store with deli, fashion, beauty care and stationery. Basically your ethical flagship store.

La Briée €

A shop specialising in French brioche from all regions. Eat in or take away. You can see the baking process in the open workshop.

Arts & Digital Culture

L'Atelier des Lumières

A venue dedicated to digital art located in a 19th-century renovated foundry. The space is often used for immersive light and sound exhibitions, taking advantage of expansive walls and ceilings.

La Cinémathèque

An often overlooked venue in Parc de Bercy, this museum is dedicated to the history of cinema and has become an important archive collection.

Small Kitchens

Mokonuts €€

Born from love, this family-run kitchen serves breakfast and refined fusion food for lunch (reservation highly recommended). You'll be charmed by Omar and Moko's warm welcome and talent.

Friendly Kitchen €

Try Fanny's vegan organic seasonal recipes, with Middle Eastern inspirations. There's lunch, dinner, brunch and gluten-free cakes. You'll also love how pretty everything looks.

Aï Hsu Table €€

A very small, exclusive address, with a limited menu. Aï serves refined Japanese family dishes, sometimes complemented by surprising ingredients. Reservation recommended.

Le Grand Bréguet €

An organic, local canteen and bar. Spacious and welcoming, it's also a venue for workshops and local events. Open all day; a great place to stop and refresh.

Crafts & Shops

Les Fleurs

In an old workshop tucked in one of the small industrial alleys, this charming design shop has a good selection of toys, accessories, jewels, homeware, clothing and stationery.

Mapoésie

Created by a designer in love with patterns and fabric, this shop sells colourful and geometrical clothes, scarves and accessories.

Creative Gastronomy

Table €€€

A discreet two-star Michelin restaurant near the Marché d'Aligre. The chef's motto: 'The way we eat decides the world we live in'.

Clamato €€

A popular, no-reservations seafood restaurant from the owners of Septime next door. Beyond the oysters and raw bar items, the small plates show off inventive ingredients.

Privé de Dessert €€

An original concept where you eat dessert first...or almost – with deceptive artistry, the chef designs starters and main courses in the shape of desserts, and vice versa.

Breaths of Fresh Air

Parc de Bercy

This beautifully landscaped park was built atop the site of a former wine depot known as the 'world's wine cellar' in the 19th century. Vineyards recall Bercy's wine-soaked history.

Bassin de l'Arsenal

Also known as the port de l'Arsenal, this pleasure-boat marina is located at the confluence of the Canal Saint-Martin and the Seine. It's flanked by a garden promenade that makes for a pretty stroll.

Square Charles Péguy

Filled with greenery and a children's playground, this terraced garden occupies a stretch of the old Petite Ceinture train line.

French Cuisine & Bistros

A l'ami Pierre €

A traditional bistro recommended by locals for its authenticity, where everybody is welcome. It serves French dishes such as snails and *andouillette* (tripe sausage).

Café de l'Industrie €

Two spacious restaurants and a wine bar with a simple but tasty menu that rarely changes: a safe bet for French food with a twist.

Bofinger €€

An iconic brasserie, serving Alsatian dishes. Go for the atmosphere and the art nouveau decor. With its mirrored walls and glass dome, it's a time-travel experience.

ELENA DIJOUR/SHUTTERSTOCK ©

Bassin de l'Arsenal

Lively Bars & Wine Cellars

Le Troll Café €

For beer connoisseurs. There's always a friendly atmosphere in this bar, which offers more than 100 different types of beer. It's appreciated by the locals and can get crowded, so plan for your rounds.

Le Gamin €€

In busy rue de Lappe, this bar specialises in whiskies and rums, with a selection of over 300 labels. Chill in the early evening; it can become festive as it goes on.

Agrology €

A deli specialising in Mediterranean products, with a tasty selection of natural wines and spirits. It's both a bar and a wine cellar, in a cosy venue off the Marché d'Aligre.

Live Music

Les Disquaires

A live-music bar with an eclectic program of events. Best for its jazz, soul and funk, African-Caribbean and Brazilian nights. A relaxed atmosphere, conveniently just a few minutes' walk from rue de Lappe.

THE ISLANDS

FOOD | CULTURE | HISTORY

- Exploring the Islands (p140)
- Notre Dame Splendour (p142)
- Silver Tower Magic (p144)
- Listings (p146)

THE ISLANDS
Trip Builder

TAKE YOUR PICK OF MUST-SEES AND HIDDEN GEMS

In the middle of Paris, on the Seine River, lie two islands: Île de la Cité, the historic heart of the city, and Île Saint Louis, an alluring island where life seems to take on a delightful, slower pace. These islands are a must for history buffs, Francophiles and all who want to experience the city's joie de vivre.

Trip Notes

Best for Exploring like a *flâneur,* revisiting history and mingling with locals.

Transport Line 4 to Cité, line 7 to Pont Marie, or the RER B or RER C to Saint-Michel Notre-Dame.

Getting around Explore the islands on foot.

Tip Carve out half a day to visit the islands; they're small but dense.

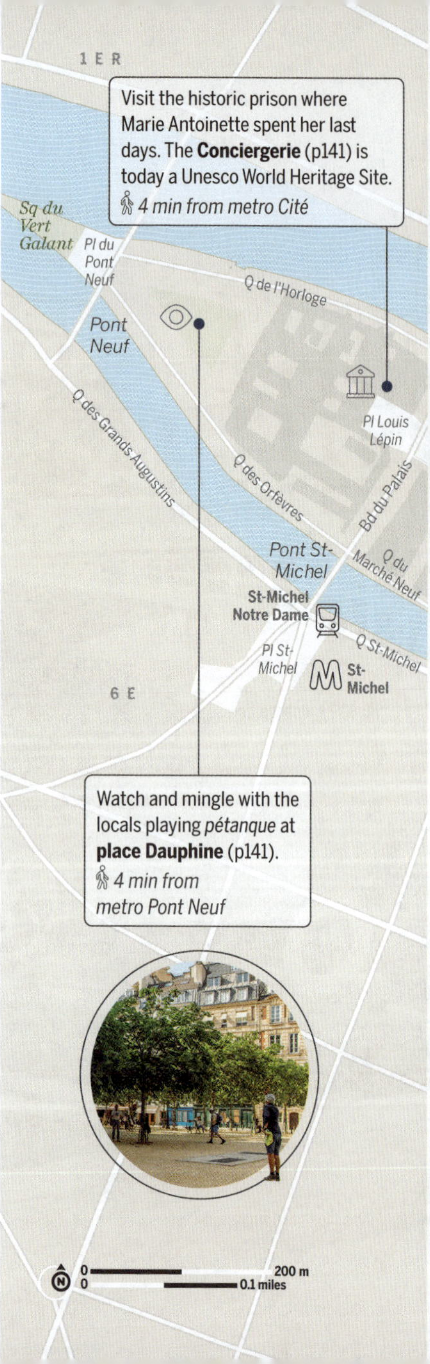

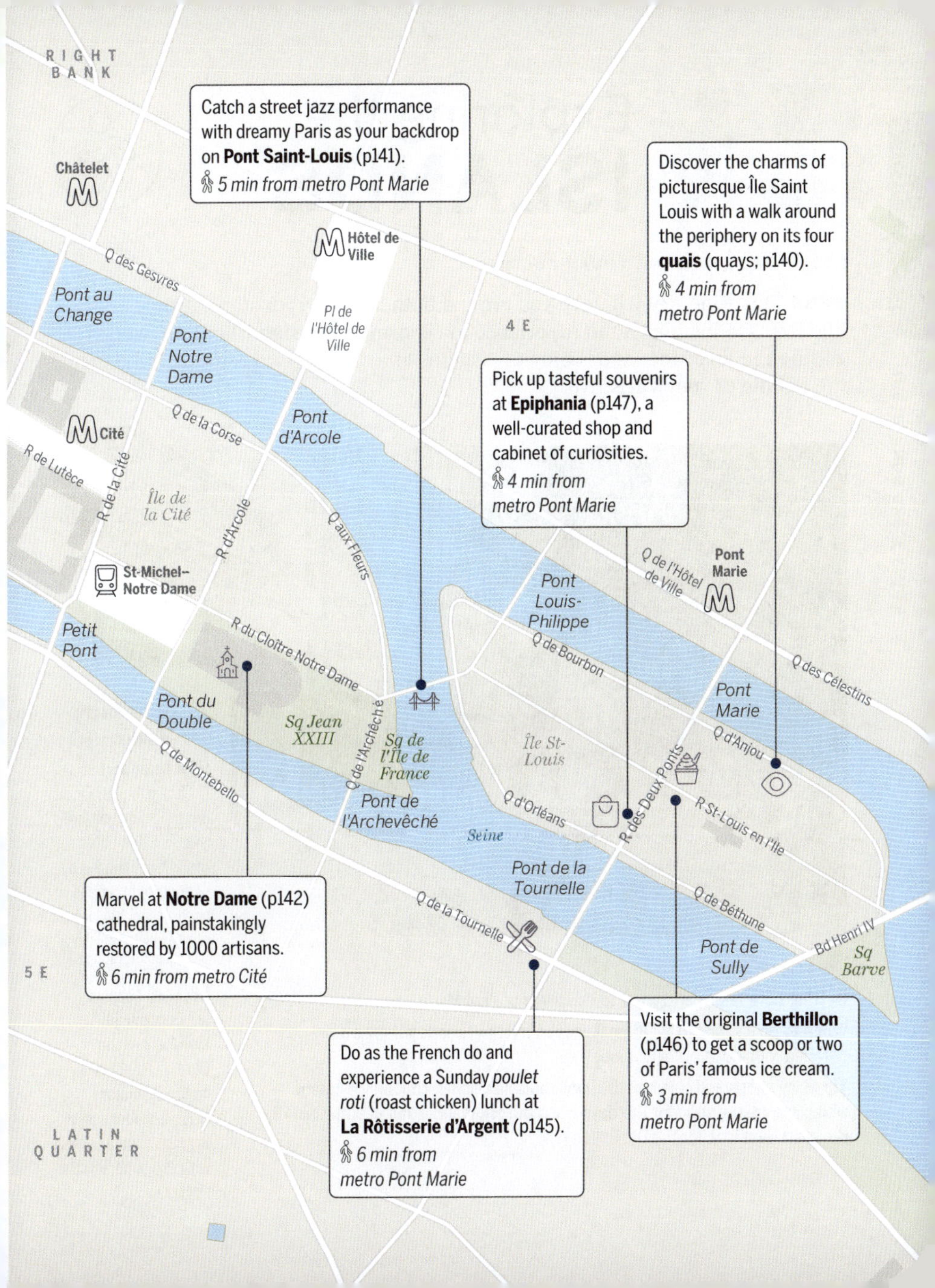
RIGHT BANK
Catch a street jazz performance with dreamy Paris as your backdrop on **Pont Saint-Louis** (p141).
5 min from metro Pont Marie
Discover the charms of picturesque Île Saint Louis with a walk around the periphery on its four **quais** (quays; p140).
4 min from metro Pont Marie
Châtelet
Hôtel de Ville
Q des Gesvres
Pont au Change
Pl de l'Hôtel de Ville
4 E
Pont Notre Dame
Pick up tasteful souvenirs at **Epiphania** (p147), a well-curated shop and cabinet of curiosities.
4 min from metro Pont Marie
Q de la Corse
Pont d'Arcole
Cité
R de Lutèce
R de la Cité
Île de la Cité
R d'Arcole
Q aux Fleurs
Q de l'Hôtel de Ville
Pont Marie
St-Michel–Notre Dame
Pont Louis-Philippe
Petit Pont
R du Cloître Notre Dame
Q de Bourbon
Q des Célestins
Pont du Double
Sq Jean XXIII
Q de l'Archêché
Sq de l'Île de France
Île St-Louis
R des Deux Ponts
Pont Marie
Q d'Anjou
Q de Montebello
Pont de l'Archevêché
Q d'Orléans
Seine
R St-Louis en l'Île
Pont de la Tournelle
Marvel at **Notre Dame** (p142) cathedral, painstakingly restored by 1000 artisans.
6 min from metro Cité
Q de la Tournelle
Q de Béthune
Bd Henri IV
Pont de Sully
Sq Barye
5 E
Do as the French do and experience a Sunday *poulet roti* (roast chicken) lunch at **La Rôtisserie d'Argent** (p145).
6 min from metro Pont Marie
Visit the original **Berthillon** (p146) to get a scoop or two of Paris' famous ice cream.
3 min from metro Pont Marie
LATIN QUARTER

24 Exploring the ISLANDS

LOCAL LIFE | WALKING TOUR | CULTURE

This itinerary will take you around both islands with stops at the highlights, allowing you to experience the charm of Parisian island life while getting the lie of the land. Enjoy the islands at a slower pace across a full day in the middle of your Paris trip.

JEROME LABOUYRIE/ SHUTTERSTOCK ©

Trip Notes

Getting here Take metro line 7 to Pont Neuf or Pont Marie.

When to go It's best to avoid weekends as the tiny islands get even more crowded with locals out and about.

Tip Many shops and cafes on Île Saint Louis also sell Berthillon ice cream, which is a great option for the days when the original Berthillon outlet (p146) is closed. Just look for the Berthillon logo.

Noteworthy Homes

Hôtel Lambert (1 Quai d'Anjou) Once inhabited by Voltaire, this Île Saint Louis mansion is owned by billionaire businessman Xavier Niel, who plans to turn it into a cultural foundation.

Hôtel de Lauzun (17 Quai d'Anjou) Members of the Club de Hashishins, including Victor Hugo and Alexandre Dumas, experimented with drugs here in the 1840s.

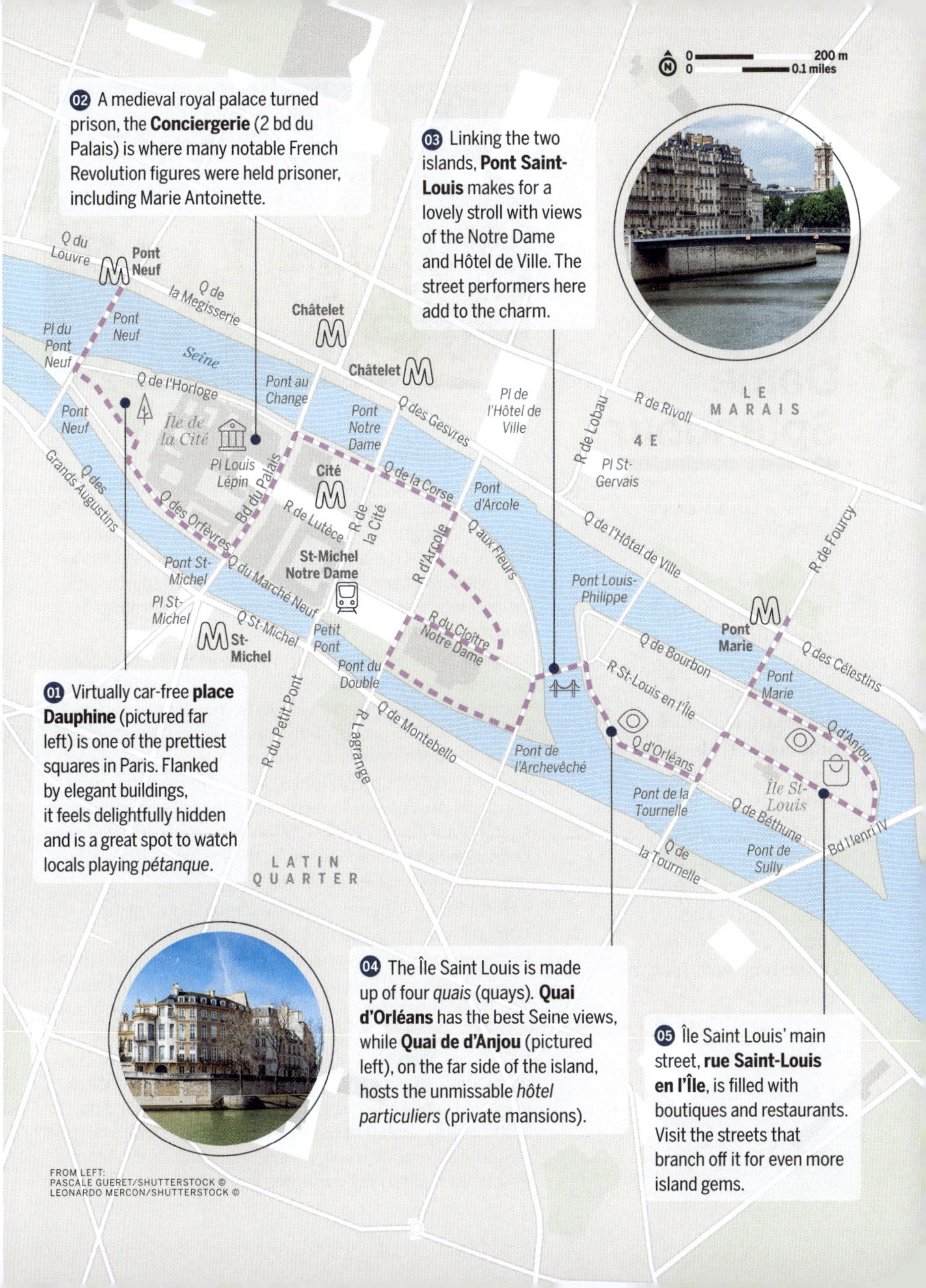

02 A medieval royal palace turned prison, the **Conciergerie** (2 bd du Palais) is where many notable French Revolution figures were held prisoner, including Marie Antoinette.

03 Linking the two islands, **Pont Saint-Louis** makes for a lovely stroll with views of the Notre Dame and Hôtel de Ville. The street performers here add to the charm.

01 Virtually car-free **place Dauphine** (pictured far left) is one of the prettiest squares in Paris. Flanked by elegant buildings, it feels delightfully hidden and is a great spot to watch locals playing *pétanque*.

04 The Île Saint Louis is made up of four *quais* (quays). **Quai d'Orléans** has the best Seine views, while **Quai de d'Anjou** (pictured left), on the far side of the island, hosts the unmissable *hôtel particuliers* (private mansions).

05 Île Saint Louis' main street, **rue Saint-Louis en l'Île**, is filled with boutiques and restaurants. Visit the streets that branch off it for even more island gems.

Notre Dame Splendour

THE BEATING HEART OF PARIS

The devastating fire of 15 April 2019 almost destroyed Notre Dame, the Gothic wonder on the Ile de la Cité. A pharaonic restoration project, enlisting 1000 artisans, has returned the much-loved cathedral to its former glory. Slated to reopen by the end of 2024, Notre Dame has wow factor aplenty.

Left Notre Dame under construction **Middle** Point Zéro des Routes de France **Right** Artist works on restoration projects

BORIS-B/SHUTTERSTOCK ©

Twelve million people can't be wrong. That was the estimated number of annual visitors to Notre Dame, a glorious vision of stained-glass windows, flying buttresses and whimsical gargoyles, prior to the fire. The cathedral is the city's geographic and spiritual heart, so much so that distances from Paris to every part of metropolitan France are measured from the cathedral square – a bronze star embedded in the forecourt indicates **Point Zéro des Routes de France**.

Construction on the cathedral began in 1163 on a sacred island site formerly occupied by an ancient Roman temple dedicated to Jupiter and later by a Romanesque basilica. It took nearly 200 years to complete the soaring masterpiece. The cathedral builders pioneered new medieval architectural techniques, such as iron reinforcements in the stone construction. The extraordinary sculpted facade, once painted in vibrant colours for an illiterate medieval public to read like a storybook, shows off the sublime balance that visitors have swooned over for centuries.

Notre Dame suffered immense damage during the French Revolution. The 28 statues of biblical kings, mistaken for French monarchs, were beheaded, and the pillaged cathedral was converted into a 'Temple of Reason'. The bells, except for the great Emmanuel bell, were melted down for ammunition. In this derelict state, the cathedral would have been demolished had it not been for the popularity of Victor Hugo's timely novel, *The Hunchback of Notre Dame,* which sparked a petition to save it. The 19th-century architect Eugène Viollet-le-Duc oversaw the restoration, embellishing the cathedral with marvellous flourishes such as the gargoyles and spire.

ZANE VERGARA/SHUTTERSTOCK ©

ANDY SOLOMAN/SHUTTERSTOCK ©

The Restoration of the Century

Following the 2019 fire that ravaged the roof and spire, the response from people all over the world was staggering: 340,000 people from 150 countries donated €846 million to rebuild the cathedral exactly as it was. The resulting construction project has been described as the *'chantier du siècle'* ('construction project of the century'). A total of 1000 specialist artisans have been employed: stonemasons rebuilding the vaults, stained-glass artists cleaning the medieval windows, and carpenters crafting the roof and spire from 2000 oak trees sourced from French forests. The project has thus been a showcase of artisanal savoir-faire.

> A total of 1000 specialist artisans have been employed: stonemasons rebuilding the vaults, stained-glass artists cleaning the windows, and carpenters crafting the roof and spire.

This epic feat will be accomplished in less than six years. The meticulous care with which the architects, artisans and scientists approached the project illustrates the fundamental importance of valorising heritage, not just for *les français* but for the entire world. Notre Dame isn't just a religious symbol and city icon, but also a place with an artistry and beauty admired by all. When you walk through the portal again, take the time not just to appreciate the precious artwork, but also to salute the craftspeople who have toiled over its restoration. Another project, to add more greenery and pedestrian zones to areas around the cathedral, is also in the works. The *parvis* (forecourt) will show off a new greener look in 2027.

Sublime Music

Beyond the art and architecture, experts have also been hard at work on restoring the cathedral's spine-tingling sound. Researchers are studying the complex acoustics in the vaulted space to reproduce and even improve the historical soundscape. Meanwhile, specialist organ artisans in three different French workshops have been cleaning the grand organ, an astonishing instrument that's the biggest in the country. The 8000 pipes have been completely dismantled. When the organ is reinstalled, the tuning will require six months – experts will do the job at night in order to have complete silence. When the cathedral reopens, concerts and organ recitals will again delight the public.

25 Silver Tower MAGIC

HERITAGE | GASTRONOMY | HISTORY

The restaurant that inspired scenes in Pixar's *Ratatouille* La Tour d'Argent (The Silver Tower) is also one of the oldest restaurants in Paris. This centuries-old establishment has fed royalty, dignitaries and celebrities from all over the world. Today, it has expanded into a mini-empire along the Quai de la Tournelle, so people on all budgets can experience the magic.

ERIC GARAULT/PARIS MATCH VIA GETTY IMAGES ©

How to

Getting here Take metro line 7 to Pont Marie.

When to go It's best to come here for lunch, so you can take in the views in daylight.

Tips All the provisions you need for your island picnics can be found at Le Boulanger de La Tour and La Petite Épicerie de la Tour. Reservations for the restaurants are required at least one week in advance.

ERICBERY/SHUTTERSTOCK ©

La Tour d'Argent This legendary, Michelin-starred restaurant offers the best bird's-eye view of the islands and monuments, including Notre Dame. At the kitchen's helm is Yannick Franques, a Meilleur Ouvrier de France. His 'Chef Imagination' lunch and dinner is an adventurous way to experience all the menu has to offer (the three-course lunch is the most affordable option and a great way to experience dining here). The wine list comes in a book that is more than 400 pages, showcasing more than 320,000 bottles in a cellar that survived WWII. Make sure you ask the staff about the special history of the place!

La Rôtisserie d'Argent This casual and homely rotisserie is La Tour d'Argent's bistro. At the menu's heart is roast chicken, but it also serves other classic French dishes such as beef fillet with bearnaise sauce. Like La Tour d'Argent, it serves duck from Challans, but at a fraction of the price, in two servings, two different ways. In the warmer months, the terrace by the Seine offers great views of Île Saint Louis.

Le Boulanger de La Tour La Tour d'Argent's bakery supplies bread for its restaurants, but is also open to the public. You'll find larger versions of the baguettes served in the Michelin-starred restaurant, classics pastries and sandwiches, such as its famed Jambon Beurre, that won't break the bank.

Left Duckling Frédéric Delair **Far left top** Crêpe preparation, La Tour d'Argent **Far left bottom** La Rôtisserie d'Argent terrace

La Tour d'Argent Menu Highlights

Pike Quenelles André Terrail Named after the current owner's grandfather, who purchased the restaurant in 1911, this is a must-try starter that comes with mushrooms and a delicious buttery, browned brioche.

Duckling Frédéric Delair One of the restaurant's specialities. Diners who order the duck receive a postcard with the bird's serial number, which also gets logged by the restaurant.

Cheese The selection exclusively highlights cheeses from the Ile-de-France region.

Crêpes Mademoiselle The servers make this dessert in front of you in the dining room on a cart. It's a performance you shouldn't miss.

Listings

BEST OF THE REST

Epicurean Gems on Île Saint Louis

La Ferme Sain-Sabin €

This no-frills cheese shop on Île Saint Louis is a great place to purchase French cheeses without feeling intimidated. The kind owner speaks English and will guide you in your selection.

Noir – Coffee Shop & Torréfacteur €

Founded in 2021, Noir is a coffee roaster with an atelier in the Saint-Ouen flea market and several coffee shops in the city, including on Île Saint Louis.

Fleuryan €

Île Saint Louis' one-stop shop for organic produce and ready-to-eat healthy meals, treats and juice. You can't miss its bright facade.

Berthillon €

Operated by the same family since the 1950s, the city's most famous ice-cream shop scoops up tempting flavours, such as salted butter caramel and wild strawberry.

Latiffe Foie Gras €

Latiffe has been supplying top chefs and gourmets all over the globe with their foie gras for more than 100 years. Its tiny Île Saint Louis boutique offers a large selection of its products.

Island Bites

Poget & De Witte €€

Named after the owners – the head of the seafood department at Galeries Lafayette Paris and an oyster fisherman – this tiny seafood shop on Île Saint Louis has the best oysters in town.

Les Fous de l'île €€

A classic spot with chicken-themed decor on Île Saint Louis that offers fresh, seasonal cuisine made with locally sourced ingredients.

Ha Noi 1988 €

Travel to Hanoi at this vibrant Vietnamese restaurant on Île de la Cité. The menu highlights northern Vietnamese cuisine – the Vietnamese coffee is a must.

Le Saint-Regis €€

This legendary Île Saint Louis institution is the picture-perfect example of an iconic Parisian bistro. Even if you don't eat here, stop by for a drink to at least experience the Saint-Regis.

Le Sergent Recruteur €€€

Chef Alain Pégouret, who trained under Joël Robuchon, has helped make Île Saint Louis a must-visit destination for fine-dining enthusiasts with his Michelin-starred restaurant.

KHANA €

This Afghan restaurant on Île Saint Louis serves up traditional dishes with modern touches. The portions are generous and the service is warm.

Le Saint-Regis

Les Deux Colombes €

This charming restaurant on Île de la Cité, with gorgeous views of the Seine and Hôtel de Ville, offers delicious comfort foods using high-quality ingredients. Its lunch *formules* (fixed-price menus) are affordable and filling.

Curious Boutiques

Epiphania

This cabinet of curiosities opened in 2021 on Île Saint Louis and is filled with well-curated souvenirs and trinkets sourced from all over the world, including some vintage finds.

Papeterie Gaubert

This *papeterie* (stationery shop) has been a Parisian institution since 1830. Its shop on Île de la Cité is a bazaar for stationery lovers. It still sells the light-blue Japanese paper that Colette sourced exclusively here by weight!

Librairie Ulysse

This bookshop on Île Saint Louis is dedicated to travel and will inspire wanderlust for days. You'll find maps, travel guides, books, magazines, postcards from all over the world and more.

Opulence Luxury & Vintage

This high end vintage shop on Île Saint Louis sells designer goods in pristine condition at fair prices. You'll find a great selection of bags, fashion jewellery, accessories and clothing from brands such as Hermès and Chanel.

Raphaël Bedos Antiquités

Visiting antique shops in Paris can be nerve-racking, but not here. This friendly gallery shop on Île de la Cité has an impressive museum-quality collection of treasures dating back to the Middle Ages.

La Sainte-Chapelle

Other Island Delights

Marché aux Fleurs – Reine-Elizabeth II

In 1808 Napoleon decided to build a flower market on Île de la Cité. Today, one of the largest flower markets in the world, here you'll find flowers, plants, garden decor, and a bird market on Sunday. Renovations are due to take place from 2023 until 2025, but the market will remain open.

La Sainte-Chapelle

This Gothic chapel, built in the mid-13th century, is widely considered the finest in France. Many visitors come for the stained-glass windows that make up the walls.

Square du Vert-Galant

Located past Pont Neuf at the tip of Île de la Cité, this park is magical. The majestic weeping willows and the secluded feel add to the appeal of the place.

Crypte Archéologique de l'Île de la Cité

Under the square in front of Notre Dame lies a subterranean museum housing ancient treasures dating back 2000 years to the Gallo-Roman period, found during archeological excavations.

26 A Day along THE SEINE

BOATS | MUSIC | SUMMER

Sightseeing cruises are a popular tourist attraction, but there are other ways to get up close and personal with the majestic river that cuts through Paris' heart. From dancing to jogging, the Seine's pedestrianised *quais* (quays) serve as a playground for Parisians. And the moored *péniches,* or river barges, double as floating restaurants and culture venues.

HEMIS/ALAMY STOCK PHOTO ©

How to

Getting here Easily accessible by metro at multiple stops.

Paris Plages This annual event pops up in summer to console those unable to escape for a coastal holiday. The 'beach' is installed on the Right Bank beneath the Hôtel de Ville and also at the Bassin de la Villette. Along with deck chairs and parasols, you'll find *pétanque* games and foosball tables.

Tip The pedestrianised *quais* can become busy with two-wheeled traffic – if you're walking, keep a lookout for bikes.

PATRICK BRUCHET/PARIS MATCH VIA GETTY IMAGES ©

Far left top Rosa Bonheur sur Seine
Far left bottom quai Saint-Bernard

Watch a Concert on a Boat Take your pick of party *péniches* (barges). **L'Improviste** is a jazz club; **Rosa Bonheur sur Seine** is a restaurant-cum-dance-hall; **Bateau Phare** is a lighthouse lounge; and **Bateau El Alamein** and **Petit Bain** are music venues. You can also catch concerts at **OFF Paris Seine**, a floating hotel near the Gare d'Austerlitz. **La Démesure Sur Seine** offers two locations for dining, dancing and live music. Many of these moored boats have terraces on terra firma, so the party can spill over onto the *quais*.

Free Floating Art Museums Near Pont des Invalides, **Fluctuart** is devoted to street art, with a permanent collection showcasing works by Invader, Keith Haring and Shepard Fairey. Enjoy cocktails with a view on the roof deck. Also free, **Le Quai de la photo** is all about contemporary photography. Moored in front of the Bibliothèque nationale de France, the barge doubles as a bar and restaurant, with small boats departing from its built-in marina.

Summer Fun The riverbanks come alive each summer with open-air dancing and pop-up *paillotes* (beach bars). Near the outdoor sculpture garden, the **quai Saint-Bernard** is a destination for tango dancing. Seasonal venues pulse in the 13e, and the vibe is also fun in the 12e at spots such as **Cargo Container Bar**.

Street Fishing

Even before the massive Seine cleanup project (p15), anglers were casting lines in the river's murky depths. A number of groups and organisations – coordinating through social media – assemble anglers on the banks for catch-and-release fishing, and sometimes competitively. Street fishing is, in fact, a new urban movement, as nature-loving urbanites have realised it's not necessary to leave Paris to partake in the sport they love. These anglers also serve as sentinels of the aquatic environment, observing first-hand the return of species such as Atlantic salmon due to the improved water quality.

THE LATIN QUARTER
CINEMA | BOOKS | CULTURE
ONVENTION NATIONALE
Experience the Latin Quarter online

- **Arab Allure** (p154)
- **Exploring the Latin Quarter** (p156)
- **The Roving Cinephile** (p160)
- **Listings** (p162)

THE LATIN QUARTER
Trip Builder

TAKE YOUR PICK OF MUST-SEES AND HIDDEN GEMS

Named after the original scholars who flocked here from all over Europe and communicated in Latin, this neighbourhood on the Left Bank remains the intellectual centre of Paris. Home to universities, bookshops and arthouse cinemas, the Latin Quarter is the best place to get a glimpse of the historically bohemian side of the city.

Trip Notes

Best for Wandering and bookshop visits.

Transport Metro to Place Monge or Cluny–La Sorbonne.

Getting around The Latin Quarter's small alleys are best explored on foot.

Tip The area is steeped in literary history. Look for James Joyce's flat (71 rue du Cardinal Lemoine) as well as Ernest Hemingway's (74 rue du Cardinal Lemoine).

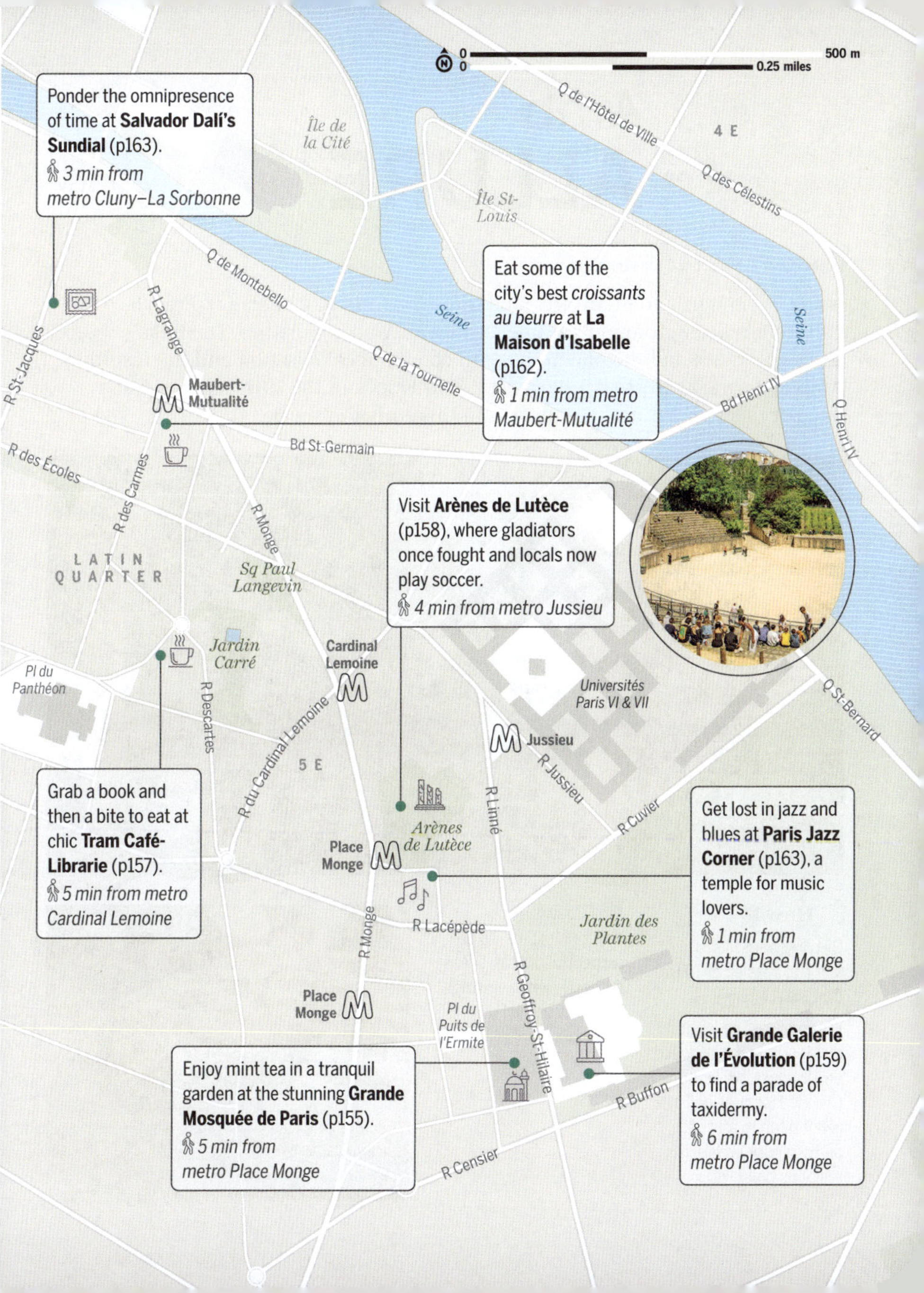
0 500 m
0 0.25 miles
Ponder the omnipresence of time at **Salvador Dalí's Sundial** (p163).
3 min from metro Cluny–La Sorbonne
Île de la Cité
Île St-Louis
Q de l'Hôtel de Ville
4 E
Q des Célestins
Q de Montebello
Seine
Q de la Tournelle
Eat some of the city's best *croissants au beurre* at **La Maison d'Isabelle** (p162).
1 min from metro Maubert-Mutualité
Seine
Bd Henri IV
Q Henri IV
R St-Jacques
R Lagrange
Maubert-Mutualité
R des Écoles
Bd St-Germain
R des Carmes
R Monge
LATIN QUARTER
Sq Paul Langevin
Visit **Arènes de Lutèce** (p158), where gladiators once fought and locals now play soccer.
4 min from metro Jussieu
Jardin Carré
Cardinal Lemoine
Pl du Panthéon
R Descartes
R du Cardinal Lemoine
Universités Paris VI & VII
Q St-Bernard
Jussieu
R Jussieu
5 E
Grab a book and then a bite to eat at chic **Tram Café-Librarie** (p157).
5 min from metro Cardinal Lemoine
R Linné
R Cuvier
Get lost in jazz and blues at **Paris Jazz Corner** (p163), a temple for music lovers.
1 min from metro Place Monge
Arènes de Lutèce
Place Monge
R Lacépède
Jardin des Plantes
R Monge
R Geoffroy-St-Hilaire
Place Monge
Pl du Puits de l'Ermite
Visit **Grande Galerie de l'Évolution** (p159) to find a parade of taxidermy.
6 min from metro Place Monge
Enjoy mint tea in a tranquil garden at the stunning **Grande Mosquée de Paris** (p155).
5 min from metro Place Monge
R Buffon
R Censier

27 Arab ALLURE

HAMMAM | ART | RESTAURANTS

From music to literature, food to *verlan* (an argot or slang), French culture has been profoundly influenced by its Arab population. The links between France and the Maghreb are anchored in colonisation and the resulting Arab diaspora, as North Africans flocked to France in the 20th century. Get a taste of this rich cultural cornucopia in this corner of the 5e.

FRANCK LEGROS/SHUTTERSTOCK ©

How to

Getting here Metro line 7 to Jussieu or 10 to Cardinal Lemoine.

When to go The Institut du Monde Arabe is closed on Mondays, while the Grande Mosquée de Paris is not open to tourists on Fridays or on Islamic religious holidays.

Tip Friday is a holy day for Muslims, so be respectful of that. Dress modestly when visiting the mosque.

PICTURE PARTNERS/SHUTTERSTOCK ©

IMAGODENS/SHUTTERSTOCK ©

Left & Far left top Grande Mosquée de Paris **Far left bottom** *Pastilla*

Institut du Monde Arabe (IMA) Jointly founded by France and 18 Middle Eastern and North African nations in 1980, with the aim of promoting cross-cultural dialogue, the IMA hosts museum galleries, concerts, film screenings and a research centre. Atop this stunning Jean Nouvel–designed landmark is an observation deck that affords views stretching across the Seine. French-Moroccan actor Jamel Debbouze is behind the chic panoramic restaurant **Dar Mima-Ziryab**, a homage to his mother Fatima. On the gourmet menu are *pastilla* (North African pie), couscous and tasty tagine.

Art Deco Mosque The **Grande Mosquée de Paris** is an oasis open to the public. Visitors can walk in and admire the gorgeous mosaics and tiles, experience the North African hammam (steam bath; women only) and enjoy mint tea with flaky pistachio pastries and orange blossom desserts in the tranquil garden. Moderate dress is required for entry.

Tunisian Tastes & Algerian Sweets There are several relaxed eateries around the mosque serving North African cuisine. **Al Mosaic**, a friendly Tunisian spot, is instantly recognisable by the street art on the wall outside: the 'Space Invader' is wearing a *chechia*, the traditional Tunisian red hat. Eat in or order takeaway dishes to eat in the **Jardin des Plantes**. To cap it off, try the delicate Algerian pastries at **Laouz** on rue Mouffetard. The *maison* enhances classic recipes with creative ingredients such as poppy and yuzu.

Amazing Architecture

The IMA's design brought international fame to architect Jean Nouvel when the building was inaugurated in 1987. He took his inspiration from traditional latticed wood windows, creating thousands of modern *mashrabiya* – photo-electrically sensitive apertures built into the glass walls that allow you to see out without being seen. These apertures are opened and closed by electric motors in order to regulate the amount of light and heat that reaches the institute's interior. A renovation when the building reached 30 years of age fixed this mechanism, which had ceased to function.

28 Exploring the Latin QUARTER

WALKING | HISTORY | GREEN SPACES

At the heart of the Latin Quarter lies the prestigious Sorbonne University, one of the world's oldest higher-education institutions, and the neighbourhood buzzes with student life. Lined with bookshops and affordable eateries, the narrow medieval streets are made for wandering.

CORTYN/SHUTTERSTOCK ©

How to

Getting here Metro to Place Monge

When to go This neighbourhood is busy all the time, but feels super packed around the middle of the day when the students are dismissed for lunch.

Tip Wear comfortable walking shoes, apply sunscreen and bring a refillable water bottle to keep yourself hydrated. The streets near place Monge are filled with speciality boutiques that are mostly frequented by locals. Let your eyes and curiosity lead you!

STEVE ESTVANIK/SHUTTERSTOCK ©

Musée de Cluny

A seven-year restoration project, unveiled in 2022, utterly transformed this much-loved museum dedicated to the Middle Ages. Filled with natural light, the building alone is a treasure – the 15th-century mansion incorporates ancient Roman baths on the lower level. The nearly 200-year-old museum is one of the city's oldest, and its collection is brimming with priceless medieval art.

ISOGOOD_PATRICK/SHUTTERSTOCK ©

The Panthéon

Completed in 1789, the neoclassical dome of the Panthéon is part of the iconic Paris skyline. It is a mausoleum for some of France's greatest citizens, including Marie Curie, Simone Veil and Voltaire. The interior is decorated with mosaics, intricate frescoes and grand paintings of French history.

Sip & Read

Tram Café-Librarie is a chic coffee shop and bookshop near the Panthéon. On one side, you'll find a curation of French books and on the other, a cafe with homemade baked goods, warm drinks and the best croque-monsieur (with truffle salt and Prince de Paris ham).

Left Panthéon interior **Above left** Musée de Cluny **Above right** Carved column capital, Musée de Cluny

Arènes de Lutèce

Cherished by local residents and unknown to most tourists, the ruins of Arènes de Lutèce date from the 2nd century CE, when Paris was named Lutetia. This Roman amphitheatre was discovered by accident in 1869 and is the city's oldest monument. Today, locals use the space where gladiators once fought as a public open space, picnicking, playing ball games and mingling with neighbours.

Rue Mouffetard

A vestige of an old Roman road, this lively market street is called 'La Mouffe' by locals. The cobblestone thoroughfare runs downhill for 650m from the Montagne Sainte-Geneviève. It's lined with boutiques, food shops, affordable restaurants, and bars filled with university students. The lower portion is home to market stalls (except on Mondays). The street served as a major inspiration for Victor Hugo when he was writing *Les Misérables*.

La Mouffe's Best Coffee Stops

Dose Get your caffeine fix at this hip coffee shop that roasts its own beans. There's a takeaway window where you can grab coffee and pastries to go, but you can also dine in for brunch. The terrace is sheltered under a covered passage with a direct view of the street – a prime spot for people-watching on La Mouffe.

Chinaski Located on an adjacent street, this restaurant named after Charles Bukowski's alter ego is a coffee shop serving brunch on weekends and a savvy bistro by night. The owner is a well-known bartender so don't miss out on its cocktails.

Far left Rue Mouffetard **Below** Grande Galerie de l'Évolution, Muséum National d'Histoire Naturelle

Natural Treasures

A collection of 13 different sites, **Muséum National d'Histoire Naturelle** is made up of zoos, museums, galleries and gardens throughout the Île-de-France region. The heart of the museum collection is in the Latin Quarter, which contains its most prominent spaces.

The 400-year-old **Jardin des Plantes** is a regal botanic garden covering 24 hectares where visitors can walk through and even study different plant species. It is France's main botanic garden and once served as a garden for medicinal plants under the authority of the king's physician.

In **Grande Galerie de l'Évolution**, you'll find an impressive parade of taxidermied animals, as well as skeletons and fossils. The building and renovated interior are themselves stunning and the museum layout is brilliant. It's a common misconception that this is a museum for children, because it's enjoyed by all ages.

For a taste of the tropics, head to the **Grandes Serres**. These sleek greenhouse structures are dedicated to four different ecosystems. For example, there's one 'desert' greenhouse where visitors will find succulents from Mexico, the Sahara, the USA and Australia, whereas the Grand Deco structure is home to the 'jungle' and filled with orchids and banana leaves.

29 The Roving CINEPHILE

CINEMA | CULTURE | BOHEMIAN

In France, especially Paris, going to the cinema to watch a film is, for many, an important part of weekly life. There are over a dozen cinemas, both mainstream and arthouse, concentrated in the Latin Quarter. Experiencing a classic or arthouse film in a historic cinema, with drinks before at an adjacent *terrasse* or cafe, is a quintessential Latin Quarter experience.

LOIC VENANCE/AFP/GETTY IMAGES ©

How to

Getting here Metro to Saint-Michel or Cluny–La Sorbonne.

When to go Check out film times and reserve your tickets in advance. Evening shows often sell out.

Tip In France, most art-house cinemas will play films in 'VOSTF', the original language, with French subtitles. If you want to catch a French film, but don't know French, check out Lost in Frenchlation (lostinfrenchlation.com), an organisation that holds screenings in Paris for French films with English subtitles.

PHOTO 12/ALAMY STOCK PHOTO ©

Le Champo Walking into the French New Wave HQ will give you the impression of following in the footsteps of François Truffaut or Claude Chabrol – a pilgrimage to the cinema of filmmakers! It's a privilege to still be able to watch films in such a symbolic theatre. Afterwards, grab a coffee at **Le Sorbon** on rue des Écoles and listen to the students debate (a favourite activity among the French).

Reflet Médicis One of the only places in Paris where you can find a good film to watch before 2pm. Make sure you check out the art deco stained glass in room 3. There's a cafe called **Le Reflet** just in front, in case you want a glass of wine while keeping an eye on the queue.

Cinéma du Panthéon Paris' oldest functioning cinema is also home to the **L'inconnu du ciné-club** event, where you can watch a secret film introduced by a secret guest. Upstairs in the salon is **Café Nouvelle Vague** with leather chairs, black-and-white pictures of famous French movie stars, and unique objects hunted down by Catherine Deneuve herself at the flea market. This is the best place to have a tea and leaf through *Les Cahiers du Cinéma,* a French magazine dedicated to film. Next door you'll find **Librairie du Cinéma du Panthéon** with a great selection of *cinélittérature* (books on cinema) and a jukebox playing film tunes.

Far left top Le Champo **Far left bottom** Cinéma du Panthéon

Paris & Cinema

Paris is absolutely crucial to cinema history, as the world's first public movie screening took place here in 1895. The concentration of cinemas in the Latin Quarter can be attributed to the fact that this neighbourhood was home to the 1950s Cineaste (filmmaker) movement. University students here also historically frequented the theatres in between classes. The May '68 protests, led by the students, helped cement film as an art form and not just entertainment. Paris is today home to 88 cinemas in total, a third of which are still independently owned.

By Manon Kerjean, *founder of Lost in Frenchlation. @lostinfrenchlation*

Listings

BEST OF THE REST

Memorable Meals

Le Reminet €€€

Tucked away in a quiet alley facing Notre Dame, this elegant bistro has been a neighbourhood fixture for 30 years. All red velvet and gilded mirrors, it oozes atmosphere.

La Bête Noire €

Homey and creative neighbourhood eatery that serves as a coffee shop with baked goods before and after lunch, and a bistro with a constantly changing lunch menu, driven by what's in season.

Han Lim €

One of the city's oldest surviving Korean restaurants, just a stone's throw from the Panthéon. This family-run place opened in 1981 and is known for its old-school Korean fried chicken and Korean bone broth soup.

Baieta €€€

When Julia Sedefdjian won her first Michelin star in 2019 at 24 years of age, she was the youngest starred chef in France. Her restaurant, the name of which means 'little kiss' in the Niçois dialect, reflects the southern origins of the sunny Mediterranean cuisine.

Kitchen Galerie Bis €€/€€€

The sibling restaurant of Michelin-starred Ze Kitchen Galerie serves up innovative French dishes with Asian touches. Think skilful additions of lemongrass bouillon and kimchi to classic French cooking.

Kodawari Ramen €

This ramen shop transports you to Japan with an interior space that is a reconstruction of Tokyo's vibrant alleys. The ramen is top-notch.

All-Day Treats

La Maison d'Isabelle €

Winner of the 2018 Best Croissant of Paris, this modest bakery is dedicated to only using organic flour and butter for its range of breads and exquisite, flaky croissants.

Fromagerie Laurent Dubois €

Laurent Dubois was the first cheesemonger to receive the Meilleur Ouvrier de France (Best Craftsman of France). His shops offer a fantastic selection of cheese, including their own cheese-pastry creations, a combination of their cheeses with other flavourful ingredients.

+82 €

This cute coffee shop sources its beans from a roaster in Jeju-do, South Korea and serves Korean-inspired sweets. Its *bingsu* (Korean-style shaved ice) and matcha cookies, made by its in-house, French-trained Korean pastry chef, are highlights.

Café Maa €

This gorgeous coffee shop with ample seating is located inside the Institut Finlandais. A great rest spot for delicious food and drink.

Red Wheelbarrow

Pierre Oteiza €

This artisanal Basque producer has the best *jambon* and saucisson you can buy. It sells grocery goods to take home, but also has fresh offerings: think sandwiches, individual charcuterie cones, and meat and cheese boards.

Books, Vinyl & Vintage

Shakespeare & Company

Located across the street from Notre Dame, this legendary shop is named after the original Shakespeare and Company bookshop, the meeting point for Hemingway's 'Lost Generation'. Note that this place gets incredibly busy. Its cafe next door offers healthy pastries, lunch and coffee.

Red Wheelbarrow

The Jardin du Luxembourg is reflected on the windows at this charming Librairie Anglophone with sliding ladders on the walls, run by the kind founder, Penelope. The shop has expanded, adding a children's bilingual bookshop called The Red Balloon.

San Francisco Books Co

This secondhand English-language bookshop near Odéon Theatre has an impressive selection of books on the city, with the best collected in a pile at the front of the shop.

Paris Jazz Corner

Hidden away on a quiet and beautiful residential street, this record shop is a temple for music aficionados. Here, you'll find an impressive jazz and blues collection of used and new vinyl and CDs.

Sous les pavés, le vintage

A quality secondhand clothing shop with two floors of higher-end pieces at affordable prices.

TELLY/SHUTTERSTOCK ©

Fontaine Saint-Michel

Abbey Bookshop

This atmospheric secondhand English-language bookshop occupies an 18th-century mansion tucked away on a pedestrian passage.

Other Neighbourhood Attractions

Fontaine Saint-Michel

The monumental Fontaine Saint-Michel is worth a quick visit before you enter or leave the neighbourhood as it's situated near the metro stations. Wall fountains are rare in Paris and this one, which depicts the struggle between good and evil, is considered the largest.

Bibliothèque Sainte-Geneviève

The world's first independent public library is open to anyone over the age of 18. Ask staff for a tour of the alluring library.

Salvador Dalí Sundial

There are 120 sundials scattered throughout Paris that often go unnoticed. This one is extraordinary because it was created and gifted by the surrealist artist Salvador Dalí himself. The artist even attended the unveiling of the sundial, accompanied by his pet ocelot and a brass band.

ST-GERMAIN DES PRÉS

HISTORY | FOOD | SHOPPING

Experience St-Germain des Prés online

- **The Chicest Shopping** (p168)
- **Left Bank Magic** (p170)
- **Painters & Paint** (p172)
- **Sweets on Rue du Bac** (p174)
- **Listings** (p176)

ST-GERMAIN DES PRÉS
Trip Builder

TAKE YOUR PICK OF MUST-SEES AND HIDDEN GEMS

This legendary part of Paris has attracted and nourished some of the world's most celebrated thinkers, artists, writers and musicians. Today it's a fashionable and upmarket neighbourhood with a creative spirit. Come for the history and art, stay for the food and shopping, and leave a bit more cultured.

Trip Notes

Best for Following the footsteps of cultural icons, eating the capital's food highlights, and shopping.

Transport Take line 4 to Saint-Germain-des-Prés station.

Getting around Best experienced on foot (or bus for longer distances).

Tip If you've ever heard that how you dress matters in Paris, it especially applies here.

Q d'Orsay
Take in one of the world's most impressive art collections at the **Musée d'Orsay** (p173).
8 min from metro Rue du Bac
Esplanade des Invalides
Indulge in a treat at the famous **Chocolat Chapon** (p175) mousse bar.
1 min from metro Rue du Bac
Shop till you drop at the world's oldest department store, **Le Bon Marché** (p169).
5 min from metro Sèvres–Babylone
N
0 500 m
0 0.25 miles

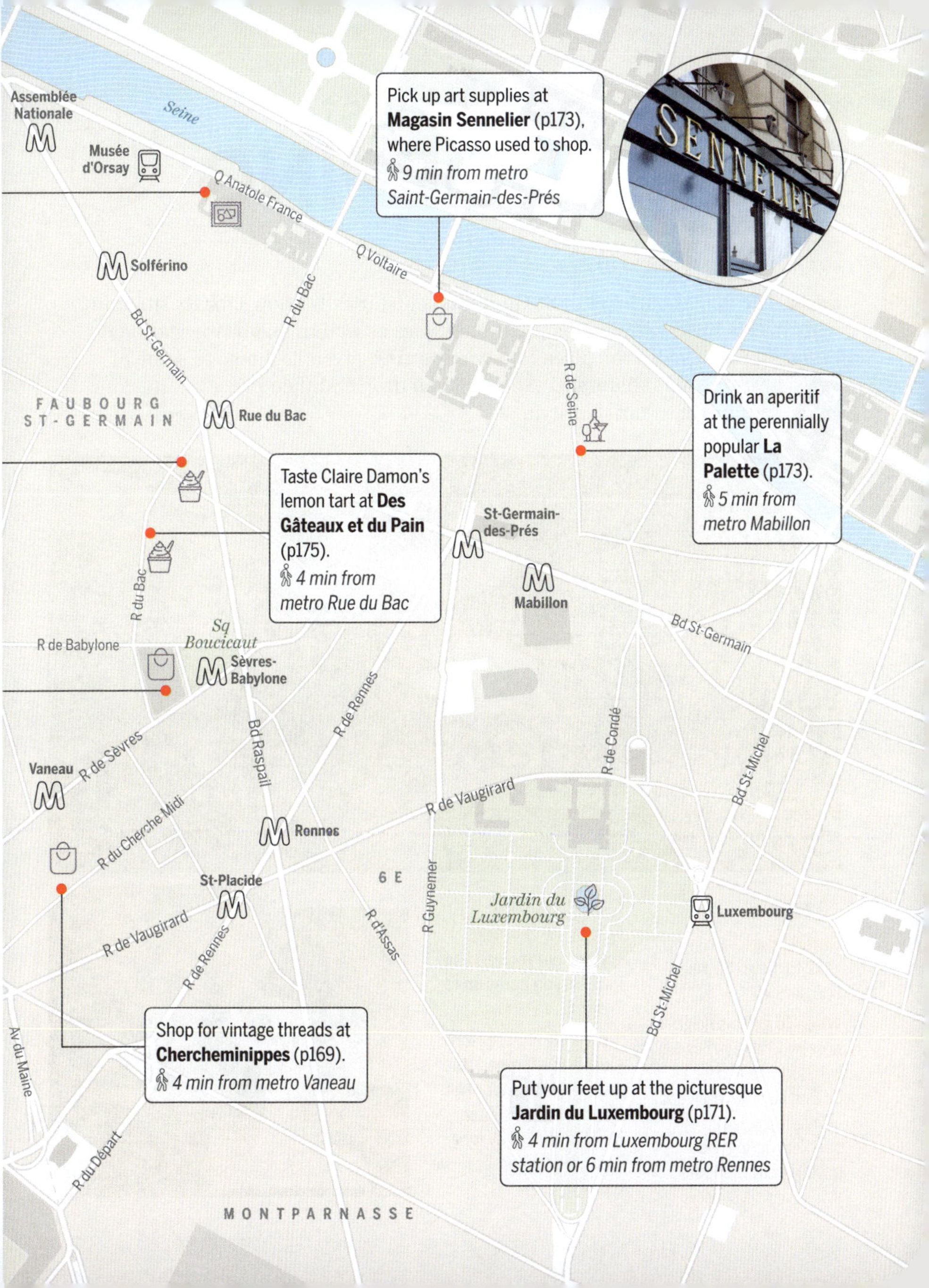

Pick up art supplies at **Magasin Sennelier** (p173), where Picasso used to shop.
9 min from metro Saint-Germain-des-Prés

Drink an aperitif at the perennially popular **La Palette** (p173).
5 min from metro Mabillon

Taste Claire Damon's lemon tart at **Des Gâteaux et du Pain** (p175).
4 min from metro Rue du Bac

Shop for vintage threads at **Chercheminippes** (p169).
4 min from metro Vaneau

Put your feet up at the picturesque **Jardin du Luxembourg** (p171).
4 min from Luxembourg RER station or 6 min from metro Rennes

30 The Chicest SHOPPING

LOCAL LIFE | DESIGN | LUXURY

The neighbourhood of St-Germain is historically known for its shopping, with streets lined with independent boutiques as well as major international brand stores. It's also the place for style spotting, given it's home to some of Paris' best-dressed inhabitants. Shop till you drop and then pause at an iconic cafe to admire chic Parisian style.

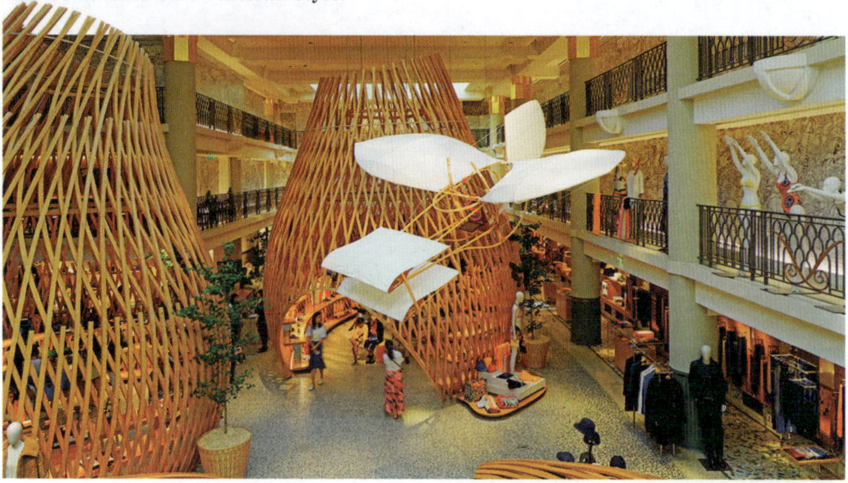

EQROY/SHUTTERSTOCK ©

How to

Getting here Take line 10 or 12 to metro Sèvres–Babylone.

When to go This neighbourhood always bustles with tourists and locals. Le Bon Marché often has *'braderie'* (clearance) sections during the government-mandated *soldes* or sale season (usually January/February and June/July) where you can find past-season items up to 70% off.

Tip During high season (June to December), the more popular shops will have a queue to enter. Don't be put off by long lines; they generally move quickly.

RANDY DUCHAINE/ALAMY STOCK PHOTO ©

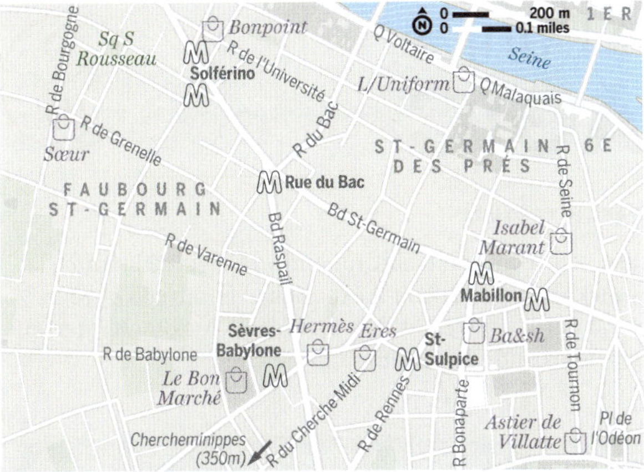

The Pick of the Shopping Crop

The world's first department store, **Le Bon Marché**, is a legendary monument to shopping, with impeccably curated pieces across multiple floors. Nearby, the **Eres** boutique shows off the luxury swimwear that was revolutionary when the brand, now owned by Chanel, was founded in 1968.

From Celine to Saint Laurent, luxe labels abound in this neighbourhood. You can also find secondhand chic. Check out the vintage selections at **Chercheminippes**. Each of the five boutiques on rue du Cherche-Midi specialises in a different theme, from haute couture to menswear.

The **Isabel Marant** boutique on rue Jacob is a destination for stylish Parisiennes. **Bonpoint**, the luxury children's clothing brand, has a 'stock' shop, or factory outlet, on rue de l'Université.

For luggage, don't miss **L/Uniform**, founded by Goyard veteran Jeanne Signoles. You can get totes monogrammed on the spot at the quai Voltaire boutique.

Ba&sh is a cult French brand that got its start in 2003 when two friends teamed up on a line of prêt-à-porter. Also popular is Parisian brand **Sœur,** which has several Left Bank boutiques, including an outlet on rue de Bourgogne.

Self-described as 'an incarnation of Parisian taste', **Astier de Villatte** is known for its ceramics inspired by centuries past. All its creations are made by artisans in its Paris atelier.

Far left top Hermès flagship store
Far left bottom Astier de Villatte

Hermès Flagship Store

The Hermès flagship store is worth a visit even if you're not planning to buy a Birkin bag. Situated inside the former swimming pool of the adjacent Hotel Lutetia, the store has preserved the original art deco mosaic floor, which is best observed with a bird's-eye view from the top floor. Pay close attention to the details as there are hidden treasures tastefully dispersed across the store, including artworks from the Hermès private collection, contemporary photographs and a special collection of exclusive objects, such as the one-of-a-kind jukebox covered in an iconic Hermès print.

31 Left Bank MAGIC

WALKING TOUR | HISTORY | ARCHITECTURE

This itinerary will take you to all the beautiful and worthwhile landmarks in the St-Germain des Prés neighbourhood. You'll experience hundreds of years of history, from stunning royal gardens to a theatre that Marie Antoinette herself visited. Put on good walking shoes and prepare to fall in love.

ANDREI ANTIPOV/SHUTTERSTOCK ©

Trip Notes

Getting here Take RER B to Luxembourg station or line 4 or 10 to metro Saint-Sulpice.

When to go Start early so you can stop and enjoy the public spaces.

Tips Bring snacks, water, sun protection and a book to read at the Jardin du Luxembourg. Watch the locals play chess on the designated chess tables. Carve out extra time to visit the art galleries of St-Germain des Prés near rue de Furstemberg.

The Drunken Boat

On rue Férou, a tiny street next to the Saint-Sulpice church, a photogenic wall is covered in Arthur Rimbaud's 'Le Bateau Ivre'. The lovely poem is about an imaginary voyage of a sinking ship, offering readers an escape. Rimbaud first recited the poem near this spot.

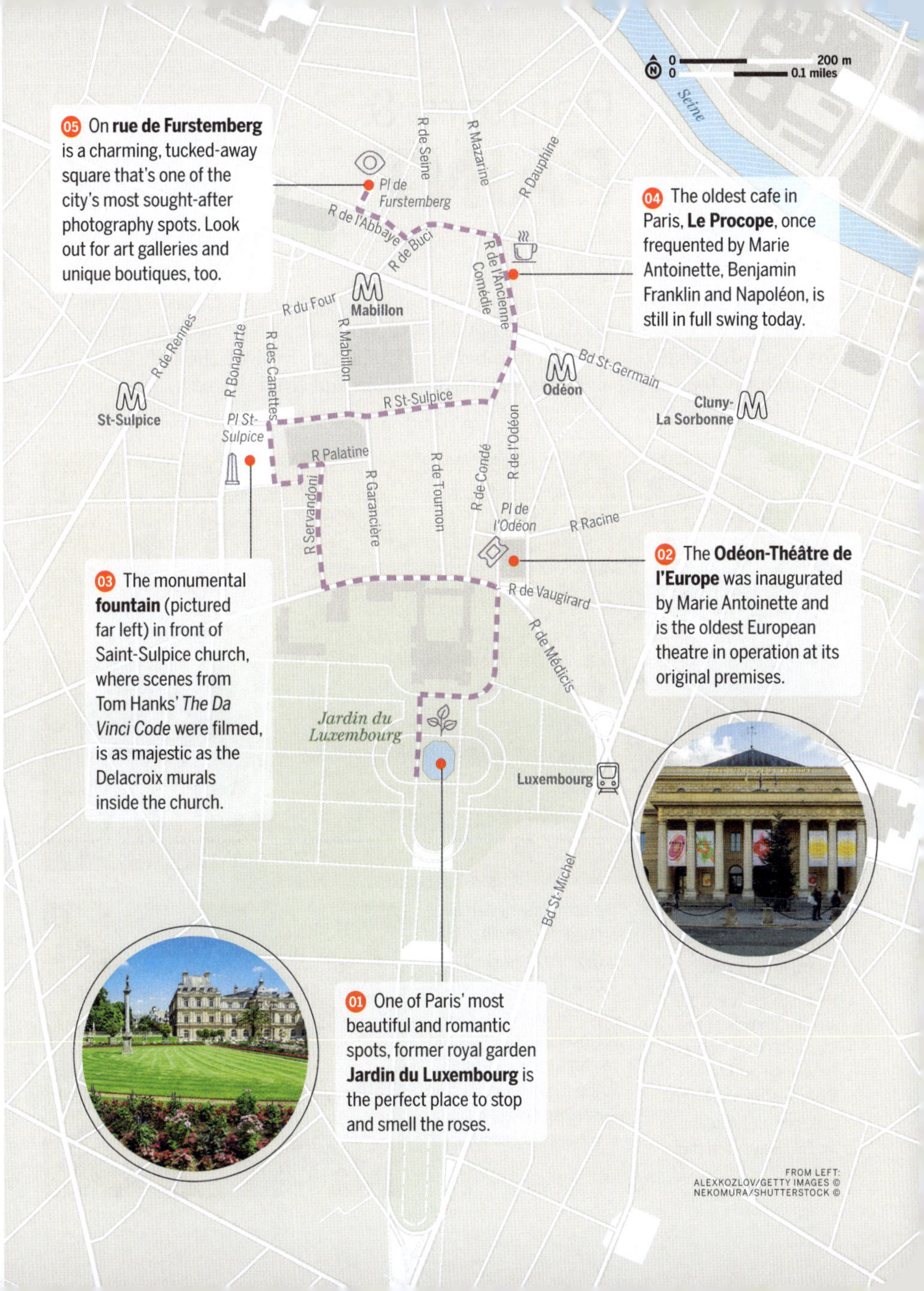

01 One of Paris' most beautiful and romantic spots, former royal garden **Jardin du Luxembourg** is the perfect place to stop and smell the roses.

02 The **Odéon-Théâtre de l'Europe** was inaugurated by Marie Antoinette and is the oldest European theatre in operation at its original premises.

03 The monumental **fountain** (pictured far left) in front of Saint-Sulpice church, where scenes from Tom Hanks' *The Da Vinci Code* were filmed, is as majestic as the Delacroix murals inside the church.

04 The oldest cafe in Paris, **Le Procope**, once frequented by Marie Antoinette, Benjamin Franklin and Napoléon, is still in full swing today.

05 On **rue de Furstemberg** is a charming, tucked-away square that's one of the city's most sought-after photography spots. Look out for art galleries and unique boutiques, too.

32 Painters & PAINT

ART | DRINKS | SAVOIR FAIRE

The Rive Gauche is the historic stomping ground of artists, tastemakers and cultural icons. To this day, the neighbourhood is an artistic hub, home to the École des Beaux-Arts and a number of art galleries. Explore the Left Bank through the lens of the painters who have studied and lived there.

HEMIS/ALAMY STOCK PHOTO ©

How to

Getting here Take the metro to Solférino.

When to go There are smaller crowds at the Musée d'Orsay between November and March. Many say the museum is busier on Tuesdays and Sundays, and that the best time to visit is around the middle of the day, when the gallery's crowd thins out for lunch.

Tips The Musée d'Orsay is closed on Mondays and remains open late (until 9.45pm) on Thursdays. Reserving tickets online in advance is encouraged.

JOEL SAGET/AFP/GETTY IMAGES ©

JOAO PAULO V TINOCO/SHUTTERSTOCK ©

Left École des Beaux-Arts **Far left top** Salle des fêtes, Musée d'Orsay **Far left bottom** Oil pastels, Magasin Sennelier

Musée d'Orsay Paris' second-most-visited museum (after the Louvre) is located in a former train station that could just as well be a palace given its beautiful beaux-arts architecture. The Impressionist galleries on the 5th floor are a place of pilgrimage. Other collection highlights include Courbet's *Un enterrement à Ornans* (Burial at Ornans), Van Gogh's self-portrait and Millet's *The Gleaners*. On the 2nd floor, take a peek into the gorgeous *salle des fêtes,* a golden party room with chandeliers.

Magasin Sennelier Nearby, on the quai Voltaire, this famous art-supply shop dates from 1887. Passionate about the chemistry of colours, Gustave Sennelier developed his own range of oil paints using pigments and binders sourced from his European travels. Artists such as Cézanne and Gauguin worked with Sennelier to create colours, and later the shop innovated with oil pastels for Picasso. To this day, the *maison* is a rendezvous point for artists who consider Sennelier paints and pastels to be *la crème de la crème*.

La Palette An institution in the St-Germain des Prés quarter, La Palette has been a popular gathering place since the early 20th century, attracting gallery owners, artists and celebrities. The cafe's decor is a testament to its history: paint-spattered palettes adorn the walls, alongside works left by artists as payment. This classified historic monument has a pavement *terrasse* that's perfect for people-watching.

Fine Arts Education

The **École des Beaux-Arts** (School of Fine Arts) is an institution in St-Germain des Prés. Founded in the 17th century as a royal academy, the prestigious school has occupied the site of a former monastery on rue Bonaparte since the 19th century. Some of the world's most famous artists have trained here, including the Impressionists Pierre-Auguste Renoir and Edgar Degas. Visitors can access the school during temporary exhibitions, the European Heritage Days and special open-house events. The building is steeped in history and atmosphere, particularly the courtyard and former **Chapelle des Petits-Augustins**, the only vestige of the old monastery.

33 SWEETS on Rue du Bac

PASTRY | ARTISAN | CHOCOLATE

Over the last few years, Paris' pastry obsession has reached new heights. Gourmets line up in long queues outside couture-style boutiques where celebrity *pâtissiers* display Instagrammable confections like jewellery under glass. Instead of a *tour de Paris* to survey the scene, get your sugar fix on the rue du Bac. This street has a concentration of shops peddling irresistible treats.

STEVEN ROTHFELD/ALAMY STOCK PHOTO ©

How to

Getting here Take line 12 to metro Rue du Bac.

When to go The area is always busy, but avoid the pre-lunch or pre-dinner crowds at La Grande Épicerie. Des Gâteaux et du Pain is closed on Tuesdays.

Tips La Grande Épicerie offers a delivery service where you can get your purchases brought to your Parisian address at a designated time. The street's chocolate shops go all out for Christmas and Easter with fantastical edible creations.

PHILIPPE PETIT/PARIS MATCH /GETTY IMAGES ©

Left Mont Blanc dessert, Angelina **Far left top** Jacques Genin chocolates **Far left bottom** Noglu cake and cereal

Pastry Icons and Sweet Desserts Running 1150m through the 7e, the rue du Bac has been drawing pastry fanatics since 1867. That's when *pâtissier* Adolphe Seugnot unveiled his speciality, a precursor of the millefeuille made with vanilla *crème pâtissière* sandwiched between layers of puff pastry. The address at 28 rue du Bac no longer exists, but today's cult favourites can be found at **Des Gâteaux et du Pain**, where Claire Damon makes sublime tarts from seasonal fruit – fans swear the 'Absolu Citron' is the city's best lemon tart. Another standout is **Philippe Conticini's boutique** on the corner of rue Varenne.

You'll also find an outpost of **Angelina** – its decadent hot chocolate is only rivalled by its signature Mont Blanc dessert, inspired by the snowcapped Alpine peak. There's even gluten-free goodies at **Noglu** and pastries with a low glycemic index at the **Oh Oui!** shop. On a hot day, try the artisanal ice cream at **Le Bac à Glaces**.

Cacao Delights Craving chocolate? You're spoiled for choice. **Chocolat Chapon** draws dessert devotees to its chocolate mousse bar. **Jacques Genin** and **Jean-Paul Hévin**, two of the city's most renowned chocolatiers, operate boutiques on this street. And the sixth-generation **Chocolat Foucher** has been in its charming location at No 126 since 1819. Wrap up your sweets crawl at the nearby **Grande Épicerie**, the gourmet food hall for Le Bon Marché department store.

Gourmet Left Bank

Situated in the 14e, **Mosuke** restaurant is so popular there's a months-long waiting list. The culinary maestro behind this Michelin-starred hot spot shares his favourite food addresses on the Left Bank.

Best boutique on the rue du Bac

La Grande Épicerie (7e)

Favourite café

Hexagone Café (14e)

Must-visit pâtisserie

Mori Yoshida (7e)

A dish to travel for

Le Camouflage by Atsushi Tanaka at the restaurant A.T. (5e)

Best lunch

Kitchen Ter(re) (5e) or Aux Plumes (14e)

A market detour

Marché Edgar Quinet (14e)

Favourite restaurant

Kitchen Galerie (6e)

With thanks to Mory Sacko, *Michelin-starred chef and TV personality. @mory_sacko_*

Listings

BEST OF THE REST

Fine Meals

Café des Ministères €€

This excellent and authentic French restaurant near the Assemblée nationale books up fast – reservations open 21 days in advance. The chef was named national champion for his *chou de Pontoise farci* (stuffed Pontoise cabbage).

Yen €€

One of the best places in the city for Japanese food can be found in the 6e. Its speciality is handmade soba, but its sashimi and Wagyu offerings are also excellent.

Le Relais de L'Entrecote €€

A favourite of locals and tourists, this chain only serves one dish: walnut salad followed by *steak frites*. Here at the oldest location, all you have to do is tell the waiter how you want your steak cooked.

Dupin €€

This restaurant near Le Bon Marché offers affordable and tasty meals using the best French ingredients. Its chocolate soufflé is an absolute must.

Colorova €€

Whether you're going for lunch, brunch or tea, Colorova near Le Bon Marché is always a good idea. Its innovative menu, combined with a chef who has a penchant for pastries, make for a memorable meal in a cosy setting.

Aux Prés €€

French celebrity chef Cyril Lignac rose to fame thanks to TV, but his businesses offer consistently excellent food. Here you'll find cocktails and his favourite dishes, such as crispy salmon sushi and lobster rolls.

Le Bon Saint Pourçain €€€

This small French restaurant on a tiny and romantic street in the 6e offers an intimate dining experience with views of the kitchen no matter where you sit.

Shu €€€

This intimate Japanese restaurant is a hidden gem that specialises in *kushiagué* (small bites of food on skewers). Its sashimi offerings are also excellent.

Small Bites

Beaupassage €€

From Pierre Hermé's tearoom-like cafe, to the trendy coffee spot Arabica, to Thierry Marx' bakery, you'll find everything you need to satisfy your snack cravings at this shopping arcade and courtyard space.

Le Chocolat Alain Ducasse €

Only good things happen when France's most prized chef decides to venture into chocolate. With two shops in the neighbourhood, you're never far from some of the best chocolate creations in Paris.

GILMANSHIN/SHUTTERSTOCK ©

Musée Rodin

Mori Yoshida €

Japanese chef Mori Yoshida's pastry shop is located near Invalides and offers French pastries with a Japanese flair. Matcha, black sesame, cherry blossom and yuzu flavours are the norm here.

Fruttini by Mo €€

This ice-cream shop's speciality is ice cream frozen in fruits and vegetables. Its offerings are seasonal and can range from a tiny fig to a whole melon.

Barthélémy Cheese €

Shop owner Nicole has been in business for more than 50 years and has some of the best suggestions for what's in season. Her beautiful shop and display alone are worth the visit.

Cocktails, Wine & Views

Chez Nous €

This inviting and chic wine bar near the Seine is a great place to experience wines and charcuterie plates. The servers are outgoing and friendly without being overwhelming.

Dame Roof €

Enjoy panoramic views from the rooftop of the Hôtel Dame des Arts while you sip a signature Spritz des Dames cocktail made with champagne, umeshu and raspberry *eau de vie*.

Silencio des Prés €€

The legendary nightclub Silencio has opened a second hot spot in St-Germain des Prés. Taking over the last available independent cinema, this space is a 360-degree theatre-and-restaurant-in-one.

More Museums

Musée du Luxembourg

The first museum to open to the public in France today hosts several popular exhibitions throughout the year and is also home to the popular Mademoiselle Angelina tearoom.

L'Officine Universelle Buly

Musée Rodin

This museum, created by the sculptor Auguste Rodin in his mansion surrounded by gardens, is now home to many of his creations as well as his art collection.

Monnaie de Paris

France's oldest institution is responsible for creating the country's coins. The institution hosts contemporary-art exhibitions in its historic building.

Unique Boutiques & Galleries

Carel

Incredibly comfortable, Carel shoes are representative of Parisian style and are a favourite of fashionable celebrities such as Alexa Chung.

Deyrolle

Opened in 1831, this whimsical shop dedicated to taxidermy is also a cabinet of curiosities and a museum.

L'Officine Universelle Buly

This gorgeous Parisian apothecary with 19th-century roots offers a wide range of products inspired by old beauty recipes.

Galerie Kamel Mennour

Visit this well-known gallery in a large private mansion to see (for free) some of the work from the contemporary artists it represents.

MONTPARNASSE & SOUTHERN PARIS

ART | VILLAGES | CHINATOWN

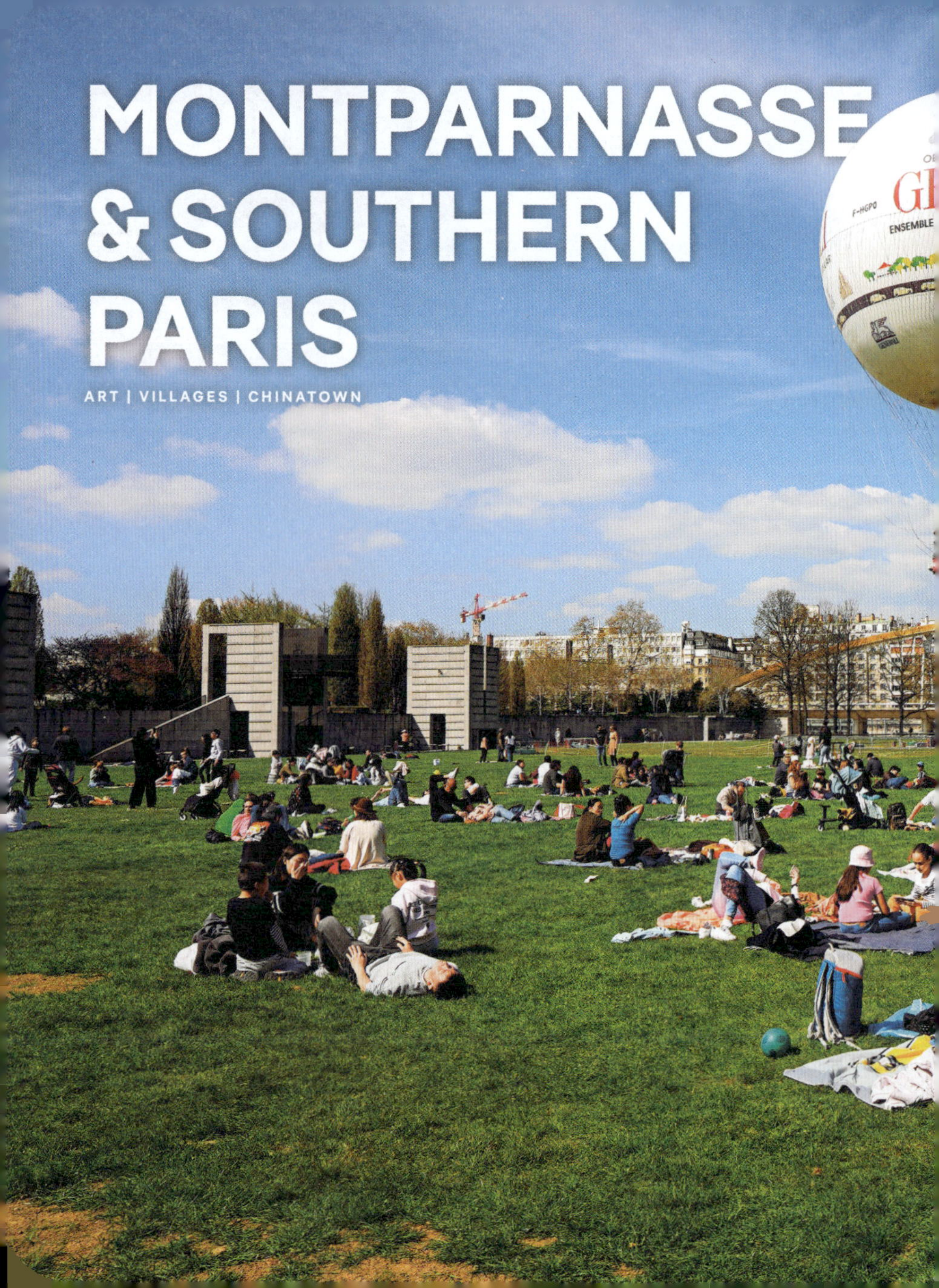

- **Massive Murals** (p182)
- **Secret Villages** (p184)
- **Bistros, Brasseries & Bouillons** (p186)
- **Asian Flavours** (p188)
- **Listings** (p190)

MONTPARNASSE & SOUTHERN PARIS

Trip Builder

TAKE YOUR PICK OF MUST-SEES AND HIDDEN GEMS

This vast swath of southern Paris is full of surprises and discoveries, and is a great place to explore if you're looking for a local experience. Unpretentious yet seductive, gritty yet full of good vibes, it's a happy mix of village-like areas, edgy street art, vast parks and striking contemporary architecture.

Trip Notes

Best for Picturesque neighbourhoods, cutting-edge architecture and vast parks.

Transport Montparnasse Bienvenüe is the metro hub for Montparnasse and the 15e. Bibliothèque François-Mitterrand and Place d'Italie are convenient 13e stops.

Getting around Walk, ride or use the metro.

Tip Hop on the T3 tram to whizz around Paris' perimeter.

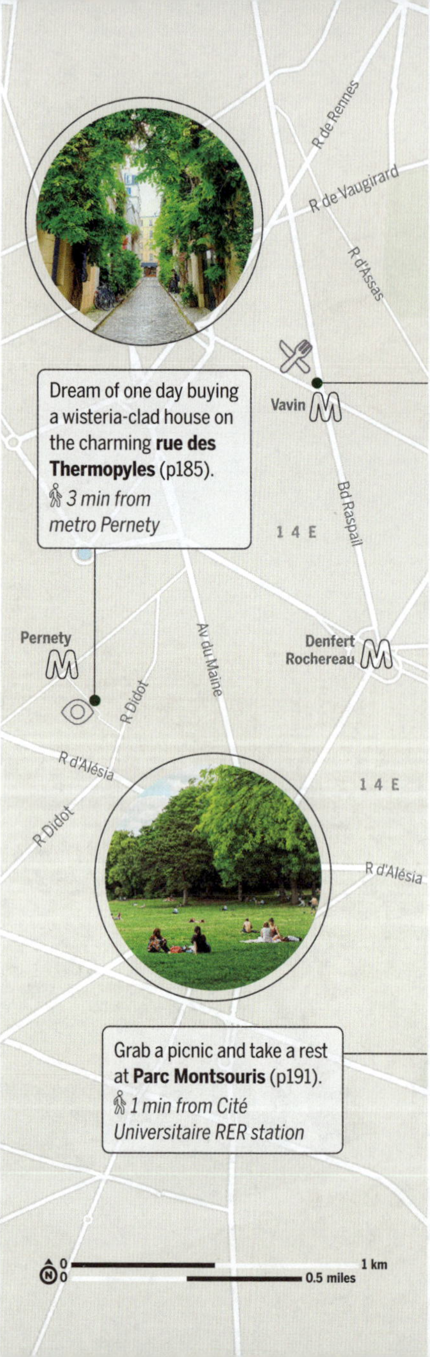

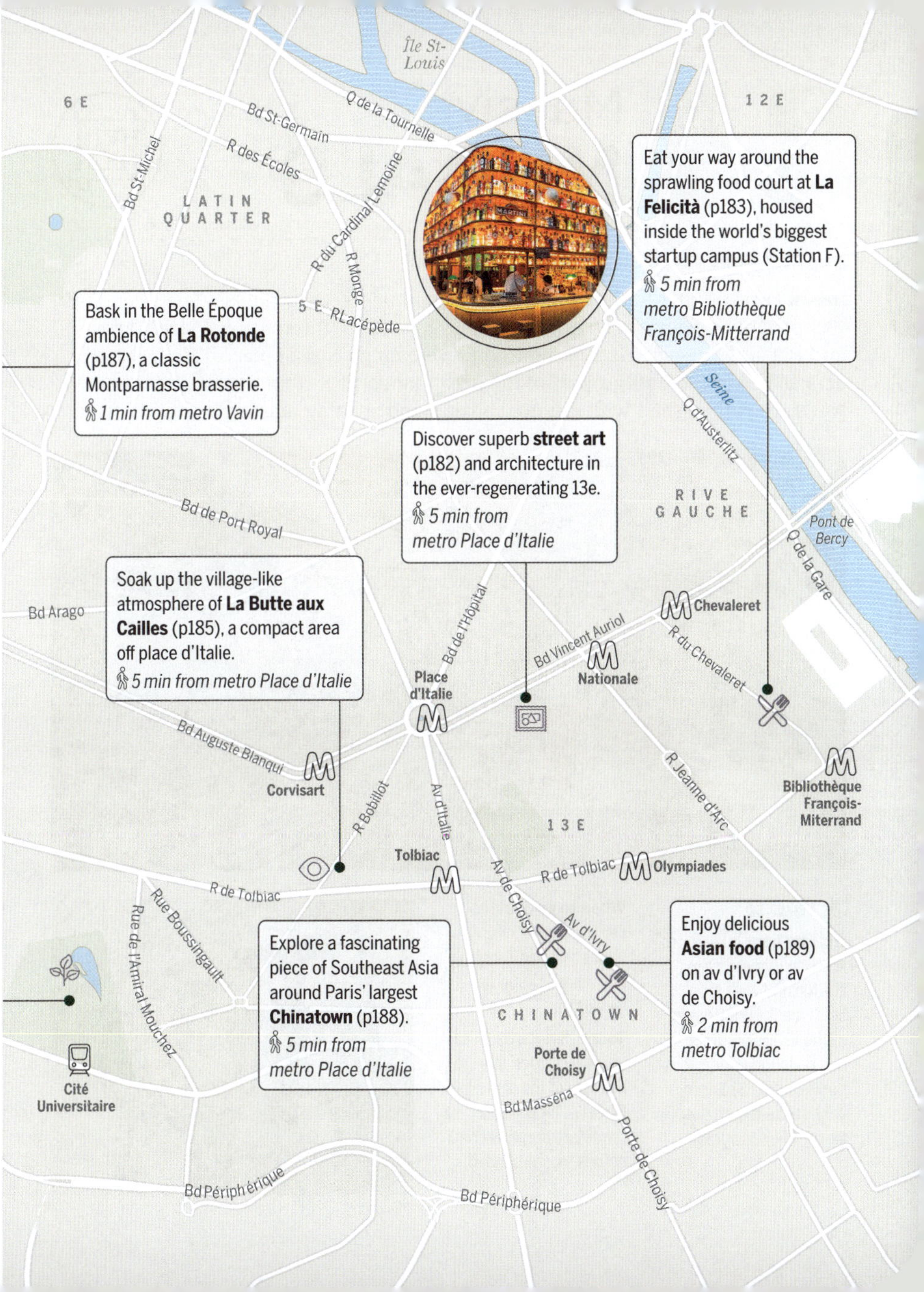

Île St-Louis
6 E
12 E
Q de la Tournelle
Bd St-Germain
R des Écoles
Bd St-Michel
R du Cardinal Lemoine
LATIN QUARTER
R Monge
5 E
R Lacépède
Eat your way around the sprawling food court at **La Felicità** (p183), housed inside the world's biggest startup campus (Station F).
5 min from metro Bibliothèque François-Mitterrand
Bask in the Belle Époque ambience of **La Rotonde** (p187), a classic Montparnasse brasserie.
1 min from metro Vavin
Seine
Q d'Austerlitz
Discover superb **street art** (p182) and architecture in the ever-regenerating 13e.
5 min from metro Place d'Italie
RIVE GAUCHE
Bd de Port Royal
Pont de Bercy
Q de la Gare
Soak up the village-like atmosphere of **La Butte aux Cailles** (p185), a compact area off place d'Italie.
5 min from metro Place d'Italie
Bd Arago
Bd de l'Hôpital
Chevaleret
Bd Vincent Auriol
Nationale
R du Chevaleret
Place d'Italie
Bd Auguste Blanqui
Corvisart
R Bobillot
Av d'Italie
R Jeanne d'Arc
Bibliothèque François-Miterrand
13 E
Tolbiac
R de Tolbiac
Olympiades
Av de Choisy
Av d'Ivry
Rue Boussingault
Rue de l'Amiral Mouchez
Explore a fascinating piece of Southeast Asia around Paris' largest **Chinatown** (p188).
5 min from metro Place d'Italie
Enjoy delicious **Asian food** (p189) on av d'Ivry or av de Choisy.
2 min from metro Tolbiac
CHINATOWN
Porte de Choisy
Cité Universitaire
Bd Masséna
Porte de Choisy
Bd Périphérique
Bd Périphérique

34 Massive MURALS

ART | CULTURE | WALKING

Paris doesn't limit itself to iconic monuments. Over the last few years, the 13e arrondissement has emerged as a playground for international street artists and is a superb open-air museum. Wherever you go east of place d'Italie, street art has become a familiar part of the urban landscape. Numerous facades and walls are embellished with graffiti, collages and striking masterpieces.

HEMIS/ALAMY STOCK PHOTO ©

How to

Getting here Take metro line 6 to Place d'Italie station and walk along bd Vincent Auriol. A map of the various murals can be found online at boulevardparis13.com – very useful to find the lesser-known murals.

When to go Beat the crowds by planning your stroll mid-morning or mid-afternoon on weekdays.

Tours It's not a bad idea to take a guided tour (in English) of the district – Street Art Tour Paris (streetarttourparis.com) comes recommended.

DIRECTPHOTO COLLECTION/ ALAMY STOCK PHOTO ©

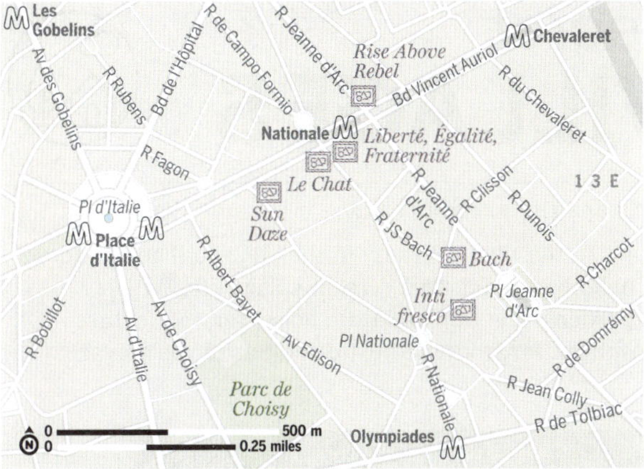

Mural Spotting in the 13e

More than 30 monumental murals enliven streets and thoroughfares in an area between av de France, rue de Tolbiac and bd Vincent Auriol, with more added every year. Moseying past a few of these cheery murals is a great way to explore less-visited neighbourhoods.

Highlights include a colourful **fresco** (13 rue Lahire) by famous artist Inti, **Bach** (57 rue Clisson), the elaborate **Sun Daze** (167 bd Vincent Auriol) by the talented twins How and Nosm, a splendid **portrait of a geisha-like woman** (169 bd Vincent Auriol) by British artist Hush on an adjacent building, **Le Chat** (corner of bd Vincent Auriol and rue Nationale) and the famous **Liberté, Égalité, Fraternité** (186 rue Nationale) by Shepard Fairey, which represents the symbol of the French Republic.

Other great works to look for include the strikingly expressive **Turncoat** (190 rue Nationale) by Londoner D*Face and the equally stunning **Rise Above Rebel** (corner of bd Vincent Auriol and rue Jeanne d'Arc), another massive mural by Shepard Fairey. On the opposite side of bd Vincent Auriol, it's impossible to miss the awesome **Dancer** (98 bd Vincent Auriol), with a strapline *'Et j'ai retenu mon souffle'* ('And I hold my breath'), by the collective Faile.

Far left top La Felicità **Far left bottom** Street art tour group

Artistic Immersion

Most colourful mural
The giant *Mona Lisa* by Okuda.

Restaurant with murals
La Felicità, inside an old train depot.

Most meaningful mural
The one by SPY, because of his conceptual approach that stands out from the others.

Best perspective
Several amazing murals can be seen between the Place d'Italie and Quai de la Gare metro stations (line 6).

Most secret mural
Spot 13, a graffiti hot spot below Lavo//matik gallery.

Most interesting street for murals
Bd Vincent Auriol.

Most poignant
The work of Borondo, showing the three ages of life.

Most elegant
The poetic and chic work of Pantonio.

By Kasia Klon, *artist and tour guide in Paris. @streetart tourparis*

35 Secret VILLAGES

PICTURESQUE | AUTHENTIC | OFF THE BEATEN TRACK

From Butte aux Cailles in the 13e to Pernety in the 14e, you'll encounter little-known, pocket-sized neighbourhoods that scream village life. With small houses, flower-filled gardens, few cars and little noise, they all feature a welcoming, bucolic atmosphere, far from the hustle and bustle you'd expect from a city this size.

HEMIS/ALAMY STOCK PHOTO ©

How to

Getting here Place d'Italie (13e), Denfert-Rochereau (14e) and Pernety (14e) are the most convenient metro stations.

Getting around Use the metro (line 6) to get from one arrondissement to the next.

When to go Weekdays are very peaceful in these neighbourhoods.

Hidden spot Explore on foot sections of the former Petite Ceinture steam railway line in the 13e, 14e and 15e, with biodiverse habitats that include forest, grassland and prairies.

JEROME LABOUYRIE/SHUTTERSTOCK ©

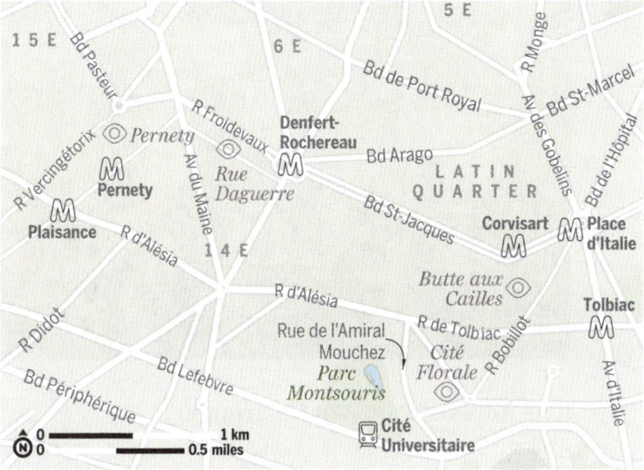

Far left top Butte aux Cailles Far left bottom Cité Florale

Choose your Neighbourhood

Paris' Best-kept Secret A stone's throw east of Parc Montsouris, the micro-neighbourhood of the **Cité Florale** is a gem to wander. Built in the 1920s, the 'Floral City' comprises five streets named after flowers and flanked with small houses with facades that are covered in ivy, wild vines and flowers.

Village Life The **Butte aux Cailles** is a compact area off place d'Italie, where cobblestone streets are lined with quaint houses. It has plenty of fabulous dining options and bars popular with students and locals. There's very little car traffic, which enhances the spirited vibe. **Petit Alsace** is an ensemble of Alsatian-style buildings that were an early example of social housing.

Bohemian Atmosphere Nestled on the outskirts of the Montparnasse train station, the **Pernety** district has retained its intimate character. With its pedestrian lanes and charming brick buildings, it's entirely different from the Haussmannian architectural style that characterises much of the rest of Paris. One of the most bucolic streets is **rue des Thermopyles**, a cobbled lane lined with potted plants and wisteria-clad houses.

Step Back in Time Paris' traditional village atmosphere thrives along **rue Daguerre** (14e). Tucked just southwest of the Denfert-Rochereau metro station, this narrow street is lined with florists, cheese shops, bakeries, greengrocers, delis and classic cafes. Sunday mornings are especially lively.

Atmospheric Streets & Squares

In the Pernety area (14e), look for **rue des Thermopyles**, where you can sample authentic, simple village life. In the 15e, **rue St Charles** (between av Emile Zola and Rond-Point St Charles) is *the* place to shop like a real Parisian. Here you'll find traditional bakeries, groceries, pastry shops, cheesemongers and delis. In the 13e, **rue de la Butte aux Cailles** has numerous traditional restaurants, including **Le Temps des Cerises**. It also features some great street art by Miss. Tic. Nearby, **Square des Peupliers** is one of the few places in Paris to see individual houses with private gardens.

By Mélanie Després, *a historian and tour guide in Paris. @visitesaufildelart*

Bistros, Brasseries & Bouillons

SINK YOUR TEETH INTO CULINARY HERITAGE

An undisputed culinary capital, Paris is a showcase par excellence for French cuisine. This is where the restaurant was invented and, to this day, chefs from all over the world come here to train. New dining trends champion small plates and global flavours, yet there's still rich tradition found in one-of-a-kind Parisian institutions.

Left Bouillon Julien **Middle** Bofinger **Right** La Mère Catherine

VIENNASLIDE/ALAMY STOCK PHOTO ©

The Roots of Parisian Gastronomy

Refined over the centuries, restaurant culture is an intrinsic part of the social fabric, an art form that's infused with ritual. These establishments, each with their own codes and decor, offer up an unchanged slice of Paris.

The restaurant concept was born in 1765 on rue des Poulies (now the rue du Louvre). That's when Mathurin Roze de Chantoiseau invited customers to sit at individual tables and choose a dish from a reasonably priced menu. Prior to this, travellers had to find sustenance at *auberges* (inns). The idea was revolutionary, and soon the area around the Palais Royal exploded with restaurants. Today, **Le Grand Véfour** is the only survivor of this 18th-century boom.

The Bouillon was baptised in 1855 when the butcher Baptiste-Adolphe Duval set up shop near Les Halles. His vast hall could accommodate 500 people at a time, and served bouillon, or broth-based recipes. Nowadays the bouillons are undergoing a renaissance with places such as **Bouillon Pigalle** and **Bouillon Republique** complementing historic spots like the **Bouillon Julien**.

Montparnasse Mecca

Dating from the 1860s, the brasserie was originally a brewery overseen by Alsatian entrepreneurs who served *choucroute* (sauerkraut) and hearty Alsatian dishes. Frédéric Bofinger pioneered with beers on tap – his eponymous **Bofinger** brasserie remains a popular fixture. Richly decorated, these bustling spaces showed off art nouveau and art deco styles. The names resonate today: **Terminus Nord**, **La Closerie des Lilas**, **Brasserie Lipp** and a legendary quartet in Montparnasse.

AGEFOTOSTOCK/ALAMY STOCK PHOTO ©

KUMAR SRISKANDAN/ALAMY STOCK PHOTO ©

It was here in the early 20th century that bohemian artists and thinkers congregated at **Le Select**, **Le Dôme**, **La Coupole** and **La Rotonde**. These Montparnasse hangouts were also the stomping grounds of 'Lost Generation' Americans such as Hemingway and Fitzgerald. Nowadays, these historic monuments are custodians of tradition, their white-aproned waiters serving seafood platters and Parisian specialities amid the grandeur so you can relive the joie de vivre of the Roaring Twenties. La Coupole's *prix-fixe* lunch menu is an affordable way to access the glamour.

Beloved Bistros

Legend has it that the bistro was born at **La Mère Catherine** in Montmartre. After Napoléon's fall in 1814, occupying Cossack soldiers – sneaking away from their posts without their officers' permission – shouted *'Bistro! Bistro!'* (Hurry! Hurry!) when ordering drinks. The bistro's origins remain murky, but the tradition is firmly established.

These small neighbourhood restaurants, offering chalkboard menus, are often decorated with a zinc-topped bar and mosaic floors. A cornerstone of community life, the bistro serves as much as a rendezvous point as a place to eat. A few soulful examples: **À l'Épi d'Or** (1e), **Le Petit Rétro** (16e), **Au Vin des Rues** (14e), **Chez Paul** (11e), **Joséphine Chez Dumonet** (6e).

In recent years, concerned citizens have sounded an alarm. Skyrocketing rents are threatening the closure of bistros such as **Les Pipos** (5e). Could it be a dying breed? Bistro owners have united to lobby for Unesco World Heritage status, recognising the bistro as part of France's 'intangible cultural heritage' – a move that could safeguard the tradition for generations to come.

The Birthplace of the Baguette

There's a lot of lore about the baguette. Was it invented because Napoléon decreed that bakers create an easily transportable bread for soldiers? Or was it a request from Fulgence Bienvenüe, the 'father of the Paris metro', so that his tunnel workers could break their bread without carrying brawl-inducing knives? Regardless of the myths, the truth remains: the wand-shaped loaf, born in Paris, has become a veritable emblem of France, and is now even recognised by Unesco. An annual Paris competition awards the city's best *boulanger* with a year-long contract to supply the bread to the Élysée presidential palace.

36 ASIAN Flavours

CHINATOWN | STROLLING | RESTAURANTS

Southeast of place d'Italie and near rue de Tolbiac is Paris' largest Chinatown. Don't let the massive tower blocks dating from the 1960s deter you from exploring this district, which feels so different from other Parisian neighbourhoods. It's a fascinating piece of Southeast Asia, with plenty of surprises, including culinary delights, colourful festivals and art.

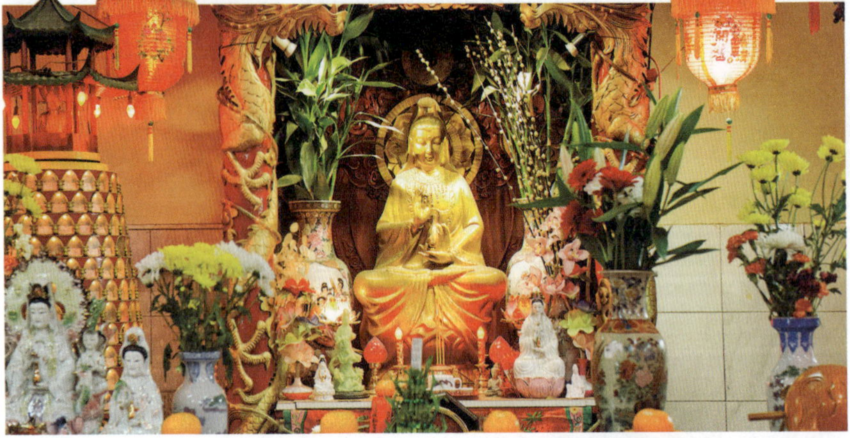

DANIEL THIERRY/GETTY IMAGES ©

How to

Getting here Take metro line 5, 6 or 7 to Place d'Italie station.

Getting around Walk along av d'Ivry, av de Choisy, rue Baudricourt and adjacent streets.

When to go Chinatown is at its liveliest on weekends.

Green spot Parc de Choisy, a soothing park off av de Choisy.

Hidden spots South of rue de Tolbiac, passage Bourgoin and passage National are two lovely paved roads flanked with private houses.

SENTELIA/SHUTTERSTOCK ©

Far left top Autel du Culte de Bouddha
Far left bottom Vietnamese pho

Asian Accents

Art & Culture If you're a fan of underground cultures, head to **La Dalle des Olympiades**, off rue de Tolbiac. This vast concrete esplanade with platformed pedestrian zones surrounded by towers has become the focal point for local K-pop dancers and skateboarders. On rue Paul Klee, **La Danse de la Fontaine Émergente** (Dance of the Emerging Fountain) is a large fountain built of stainless steel, plastic and glass, designed by French-Chinese sculptor Chen Zhen. Completed in 2008, it looks like a giant stylised dragon winding its way across the square, emerging from and submerging into the concrete pavement. High-pressure water flows inside the sculpture. The most unusual sacred site in Paris must be the **Autel du Culte de Bouddha** (37 rue du Disque), a small yet colourful Buddhist temple hidden in an underground car park beneath a tower block.

Food & Shopping For any Asian food you can imagine, as well as many decorative and household items, shop at **Tang Frères** (48 av d'Ivry), the biggest Asian store in Paris (and possibly Europe). Nestled beneath the towers on av d'Ivry and av de Choisy, you'll find great Vietnamese pho noodle bars, family-run restaurants serving homemade dumplings and spicy soups, and traditional Chinese pastry shops. Some of them have terraces that are great for a bout of people-watching.

Chinese New Year

The best time to immerse yourself in Chinatown is during Chinese New Year (also known as Spring Festival), usually in late January or February. With about 2000 participants and more than 200,000 spectators, it's one of the most spectacular events in the city. Celebrations typically last about two weeks and feature colourful parades as well as lion and dragon dances. Expect brightly lit red lanterns, firecrackers and performances by ribbon dancers, drummers, cymbal players and acrobats wearing traditional costumes. It kicks off in front of Tang Frères supermarket on av d'Ivry. For exact dates, check mairie13.paris.fr/culture.

Listings

BEST OF THE REST

Asian Delights

Camly – Bo Bun 2 Go €

Halfway between place d'Italie and the Bibliothèque nationale de France, this great little restaurant serves up some of the 13e's best Vietnamese cuisine in a sleek interior.

Pho Bành Cúon 14 €

This small, buzzy restaurant (also known as Pho 14) right in Chinatown is wildly popular with in-the-know locals for its super-fresh and astonishingly cheap pho.

Thieng Heng €

This takeaway joint in the heart of Chinatown dishes up giant banh mi, which have earned Thieng Heng a cult following.

Misso €

A terrific spot for takeaway Korean food by a Seoul-born chef in the Butte aux Cailles.

Exciting Neobistros

Simone Le Resto €€

A generous smattering of pavement terrace tables flags this vibrant neobistro north of place d'Italie. Inventive menus are created in the open kitchen from high-quality products.

Le Sévéro €€

Steaks served with sensational *frites* (fries) are the mainstay of this upmarket bistro not far from Montparnasse; other meat specialities include black pudding and pigs' trotters.

Le Beurre Noisette €€

This eatery with a convivial chocolate-toned dining room in the heart of the 15e prepares meat dishes accompanied with *beurre noisette* (brown butter sauce).

Stylish Swimming Pools

Piscine de la Butte aux Cailles

Built in 1924, this art deco swimming complex – a historic monument – has a spectacular vaulted indoor pool and, since 2017, Paris' only Nordic (open-air) pool. Near place d'Italie.

Piscine Joséphine Baker

Floating on the Seine off the Bibliothèque nationale de France, this striking swimming pool, named after the 1920s American singer, is popular in summer when the roof slides back.

Arts, Culture & Galleries

Bibliothèque nationale de France

Designed with four glass towers shaped like half-open books, the François-Mitterrand site of the National Library hosts superb temporary exhibitions.

Galerie Itinerrance

Testament to the 13e's ongoing creative renaissance, this gallery showcases graffiti and street art, and can advise on street-art tours of the neighbourhood. South of the 13e.

Manufacture des Gobelins

Les Docks

Framed by a wave-like glass facade, this transformed Seine-side warehouse off the Bibliothèque nationale de France is home to the French fashion institute. Other draws include huge riverside terraces and a popular Australian rooftop bar.

La Fab

French fashion designer and art collector agnès b opened this gallery in a striking new building in 2020. Her collection of contemporary works is presented in themed exhibitions.

Manufacture des Gobelins

This renowned factory has been weaving tapestries on specialised looms since the 18th century. The factory is open for guided tours, and the Galerie des Gobelins hosts exhibitions.

Musée de la Libération de Paris

Across from the entrance to Les Catacombs, this history museum is devoted to the WWII German occupation of Paris, with a focus on the Resistance and its leaders.

Breads & Sweets

Laurent Duchêne

This boulangerie at the foot of the Butte aux Cailles is overseen by a baker awarded Meilleur Ouvrier de France, and the croissants are considered some of the best in Paris.

Wonderland Pâtisserie

From edible baobab trees to the merry-go-round-inspired 'Fantasia', the pastries are works of art at this 14e hot spot.

Green Spaces

Parc Montsouris

South of the 14e, this sprawling lakeside park, planted with horse chestnut, yew, cedar, weeping beech and buttonwood trees, is a delightful picnic spot and has endearing playground areas.

Parc Georges Brassens

Parc Georges Brassens

This park in the 15e has a large central pond bordered by lawns, and gardens featuring roses and medicinal and aromatic plants. The sloping hill is home to a vineyard.

Parc André Citroën

In this urban park west of the 15e, the central lawn is flanked by greenhouses, dancing fountains, an elevated reflecting pool and smaller gardens.

Wine, Beer & Music

Poinçon €

Half trendy bar and half slick bistro bathing in a warm atmosphere, Poinçon occupies a delightfully restored 1867 train station that was part of the Petite Ceinture.

Félicie €

This unpretentious neighbourhood cafe in the 14e, with a big heated pavement terrace, fun-loving staff and a laid-back vibe, is a quintessentially Parisian spot to hang out any time of day.

Bateau El Alamein €

Strung with terracotta pots of flowers, this deep-purple boat has a Seine-side terrace for sitting amid tulips and enjoying live bands. Off the Bibliothèque nationale de France.

DAY TRIPS

NATURE | OUTDOORS | ART

- **A Costumed Affair** (p196)
- **Artist Villages** (p198)
- **Parisian Paddleboarding** (p200)
- **Suburban Culture & Nature** (p202)
- **A Forest Hike & Palace** (p204)

DAY TRIPS
Trip Builder

TAKE YOUR PICK OF MUST-SEES AND HIDDEN GEMS

Although you could spend years in Paris without running out of things to see and do, there's also a wealth of sights and activities just a short train ride away. Escape hectic city life for a day to explore magnificent châteaux, tranquil forests and inspiring artist villages.

Trip Notes

Best for Grand palaces, sporty excursions and getting back to nature.

Transport and getting around Most places are easy to reach by train. Hiring a bike can be a pleasant option for getting around, while a car can give access to otherwise-hard-to-reach side stops.

Tip Be aware that châteaux and gardens are often closed on Mondays.

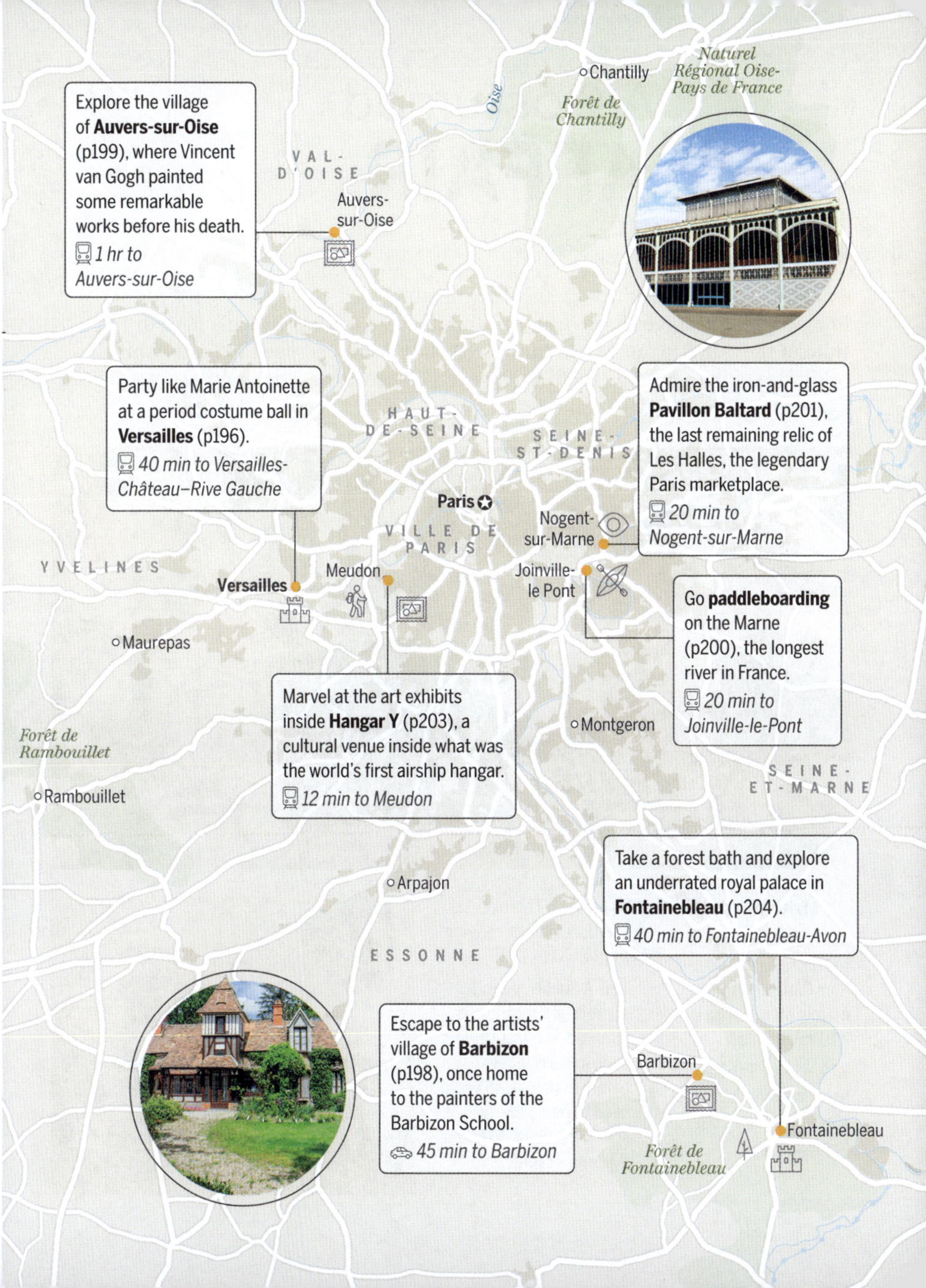
Explore the village of **Auvers-sur-Oise** (p199), where Vincent van Gogh painted some remarkable works before his death.
1 hr to Auvers-sur-Oise
Party like Marie Antoinette at a period costume ball in **Versailles** (p196).
40 min to Versailles-Château–Rive Gauche
Admire the iron-and-glass **Pavillon Baltard** (p201), the last remaining relic of Les Halles, the legendary Paris marketplace.
20 min to Nogent-sur-Marne
Go **paddleboarding** on the Marne (p200), the longest river in France.
20 min to Joinville-le-Pont
Marvel at the art exhibits inside **Hangar Y** (p203), a cultural venue inside what was the world's first airship hangar.
12 min to Meudon
Take a forest bath and explore an underrated royal palace in **Fontainebleau** (p204).
40 min to Fontainebleau-Avon
Escape to the artists' village of **Barbizon** (p198), once home to the painters of the Barbizon School.
45 min to Barbizon
Chantilly
Naturel Régional Oise-Pays de France
Forêt de Chantilly
Oise
VAL-D'OISE
Auvers-sur-Oise
HAUT-DE-SEINE
SEINE-ST-DENIS
Paris
VILLE DE PARIS
Nogent-sur-Marne
Joinville-le Pont
YVELINES
Versailles
Meudon
Maurepas
Montgeron
Forêt de Rambouillet
Rambouillet
SEINE-ET-MARNE
Arpajon
ESSONNE
Barbizon
Fontainebleau
Forêt de Fontainebleau

37 A Costumed AFFAIR

HISTORY I PALACE I DANCE

As you wander through the extravagant Palace of Versailles, it's fun to imagine what it might have been like to attend lavish formal balls here in the time of the Sun King or Marie Antoinette. But there's no need to limit yourself to daydreaming – for one night each year, you can travel back in time and experience it at the Fêtes Galantes.

LUDOVIC MARIN/AFP/GETTY IMAGES ©

How to

Getting here RER line C to Versailles Château–Rive Gauche, approximately 40 minutes, then a 10-minute walk.

When to go The ball is held on a Monday in late May/early June from 7pm to midnight.

How much There are several ticket levels, ranging from €170 to €595.

Tips A quality, period-appropriate costume is required. The last RER back to Paris leaves before midnight, so you'll need to hire a car, or spend the night, to catch the entire event.

HEMIS/ALAMY STOCK PHOTO ©

FRANCK LEGROS/SHUTTERSTOCK ©

Left Hall of Mirrors, Château de Versailles **Far left top** Fêtes Galantes **Far left bottom** Private apartment of Madame de Pompadour

As one of the most-visited attractions in France, the awe-inspiring **Château de Versailles** receives nearly 10 million visitors every year. Unsurprisingly, it's usually a very crowded and chaotic place. But there's a way to experience Versailles in an intimate, magical way.

Each year since 2015, the **Fêtes Galantes** costume ball has been held at the palace in the late spring. The ball is always centred on a theme, such as 'Marie Antoinette and Fashion', and the evening is immersive, with presenters and attendees in full, elaborate 18th-century costume.

The participants, who come from around the world, are allowed to visit some palace rooms not usually open to the public, such as the private apartments of Madame du Barry and Madame de Pompadour. The evening includes live baroque music concerts, demonstrations of period entertainments and games, and even dancing lessons – in case you're not already well-versed in the minuet. After a buffet of dainty hors d'oeuvres and bite-sized sweets, guests head to the dazzling Hall of Mirrors to try out their new baroque dance moves at the grand ball.

Once the ball draws to a close, the evening ends with a spectacular fireworks show, viewed through the floor-to-ceiling windows of the Hall of Mirrors.

Go for Baroque: Event Tips

I've been to this exceptional event several times; here is my advice for the best experience. It's worth investing in a high-quality, historically accurate costume and accessories – either high-end hire or from a professional costume designer. Arrive early in the afternoon so you'll have time to enjoy the beautiful gardens of Versailles and take photos there in costume. Ideally, get a hotel room near the château so you can get dressed there in comfort and then arrive on foot. Book tickets well in advance – it's a very popular event!

By Olympe de Bagatelle, *costume maker, 18th-century fashion expert and wig designer. @decorum_et_bagatelle*

Artist Villages

COUNTRYSIDE AS MUSE

A revolutionary invention in the 19th century changed the art world forever. With transportable metal paint tubes, artists could take the train from Paris to find inspiration in the countryside. They painted *en plein air* in bucolic settings that continue to inspire today. Follow in the footsteps of the great artists.

Left Monet's garden, Giverny **Middle** Fontainebleau Forest **Right** Notre-Dame-de-l'Assomption, Auvers-sur-Oise

OLEG BAKHIREV/SHUTTERSTOCK ©

Giverny

It was Claude Monet who put the tiny Seine-side village of Giverny on the map. The artist settled here with his family in 1883 and stayed until his death in 1926. Designed with great care as a floral composition, the gardens at his home were planted in order to be painted, showing off a different colour palette with each season. Today, **Monet's house and garden** is an incredibly popular attraction, with the famous water lily ponds drawing visitors from all over the world. The brilliant hues inside the house are just as stunning as the floral masterpiece outside. The property is generally open from 1 April through to 1 November, and there's no bad time to visit. Even in autumn, the gardens are festooned with flowers. Online booking is highly recommended.

Barbizon

The Forest of Fontainebleau inspired a group of 19th-century painters, including Jean-Francois Millet, Camille Corot and Théodore Rousseau, who set up shop in the village of Barbizon at the forest's edge. Known as the Barbizon School, they paved the way for the Impressionists such as Monet, Sisley and Renoir, who later also visited Fontainebleau to paint woodland scenes *en plein air.* Nowadays the gallery-lined village makes for a picturesque countryside escape and immersion in the artists' world. The **Auberge Ganne**, which once hosted many of the period's painters, now houses a small art museum where you can see traces of the artists' sketches on the bedroom walls. The original grocery shop and dining room are re-created on the ground floor, while the upstairs rooms display the paintings of the museum's permanent collection.

RAZVAN/GETTY IMAGES ©

JEROME LABOUYRIE/SHUTTERSTOCK ©

Auvers-sur-Oise

North of Paris, the charming hamlet of Auvers-sur-Oise is where Vincent van Gogh painted some of his greatest works, including the nearby wheat fields and the church of Notre-Dame-de-l'Assomption, before his alleged suicide in 1890. He rented a room at the Auberge Ravoux, which today serves as a museum called **Maison de Van Gogh**. You can enjoy a glass of wine and charcuterie and cheese plates in the original dining room. The artist's simple attic room has been left unchanged since his death. It was an incredibly prolific period – van Gogh lived here for 70 days and created 80 paintings. See the scenes that inspired him on a stroll through the village and fields. You can also see the cemetery where van Gogh lies next to his brother, Theo. A trip to the village isn't complete without a stop at the **Château d'Auvers**, which houses an interactive museum devoted to Impressionism. Learn about the art movement through multimedia exhibits, giant projections and special effects.

The charming hamlet of Auvers-sur-Oise is where Vincent van Gogh painted some of his greatest works, including the nearby wheat fields.

Aubervilliers

A showcase of today's contemporary talent, the 'artistic incubator' known as **Poush** moved from Clichy in Paris to this Parisian suburb in 2022. Inside a formerly vacant perfume factory, 225 artists make magic in the workshops, which visitors can see during the Wednesday evening open-house.

Fontainebleau

The forest that inspired the Barbizon School was also the birthplace of nature tourism. Once a royal hunting ground, Fontainebleau Forest is where the world's first marked walking trails were developed. In 1842, a former soldier named Claude-François Denecourt pioneered hiking as a leisure activity by creating a network of more than 100km of forest paths; his *sentiers bleus* are still marked today with blue lines painted on trees and rocks – known as the Denecourt-Colinet trails. In 1861, more than 10 years before Yellowstone became the world's first national park, part of Fontainebleau Forest became the world's first nature reserve.

38 PARISIAN Paddleboarding

RIVER | OUTDOORS | SPORTS

Just 20 minutes from central Paris, a serene stretch of the Marne River has served as an aquatic playground for Parisians since the 19th century. Nautical clubs developed along the banks, offering canoes and rowboats, creating the festive and leisurely Eldorado du Dimanche (Sunday's Eldorado) depicted in the 1929 film. Continue the tradition today with an active day on the water.

BENSLIMAN HASSAN/SHUTTERSTOCK ©

How to

Getting here Take the RER A to the Joinville-le-Pont station.

When to go Paddle-boarding sessions take place on Sundays, May to September. Open year-round, but contact Le Grand Huit for precise seasonal information.

How much Paddleboarding costs €29 (for 1¾ hours).

Tip Wear shorts and go with bare feet. In the colder months, you can borrow a wetsuit and wear old sneakers. The minimum age is 10 years old.

HEMIS/ALAMY STOCK PHOTO ©

HEMIS/ALAMY STOCK PHOTO ©

When the Paris–Mulhouse railway line was inaugurated in 1839, **Nogent-sur-Marne** was suddenly linked to the capital, attracting Parisians in droves to the banks of the Marne. They'd rent boats for a leisurely tour and picnic among the islands. Artists such as Raoul Dufy captured the moment on their canvases. In *The Ladies' Delight* (1883), Emile Zola wrote about **Chez Jullien**, a *guingette* (riverside dance hall) that is now a music school. Water sports even got competitive through clubs such as Société d'Encouragement du Sport Nautique (Encou), situated on the Île des Loups since 1879.

Partake in today's popular pursuit by signing up for a stand-up paddleboard session with Le Grand Huit. Beginners shouldn't be put off: the outing is supervised by a guide who doubles as a teacher, providing tips for novices and experienced boarders alike.

This Seine tributary is actually the longest river in France, and you're privy to a serene scene. Admire the willow trees at the water's edge, songbirds flying over the **Île Fanac** and magnificent art nouveau villas lining the riverbanks, while seasoned kayakers practise their moves through slalom gates.

Post-paddle, head to one of the *guingettes* such as **Chez Gégène**, which predates WWI. Les Maquereaux, which operates several popular Paris restaurants, has a *guinguette* on a boat. **La Guinguette des Maquereaux** evokes the playful vibe found here since the 19th century.

Left Île Fanac **Far left top** Paddle-boarding the Marne **Far left bottom** Chez Gégène

ⓘ Market Memento

Walk a few steps from the Nogent-sur-Marne station and you come face to face with a vestige of old Paris. The **Pavillon Baltard** is the last remaining relic of Les Halles, the sprawling city-centre marketplace. Commissioned by Napoléon III, the architect Victor Baltard designed a complex of 10 iron and glass pavilions – demolished in the 1970s when the wholesale market was moved to Rungis. The only survivor was Pavilion No 8, which housed the poultry and egg market. Dismounted and reassembled here, it serves today as a concert hall and events space.

39 SUBURBAN Culture & Nature

FOREST | LAKE | ART

You don't have to travel far in the Greater Paris region for a total change of scene. Right on the capital's doorstep, the hilly suburb of Meudon is a destination for both culture and hikes in the woods. It's the closest forest to Paris, and it's threaded with trails looping past ponds rich in flora and fauna.

How to

Getting here The RER C links the Champ de Mars-Eiffel Tower station and the Val de Fleury station in Meudon in 12 minutes.

When to go Hangar Y is open 10am to 8pm on weekends, holidays and every day during the Paris region's school holidays. The venue's surrounding park is open every day.

How much The ticket for Hangar Y, including entrance to the park, starts at €10.

Rabelais & Rodin Meudon has a long history in the arts. The great Renaissance writer François Rabelais once lived here, as did the composer Richard Wagner and sculptor Auguste Rodin. The newest cultural and arts venue is **Hangar Y**, housed inside what was the world's first airship hangar. Constructed from dismantled buildings from the 1878 Exposition Universelle, the hangar had been left vacant for 70 years. It was reborn in March 2023 as a hybrid public space with a thrilling artistic program. Overlooking the pond, a lively restaurant is operated by the popular Le Perchoir group.

Forest Rambling After a morning culture fix, set out for a hike in the **Forêt domaniale de Meudon**, a haven of centuries-old oak and chestnut trees with 16.5km of trails. Pack a picnic to enjoy by one of the ponds, which are lush with reeds and waterlilies. You'll spy herons, cormorants and the occasional coypu. Another surprising find: a megalith called the **Pierre aux Moines menhir** that dates from the late Stone Age.

Beer with a View Post-hike, head back into Meudon. Once the site of a royal château and gardens, the **Meudon Observatory** has a terrace with some of the region's best views of Paris. Grab a seat at **La Loggia** cafe and sip a local beer from the Rive Droite Rive Gauche microbrewery while admiring the vistas.

Above left Forêt domaniale de Meudon **Far left top** Hangar Y **Far left bottom** Villa des Brillants

The Sculptor's Villa

The Rodin Museum in Paris' 7e draws crowds, but many visitors are unaware of a second location in Meudon. The sculptor lived the last 20 years of his life at the **Villa des Brillants**, now a museum offering insights into Rodin's everyday life. Important oeuvres are displayed in the studio where he worked – the light-filled plaster gallery shows the stages of sculpture creation. In the expansive gardens surrounding the villa, you can pay your respects at the artist's tomb, topped by his famous *The Thinker* sculpture.

40 A Forest Hike & PALACE

NATURE I PALACE I HISTORY

While the Château de Versailles is constantly thronged by hordes of visitors, there's another royal palace just outside Paris that's equally grand, with the added benefits of being far less crowded and surrounded by an expansive forest. Hop on the train and head to Fontainebleau for a day of grandeur and peaceful rambling in nature.

BENSLIMAN HASSAN/SHUTTERSTOCK ©

How to

Getting here Transilien R Montargis or Montereau train from Gare de Lyon to Fontainebleau-Avon (40 minutes), then line 1 Les Lilas bus to the château (10 minutes). A Navigo day pass for zones 1–5 is the most cost-efficient option as it includes metro, train and bus.

When to go The château is open daily except for Tuesdays. Admission is free on the first Sunday of every month; pre-booking is recommended.

Tip Bring a picnic lunch for the hike.

ANTON_IVANOV/SHUTTERSTOCK ©

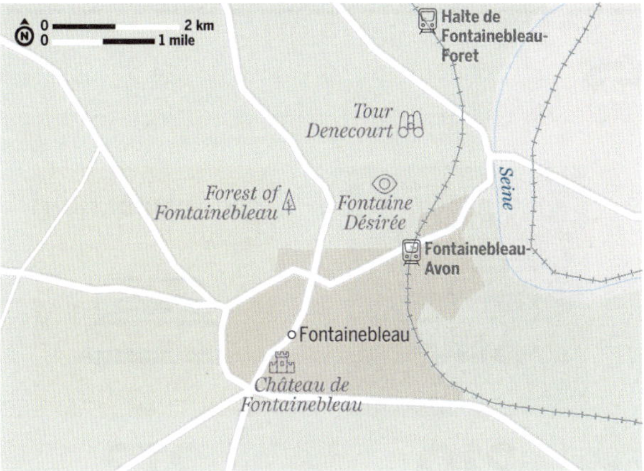

Get some Fresh Air in a Tranquil Forest The **Forest of Fontainebleau** has more than 400km of well-marked hiking trails ranging from easy to strenuous. As you exit the Fontainebleau-Avon station, you can turn left and walk straight up into the forest in less than five minutes. From the forest's edge, you can follow the blue Denecourt-Colinet No 2 trail signs up to the **Tour Denecourt** lookout tower for a scenic view. This moderate route of about an hour passes several 19th-century fountains. One of them, the **Fontaine Désirée**, has a stone table and benches – the perfect stopping point for a picnic lunch. Note that no forest maps are sold at the train station, so it's best to download offline hiking routes before arriving. On Saturday and Sunday mornings, some of the Montargis trains stop in the forest (Halte de Fontainebleau-Forêt), approximately 4km from Fontainebleau-Avon, if you want to get off earlier and hike down through the forest to the town.

Explore a History-rich Château While not nearly as well known as Versailles, the **Château de Fontainebleau** holds a more important place in French history as it was inhabited by every French monarch for nearly 800 years after its beginnings in the 12th century. With more than 1500 rooms, the sprawling complex is a fascinating melange of architectural styles, from medieval and Renaissance to rocaille and neoclassical. Famous residents have included Thomas Becket, Catherine de' Medici, Louis XIV, Marie Antoinette and Napoléon.

Far left top Fontainebleau Forest
Far left bottom Council chamber, Château de Fontainebleau

Historic Gardens

The château's extensive gardens and park also deserve a visit, and admission to them is free. Covering more than 120 hectares, they include a grand canal, an extensive formal 17th-century French garden created by André Le Nôtre (who also designed the gardens of Versailles) and an informal, English-style garden built in 1812. The grounds can be explored on foot, aboard the miniature train that runs through the estate or by horse-drawn carriage. The train rides include an audio guide in several languages. You can also hire small rowboats for excursions on the large carp pond.

Practicalities

ARRIVING 208

GETTING AROUND 210

ACCOMMODATION 212

SAFE TRAVEL 214

MONEY 215

RESPONSIBLE TRAVEL 216

ESSENTIALS 218

LANGUAGE 220

Right Batobus (p210)

BATOBUS
PARIS
P016593F
IVOLI

EASY STEPS FROM THE AIRPORT TO THE CITY CENTRE

Most international airlines fly to Aéroport de Charles de Gaulle, which is 28km northeast of central Paris. In French it is commonly called 'Roissy' after the suburb in which it's located. Inter-terminal shuttle services are free. The airport is linked to the city by rail, buses and taxi services.

AT THE AIRPORT

MIHAI_ANDRITOIU/SHUTTERSTOCK ©

MONEY
ATMs are located throughout the terminals. They accept foreign cards and have multiple language options. International currency exchange services *(bureaux de change)* are located in the arrivals areas of each terminal, though you'll probably get better rates at banks in the city centre.

SIM CARDS
You'll get a better deal buying a SIM in the city. It's also hard to find advice on the best packages and set-up at the airport. To buy one immediately, get a local SIM *(mobicarte)* at a Relay shop (in each terminal).

WI-FI At the airport, wi-fi is available for free *(gratuit)*; there are faster premium services for an extra charge.

CHARGING STATIONS Lockable charge boxes are free and available throughout the airport. Don't forget to collect your phone afterwards!

MORE INFORMATION The website parisaeroport.fr has details of airport facilities and transport services.

CUSTOMS REGULATIONS
Limits from non-EU countries include: 16L of beer, 4L of wine, 1L of spirits over 22% ABV or 2L not exceeding 22% ABV, 200 cigarettes, 50 cigars or 250g of tobacco. Total value cannot exceed €430 (plane or ferry arrivals; €300 by car, train or other arrivals). From EU countries, limits only apply for excessive amounts; see douane.gouv.fr.

GETTING TO THE CITY CENTRE

Train RER B €11.45, one hour, every 15 minutes. Central Paris stops include Gare du Nord, Châtelet–Les Halles and St-Michel–Notre Dame. From T1, take the free CDGVAL shuttle-train to the station at T3. Buy tickets using cash or credit cards from ticket machines (English-language option) or ticket counters.

Bus Roissybus €16.20 to Paris-Opéra, 60 to 90 minutes, every 15 to 30 minutes 5.15am to 12.30am. Buy tickets from all three terminals' bus stops, the driver or airport train stations.

Noctilien night buses N140 and N143 to Gare du Nord and Gare de l'Est, €8, 60 to 90 minutes, every 30 to 60 minutes 12.30am to 5.30am.

HOW MUCH FOR A...

taxi
€55–62
40–80 minutes

train
€11.45
60 minutes

bus
€16.20
60–90 minutes

Local buses
Cheaper but slower daytime services are bus 350 to Porte de la Chapelle (€2.10, 70 minutes) and bus 351 to Nation (€2.10, 80 minutes).

Rideshare
Uber services cost around €49; rates can be much higher during surge periods. Follow pick-up instructions as directed on your app.

Taxi Allow 40 to 80 minutes to central Paris, depending on traffic. Take an official taxi from the clearly marked ranks at each terminal's Arrivals level. Taxis charge a fixed price of €55 to the Right Bank and €62 to the Left Bank; fares increase by 15% from 7pm to 7am and on Sundays. Credit cards accepted.

OTHER POINTS OF ENTRY

Aéroport d'Orly Paris' second airport, Orly, is located 19km south of central Paris. The easiest transport options are the Orlybus to Paris' place Denfert–Rochereau (€11.20, every 15 to 20 minutes 6am to 12.30am) or taxi (Left/Right Bank €35/41; fares increase by 15% 7pm to 7am and on Sundays).

Aéroport de Beauvais Serving some low-cost airlines, Beauvais airport is 75km north of Paris. Shuttle buses to Paris' Porte Maillot (€16.90) meet flights.

Gare du Nord The terminus for northbound domestic trains as well as several international services. Located in northern Paris and linked to Paris' metro/RER and bus network. The London–Paris **Eurostar** (eurostar.com) line runs to/from St Pancras International; voyages take 2¼ hours. Eurostar has also taken over the routes formerly operated by Thalys. These trains pull into Paris' Gare du Nord from Brussels, Amsterdam and Cologne.

Other mainline train stations Paris is the central point in the French rail network, SNCF. In addition to Gare du Nord, the train stations Gare d'Austerlitz, Gare de l'Est, Gare de Lyon, Gare Montparnasse and Gare St-Lazare handle traffic to different parts of France and Europe. Each is well connected to the Paris public-transport system.

TRANSPORT TIPS TO HELP YOU GET AROUND

With its broad boulevards, charming backstreets and beautiful Unesco World Heritage–listed riverbanks, Paris is ideal for walking. Thanks to largely flat terrain and expanding bike lanes, cycling is an increasingly popular way to get around. The city's efficient, inexpensive public-transport network also makes it easy to explore far and wide.

€2.10 per metro & bus ride

FREE

Children under 10/four half price/free

Day pass from €8.45

TAXI & RIDESHARE

Find taxis at official stands or via companies such as Taxis G7 (g7.fr). The *prise en charge* (flagfall) is €2.60 (€4 to order immediately, €7 in advance); minimum journey cost is €7.30. Per kilometre tariffs are €1.14 to €1.53, depending on the time of day; there are supplements for a fifth passenger and luggage. Alternatively, use Uber (uber.com/fr/cities/paris).

BICYCLE

Cycle lanes continue to roll out across Paris. The Vélib' (velib-metropole.fr) bike-share scheme has more than 20,000 bikes, both classic (aka mechanical; green) and electric (blue) at 1400 stations citywide. Purchase a subscription online (EU credit cards only) or at docking stations. There are single-trip, day and multiday pass options (from €3), with rates charged in 30-minute increments (from €1).

WALK

Easily navigable, Paris is a walker's paradise. If you need to recharge your phone while you're out exploring the city, outlets can be found in the public bus kiosks.

BUS

With no stairs, buses are widely accessible. Normal rides (one or two bus zones) cost one metro ticket. Noctilien buses operate at night.

BOAT

Combining scenery and convenience, the Batobus (batobus.com; 24-hour pass €19) is a handy hop-on, hop-off service stopping at nine key destinations along the Seine.

RATP

Paris' integrated public-transport system, which includes the metro, RER suburban trains and buses, is operated by Régie Autonome des Transports Parisiens (RATP).

Visit ratp.fr for transport maps and a journey planner.

METRO & RER ESSENTIALS

Metro and RER network The fastest transport option, Paris' underground rail network consists of two separate but linked systems: the metro and the Réseau Express Régional (RER). Paris' metro has 14 numbered lines (currently being expanded to 18 as part of the Grand Paris Express project) and the RER has five main lines (though visitors usually only need to use lines A, B and C).

Operating hours Services usually run from around 5.30am to between 12.35am and 1.15am (2.15am on Friday and Saturday).

Zones There are five concentric transport zones radiating from Paris (zone 5 being the furthest out); if you travel from Charles de Gaulle Airport to Paris, for instance, you will need a ticket for zones 1 to 5.

Duration and transfers One t+ fare lets you travel between any two metro stations (no return journeys) for a period of 1½ hours, no matter how many transfers are required, and the RER zone 1, encompassing central Paris.

Tickets Paris is phasing out paper tickets. A Navigo Easy contactless card (€2; valid for 10 years) allows infrequent transport users, including visitors, to prepay for journeys (single t+ tickets €2.10; banks of 10 €16.90) by topping up the card. Navigo Easy can be used on the metro, RER (within the applicable zones), buses, trams and the Montmartre funicular. Airport buses Roissybus (€12) and Orlybus (€10.05) can be added on (which is cheaper than buying without the card). Navigo cards and top-ups are sold at metro/RER station ticket windows, RATP-affiliated outlets (eg tobacconists) and Charles de Gaulle Airport train stations.

Day passes A Forfait Navigo Jour (unlimited-use day pass) can be loaded onto Navigo Easy cards. It costs €8.45 for two zones up to €20.10 for five zones.

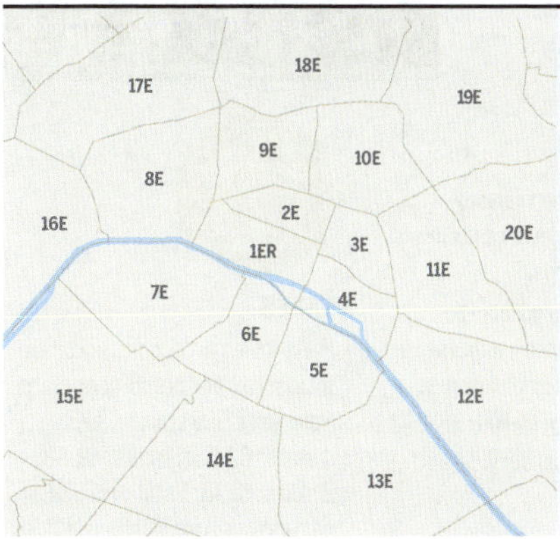

ARRONDISSEMENTS

Within the *périphérique* (ring road), Paris' 20 *arrondissements* (city districts) are numbered clockwise in a spiral from the centre and form part of all Parisian addresses.

Above Navigo card and transport tickets

UNIQUE AND LOCAL WAYS TO STAY

Paris' accommodation options span hip hostels, B&Bs, apartments and charming inexpensive hotels to boutique gems, lifestyle hotels and opulent palaces. Generally any savings from staying outside central Paris are negated when travel time and costs are considered – choose lodgings in Paris' arrondissements to instantly soak up Parisian life.

Find a place to stay in Paris

HOW MUCH FOR A NIGHT IN...

hostel dorm bed **from €25**

boutique midrange hotel **from €145**

private studio apartment **from €125**

HOSTELS

Paris is home to some state-of-the-art, new-generation hostels such as Generator, near Canal St-Martin, and, close by, two by St Christopher's Inns. Only Hostelling International (HI) *auberges de jeunesse* (youth hostels) require membership cards.

B&BS

Bed-and-breakfast accommodation (*chambres d'hôte* in French) offers an immersive way to experience the city. Paris' tourist office maintains a list of B&Bs.

APARTMENTS

As well as home-share sites such as Airbnb, Paris has a number of *résidences de tourisme* (serviced apartments, aka 'aparthotels'), such as the Citadines chain. Rental agencies such as Paris Attitude list pre-inspected furnished residential apartments for short to medium stays.

HOTELS

In Paris, hotel rooms are typically small by international standards, and cheaper properties may not have lifts or air-conditioning. Upper midrange and top-end hotels often have restaurants and bars on-site (but breakfast is rarely included in the price).

BOOKING

Accommodation is in high demand in Paris, particularly during peak times (April to October, as well as public and school holidays). Reservations are essential at these times, but are also recommended year-round.

Prices are invariably cheaper online, especially on the hotels' own websites.

Booking websites:

lonelyplanet.com/france/paris/hotels Reviews of Lonely Planet's top choices.

en.parisinfo.com/where-to-sleep-in-paris Search accommodation by categories of interest.

parisattitude.com Vetted apartments, professional service and reasonable fees.

TAXES

Paris levies an accommodation tourist tax per person per night. Palaces: €5; 5 stars: €3.75; 4 stars: €2.88; 3 stars: €1.88; 2 stars: €1.13; 1 star and B&Bs: €1; unrated/unclassified: €2.88.

WHERE TO STAY, IF YOU LOVE...

Monuments, museums and elegant streetscapes Eiffel Tower & Western Paris (p32) Upmarket residential area with limited nightlife close to Paris' iconic tower and museums.

→ **Parisian icons and superb shopping** Champs-Élysées & Grands Boulevards (p48) Luxury hotels, flagship boutiques and department stores, gastronomic restaurants and glamorous nightlife.

Artistic treasures and epicurean treats The Louvre & Les Halles (p64) Epicentral location, excellent transport links to all parts of Paris, major museums, fashion and food shopping galore. Midrange to high-end properties are the mainstay.

Lofty views and lively multicultural quarters Montmartre & Northern Paris (p78) Hilly streets, village charm and multicultural communities. Good budget options; many places to look out over Paris.

Hip boutiques and buzzing nightlife Le Marais, Ménilmontant & Belleville (p102) History-steeped streets and secret squares, some standout museums, and copious drinking and dining choices. The hub of Paris' LGBTIQ+ scene. Very central.

↓ **Bustling markets and creative spaces** Bastille & Eastern Paris (p120) Vibrant local neighbourhood blending tradition and innovation. Loads of restaurants, drinking and nightlife venues, and small shops. Diverse accommodation offerings.

Heart-of-Paris location and architectural masterpieces The Islands (p136) The Île de la Cité is dominated by Notre Dame; limited high-end accommodation centres on the peaceful, romantic Île St-Louis.

Jazz clubs, literary connections and late-opening bookshops The Latin Quarter (p150) Energetic student area with scores of eating, drinking and entertainment options. Good mix of accommodation styles.

Stylish shopping and sophisticated dining St-Germain des Prés (p164) Quintessentially Parisian neighbourhood close to the Seine with proximity to the Jardin du Luxembourg. Accommodation skews to the high end.

Street art, expansive parks and Paris' largest Chinatown Montparnasse & Southern Paris (p178) Villagey pockets and lots of green space. Some areas out of the way. Good value-for-money accommodation.

Far left Hôtel Lutetia (p169), St-Germain des Prés
Left Marché d'Aligre (p132) **Above** Cartier, Champs-Élysées

SAFE TRAVEL

In general, Paris is a safe city – streets are mostly well-lit and random street assaults are rare. Travellers should watch for petty theft and scams, be alert when using ATMs and avoid being caught up in street protests.

PETTY THEFT Always be on your guard for pickpockets and take precautions: don't carry more cash than you need, and keep credit cards and passport concealed. On cafe and restaurant terraces, avoid placing your jacket containing your wallet or handbag over the back of your chair, and don't leave your phone unattended on the table.

SCAMS Common 'distraction' scams employed by pickpockets include fake petitions, scammers pretending to 'find' a gold ring (after subtly placing it on the ground), dropping or spilling items, or tying friendship bracelets on your wrist. Such scams are particularly prevalent where there are crowds of tourists, such as around Sacré-Cœur and the Eiffel Tower.

METRO SAFETY Stay alert for petty theft at stations and aboard trains. Metro stations best avoided late at night include Châtelet–Les Halles, Château Rouge, Gare du Nord, Strasbourg St-Denis, Réaumur Sébastopol, Stalingrad and Montparnasse Bienvenüe. Marx Dormoy, Porte de la Chapelle and Marcadet–Poissonniers can be sketchy day and night.

WALKING
A slew of new cycling lanes in the city has changed traffic patterns, meaning pedestrians should take care to heed traffic lights and also look both ways before crossing streets to avoid car and bike traffic.

INSURANCE
Travel insurance covering theft, loss and medical problems is vital. EU, Switzerland, Iceland, Norway and Liechtenstein citizens get free or reduced-cost, state-provided healthcare with the European Health Insurance Card (EHIC).

Medical services A local *pharmacie* (chemist) can help with minor health concerns. For serious problems, go to *urgences* (A&E) departments at Paris' *hôpitaux* (hospitals; aphp.fr/urgences). Call 15 for ambulance (SAMU) services.

Street protests *La manif* (an abbreviation of *manifestation*) is a common occurrence in France. Visitors should take care if encountering one, as they can turn violent.

QUICK TIPS TO HELP YOU MANAGE YOUR MONEY

CREDIT CARDS Visa/Carte Bleue is the most widely accepted credit card in Paris, followed by MasterCard (Eurocard). Amex cards are only accepted at more upmarket establishments. Some non-EU-issued cards can't be used at automated machines (eg at a metro station or museum) – ask your bank for advice before you leave.

ATMS

ATMs (*distributeur automatique de billets* in French) are widespread. Check if/how much they charge for international cash withdrawals with your bank before you travel.

DYNAMIC CURRENCY CONVERSION

The local-currency payment option (DCC; dynamic currency conversion) is always cheaper for credit-card transactions and ATM withdrawals.

CURRENCY

Euro

HOW MUCH FOR A...

baguette **around €1.20**

glass of wine **from €2.50**

two-course bistro *menu* **from €17**

TIPPING

Taxis Round up to the nearest €1.

Restaurants Bills include a service charge; leave a few extra euros for good service.

Bars/cafes For table service, tip as you would in a restaurant.

Hotels Tip bellhops €1 to €2 per bag. Not expected for concierge, cleaners or front-desk staff.

TVA France's value-added tax (VAT), known as TVA *(taxe sur la valeur ajoutée)*, is 20% on most goods and services. Prices are generally TTC (*toutes taxes comprises;* 'all taxes included').

CASH

Cash isn't a good way to carry money; it can be stolen and you often won't get the best exchange rates. French vendors rarely accept bills larger than €50.

CURRENCY EXCHANGE

Check the latest exchange rates on websites such as xe.com. In Paris, *bureaux de change* are usually more efficient, open longer hours and give better rates than banks.

TAX REFUNDS

Non-EU residents over 16 who are visiting France for less than six months can often claim a TVA refund, provided the purchase amount is over €100 and made over a maximum of three days at a retailer that offers tax-free shopping (present your passport for eligibility). The retailer will provide a slip with a barcode that can be scanned at PABLO electronic terminals prior to check-in at the departure port. For more information, visit douane.gouv.fr/fiche/eligibility-vat-refunds.

POSITIVE-IMPACT TRAVEL

Positive, sustainable and feel-good experiences around the city

CHOOSE SUSTAINABLE VENUES

Dine farm to fork at Le Perchoir Porte de Versailles (leperchoir.fr/location/le-perchoir-porte-de-versailles) at Europe's largest urban rooftop farm, the 14,000-sq-metre, biodiverse Nature Urbaine.

Chart your own course and explore Paris' waterways by renting an electric-powered boat (no licence required) from Marin D'Eau Douce (boating-paris-marindeaudouce.com).

Take an upcycling workshop at eco-conscious cultural centre La Recyclerie (larecyclerie.com) inside a repurposed steam-train station, where the cafe utilises produce from its own urban farm on the tracks.

Look out over Paris from 150m up in the air aboard the helium-filled Ballon de Paris (ballondeparis.com). Tethered in the Parc André Citroën, this aerial sightseeing balloon monitors Paris' air quality.

Above La Recyclerie **Right** Cityscoot moped

VIENNASLIDE/ALAMY STOCK PHOTO ©, VICTOR VELTER/SHUTTERSTOCK ©

GIVE BACK

Catch zero-waste, renewable-energy-powered festival We Love Green (welovegreen.fr; June) at Paris' eastern forest, the Bois de Vincennes, combining a Think Tank 'ideas laboratory' raising awareness of ecological issues with artisan producers and indie, electro and hip-hop acts.

Snap up bargain-priced unsold items at merchants such as bakeries via the app Too Good to Go (toogoodtogo.fr), which helps prevent food waste.

Take part in workshops, events and more through the Paris Good Fashion (parisgoodfashion.fr) initiative focused on improving sourcing, traceability, ecofriendly processes and circular economies as part of the city's aim to become the world's most sustainable fashion capital by 2024.

SUPPORT LOCAL

Buy fresh produce at Paris' *bio* (organic) markets, such as Marché Raspail (Sunday), Marché Biologique des Batignolles (Saturday), Marché Biologique Brancusi (Saturday) and Marché Biologique Place du Père Chaillet (Wednesday and Saturday).

Make over your wardrobe at Sézane (sezane.com), a cult-status label that donates many of its proceeds to its own children's charity, Demain.

Browse exquisite handcrafted items, all made in French designers' studios, at Empreintes (empreintes-paris.com).

LEARN MORE

Discover black Paris on a guided tour with Entrée to Black Paris (entreetoblackparis.com).

Take a walking tour of Paris' multicultural northeastern neighbourhoods with Ça Se Visite! (ca-se-visite.fr).

Learn about Islamic culture on Institut des Cultures d'Islam (institut-cultures-islam.org) tours.

Understand Paris' sustainability through tourist-office initiatives (parisjetaime.com/eng/discover-paris/paris-by-theme/sustainable-tourism-paris-i040).

LEAVE A SMALL FOOTPRINT

Cycle through the city with Paris' bike-share scheme Vélib', which has thousands of classic and electric bikes at docking stations citywide for low-impact travel.

Zoom around with Cityscoot (cityscoot.eu; per minute from €0.28), a similar scheme with the electric equivalent of 50cc mopeds, located via an app.

Look out for the highly anticipated 'flying water taxis' (electric hydrofoils) from SeaBubbles (seabubbles.fr).

CLIMATE CHANGE & TRAVEL

It's impossible to ignore the impact we have when travelling, and the importance of making changes where we can. Lonely Planet urges all travellers to engage with their travel carbon footprint. There are many carbon calculators online that allow travellers to estimate the carbon emissions generated by their journey; try resurgence.org/resources/carbon-calculator.html. Many airlines and booking sites offer travellers the option of offsetting the impact of greenhouse gas emissions by contributing to climate-friendly initiatives around the world. We continue to offset the carbon footprint of all Lonely Planet staff travel, while recognising this is a mitigation more than a solution.

RESOURCES

paris.fr/pages/les-marches-parisiens-2428

velib-metropole.fr

en.parisinfo.com/what-to-see-in-paris/sustainable-tourism-in-paris

littleafrica.fr

ESSENTIAL NUTS-AND-BOLTS

ACCESSIBLE TRAVEL

Access can be difficult in Paris for *visiteurs handicapés* (visitors with disabilities) but things are improving.

Buses are an alternative to the mostly inaccessible metro for those in a *fauteuil roulant* (wheelchair). Taxis G7 (g7.fr) has vehicles equipped for passengers with disabilities.

The 'Tourisme & Handicap' initiative identifies hotels, restaurants, museums and cultural attractions that have facilities for those with physical, cognitive, visual and/or hearing disabilities; all display the label at their entrances.

The main tourist office has a service called ACCEO, which makes it possible for people who are deaf or hearing impaired to ask for information.
A French sign-language operator helps users to communicate via a webcam, microphone and speakers. Instant speech transcription is available, too. Visit en.parisinfo.com/accessibility.

Download the Accessible Paris guide (en.parisinfo.com/what-to-see-in-paris/visiting-paris-with-a-disability/accessible-paris-guide).

Online FACIL'iti (facil-iti.com) lets you customise parisinfo.com according to motor, sensory and/or cognitive needs.

Search a database of accessible venues on jaccede.com and its app.

FAST FACTS

Time Zone
GMT+1

Country Code
33

Electricity
220V/50Hz AC

GOOD TO KNOW

Many nationalities require ETIAS pre-travel authorisation; see ec.europa.eu.

On escalators, stand on the right and walk on the left; on footpaths, walk on the right.

France uses the metric system for weights and measurements.

Parisians don't speak loudly – keep your voice at a similar volume.

The legal drinking age in France is 18; some areas in Paris restrict alcohol consumption in public places after certain hours.

GREETINGS

Greet/farewell anyone you interact with – eg shopkeepers – with *'bonjour* (*bonsoir* at night)*/au revoir'*. The custom of *la bise* (cheek-kissing) lessened during the pandemic.

TOURIST INFORMATION

Paris' main tourist office (parisinfo.com) is at the Hôtel de Ville. It sells tickets for tours and several attractions, plus museum and transport passes.

TOILETS
Cafes don't appreciate non-customers using their facilities; try big hotels and major department stores.

TELEPHONE
Calling abroad from Paris, dial France's international access code (00) before the country code.

SMOKING
Banned in indoor public spaces (including hotel rooms), but permitted on pavement terraces.

OPENING HOURS
Bars and cafes typically open 7am to 2am, museums 10am to 6pm (closed Monday or Tuesday), restaurants noon to 2pm and 7.30pm to 10.30pm (days vary), and shops 10am to 7pm Monday to Saturday. Smaller shops may close for lunch and sometimes Mondays.

FAMILY TRAVEL

The tourist office (parisinfo.com) lists museums and activities for kids.

Most restaurants welcome children; many offer a *menu enfant* (children's menu).

Under 18s (or a younger cut-off age) receive discounted or free entry to sights.

Rent strollers, car seats, high chairs, travel beds and more from companies such as Kidelio (kidelio.com).

Go to Paris Mômes (parismomes.fr) for Parisian kid culture (up to 12 years).

Hotels can often organise baby-sitters for guests.

WI-FI
Many cafes and bars in Paris have free wi-fi for customers. Free wi-fi is also available in hundreds of public places, including parks, libraries and municipal buildings; look for a purple 'Zone Wi-Fi' sign. To connect, select the 'PARIS_WI-FI_' network. Locations are mapped at paris.fr/wifi.

OLRAT/SHUTTERSTOCK ©

LGBTIQ+ TRAVELLERS

The main nightlife hub is Le Marais, especially the areas around rue Ste-Croix de la Bretonnerie and rue des Archives, and eastwards to rue Vieille du Temple. Châtelet also has several popular bars and clubs.

Pride takes place around late June, headlined by the Marche des Fiertés parade.

Guided tours are operated by the Gay Locals (thegaylocals.com); its website is also a good resource for venues.

The Centre LGBT Paris-Île de France (centrelgbtparis.org) has information for LGBTIQ+ travellers.

LANGUAGE

Standard French is taught and spoken throughout France. This said, regional accents and dialects are an important part of identity in certain regions, but you'll have no trouble being understood anywhere if you stick to standard French, which we've used in this chapter.

The sounds used in spoken French can almost all be found in English. There are a couple of exceptions: nasal vowels (represented in our pronunciation guides by *o* or *u* followed by an almost inaudible nasal consonant sound *m*, *n* or *ng*), the 'funny' *u* (*ew* in our guides) and the deep-in-the-throat *r*. Bearing these few points in mind and reading our pronunciation guides below as if they were English, you'll be understood just fine.

BASICS

Hello.	*Bonjour.*	bon·zhoor
Goodbye.	*Au revoir.*	o·rer·vwa
Yes./No.	*Oui./Non.*	wee/non
Please.	*S'il vous plaît.*	seel voo play
Thank you.	*Merci.*	mair·see
Excuse me.	*Excusez-moi.*	ek·skew·zay·mwa
Sorry.	*Pardon.*	par·don

What's your name?
Comment vous appelez-vous? — ko·mon voo·za·play voo

My name is ...
Je m'appelle ... — zher ma·pel ...

Do you speak English?
Parlez-vous anglais? — par·lay·voo ong·glay

I don't understand.
Je ne comprends pas. — zher ner kom·pron pa

TIME & NUMBERS

What time is it?	*Quelle heure est-il?*	kel er ay til
It's (10) o'clock.	*Il est (dix) heures.*	il ay (deez) er
It's half past (10).	*Il est (dix) heures et demie.*	il ay (deez) er ay day·mee.

morning	*matin*	ma·tun
afternoon	*après-midi*	a·pray·mee·dee
evening	*soir*	swar
yesterday	*hier*	yair
today	*aujourd'hui*	o·zhoor·dwee
tomorrow	*demain*	der·mun

1	*un*	un	**6**	*six*	sees
2	*deux*	der	**7**	*sept*	set
3	*trois*	trwa	**8**	*huit*	weet
4	*quatre*	ka·trer	**9**	*neuf*	nerf
5	*cinq*	sungk	**10**	*dix*	dees

EMERGENCIES

Help!	*Au secours!*	o skoor
Leave me alone!	*Fichez-moi la paix!*	fee·shay·mwa la pay
Call the police!	*Appelez la police.*	a·play la po·lees
I'm lost.	*Je suis perdu/perdue.*	zher swee pair·dew (m/f)

Index

A

accessible travel 218
accommodation 212-13
activities 18-25
airports 208, 209
Aligre 132-3
amusement parks 47
Arc de Triomphe 54
archaeological sites & ruins 11, *see also* historic buildings & sites
  Arènes de Lutèce 158
  Crypte Archéologique de l'Île de la Cité 147
  Pierre aux Moines menhir 203
architecture 13, 155
arrondissements 211
art galleries, *see* museums & galleries
arts & cultural centres 9
  Commune Libre d'Aligre 133
  Gaîté Lyrique 76
  Grand Palais 54-5
  Ground Control 125
  Hangar Y 203
  Institut du Monde Arabe (IMA) 155
  La Villette 100
  Le Hasard Ludique 92-3
  Les Docks 191
  Maison Européenne de la Photographie (MEP) 119
  Pavillon Élysée 54
  Point Éphémère 98
  Poush 199
  Viaduc des Arts 125
ATMs 208, 215
Aubervilliers 199
Auvers-sur-Oise 199

B

Barbizon 198
basilicas, *see* churches & cathedrals
Bassin de la Villette 90-1
Bastille 120-35, **122-3**
  activities 124-5
  drinking & nightlife 135
  entertainment 135
  food 125, 132-3, 134-5
  planning 122-3
  shopping 132-3, 134
bathrooms 219
beaches 19, 148
beer 9, 100, 135, 191, 203
Belleville 102-19, **104-5**
  drinking & nightlife 119
  food 118
  history 114-15
  planning 104-5
bicycle travel 210, 217
boat trips 38, 90-1, 200-1, 210
books 30, 97
bookshops 15, 157, 163
bouquinistes 15
bridges 141
Buddhist temples 189
Buren, Daniel 73
bus travel 209, 210
business hours 6, 28, 219
Butte aux Cailles 185

C

cabaret 63, 83, 84, 85, 101
canals 91, 98-9
cemeteries 116-17
Champs-Élysées 48-63, **50-1**
  drinking & nightlife 58-9, 63
  food 54, 62-3
  planning 50-1
  shopping 60-1, 62
Chateau Rouge 94-5
children, travel with 47, 219
Chinatown 188-9
churches & cathedrals
  La Saint-Chapelle 147
  Notre Dame 142-3
  Sacré-Cœur 100
cinemas 19, 63, 95, 161
Cité Florale 185
climate 18-25
climate change 217
clothing 29
Colette 87
credit cards 215
cultural centres, *see* arts & cultural centres
currency 215
customs regulations 208
cycling 210, 217

D

Dalida 87
dance halls 83, 91, 201
dangers 214
day trips 192-205, **194-5**
de Lenclos, Ninon 108

disabilities, travellers with 218
drag shows 84, 85
drinking & nightlife 23, *see also individual locations*

E

eastern Paris 120-35, **122-3**
  activities 124-5
  drinking & nightlife 135
  entertainment 135
  food 125, 132-3, 134-5
  planning 122-3
  shopping 132-3, 134
emergencies 214, 219
Eiffel Tower 36-9
etiquette 28, 29, 218
events, *see* festivals & events

F

family travel 47, 219
farms 126-7
festivals & events 18-25
  Africolor 22
  Banlieues Bleues 24
  Bastille Day 18
  Chinese New Year 189
  Easter 24
  Epiphany 23
  Festival d'Automne 21
  Fête de la Musique 18
  Fête des Vendanges de Montmartre 20
  Fêtes Galantes 197
  Foire du Trône 24
  French Open 25
  Illuminations de Noël 22
  Journées Européennes du Patrimoine 20
  La Nuit Européenne des Musées 25
  Marathon International de Paris 24
  New Year's Eve 22
  Paris Plages 19, 148
  Portes Ouvertes des Ateliers d'Artistes de Belleville 25
  Salon du Chocolat 21
  Tour de France 19
films 31
fishing 149
Fontainebleau 199, 204-5
food 6-7
  African cuisine 95
  Asian cuisine 27, 188-9, 190
  baguettes 187
  bread 145, 187, 191
  cafes 11, 72-3
  cheese 101, 130-1
  Chinese cuisine 118
  chocolate 21, 40, 47, 101, 175
  delis 75
  North African cuisine 155
  pastries 7, 63, 75, 77, 110, 145, 174-5, 191
  saffron 126
  seafood 75
  snails 75
  urban farms 126-7
Forêt domaniale de Meudon 203
fountains 163, 205
French language 28, 220

G

galleries, *see* museums & galleries
gardens, *see* parks & gardens
gay travellers 119, 219
Giverny 198
Goutte d'Or 94-5
Grands Boulevards 48-63, **50-1**
  drinking & nightlife 58-9, 63
  food 54, 62-3
  planning 50-1
  shopping 60-1, 62
guingettes 83, 91, 201

H

hiking 203, 204-5
historic buildings & sites, *see also* archaeological sites & ruins
  Arc de Triomphe 54
  Champs-Élysées 52-5
  Conciergerie 141
  Coulée verte René-Dumont 124-5
  Couvent des Récollets de Paris 99
  École des Beaux-Arts 173
  Eiffel Tower 36-9
  Grand Palais 54-5
  Hôpital Saint-Louis 99
  Hôtel de Lauzun 140
  Hôtel Lambert 140
  Hôtel Lamoignon 109
  Journées Européennes du Patrimoine 20
  Le Procope 11
  Magasins Généraux 91
  Monet's House and Garden 198
  Opéra 56-7
  Palais Garnier 56-7
  Panthéon 157
  Pavillon Baltard 201
  Pavillon Élysée 54
  Pavillon Ledoyen 54
  Père Lachaise 116-17
  Petit Alsace 185
  Petit Palais 54-5
  Petite Ceinture 93

000 Map pages

Point Zéro des Routes de France 142
rue Saint-Jacques 11
Temple de la Sibylle 91
Village Saint-Paul 107-8
history 10-11
art 198-9
Belleville 114-15
black Paris 96-7
cinema 161
food 186-7
Le Marais 106-9, 110-11
holidays 19, 21, 24, 25

I

ice skating 23
Île aux Cygnes 15, 47
Île de la Cité 136-47, **138-9**
food 144-5, 146-7
planning 138-9
shopping 147
walking tours 140-1, **141**
Île Saint Louis 136-47, **138-9**
food 144-5, 146-7
planning 138-9
shopping 147
walking tours 140-1, **141**
immigration 96-7, 114-15
internet resources 9, 31, 69, 217, 218, 219
itineraries 26-7

J

jazz 77, 88-9, 149, 163
Jewish quarter 110-11

L

language 220
Latin Quarter 150-63, **152-3**
entertainment 160-1
food 155, 157, 158, 161, 162-3
planning 152-3
shopping 158, 163
Le Marais 102-19, **104-5**
drinking & nightlife 119
food 110, 118
history 106-9, 110-11
planning 104-5
shopping 119
Les Halles 65-77, **66-7**
drinking & nightlife 76-7
food 72-3, 74-5, 76-7
planning 66-7
shopping 74-5, 77
LGBTIQ+ travellers 119, 219
libraries 76, 119, 163, 190
live music 89, 135, 149
lookouts, *see* viewpoints
Louvre 68-71

M

markets 7, 217
Les Halles 74-5
Marché aux Fleurs – Reine-Elizabeth II 147
Marché aux Puces de Saint-Ouen 88-9
Marché d'Aligre 132-3
Marché Dauphine 89
Marché des Enfants Rouges 109
Marché Le Passage 89
Marché Paul Bert 89
Marché Président Wilson 39, 47
Montorgueil 74-5
Saint-Eustache Market 75
medical services 214
Ménilmontant 102-19, **104-5**
drinking & nightlife 119
food 118
planning 104-5
metro travel 12, 210, 211, 214
Meudon 202-3
Monet, Claude 198
money 208, 215
Montmartre 78-101, **80-1**
drinking & nightlife 82-5, 92-3, 100, 101
entertainment 84, 88-9, 101
food 84, 93, 100, 101
planning 80-1
shopping 88-9
Montparnasse 178-91, **180-1**
food 186-7
planning 180-1
monuments & statues
Hôtel de la Marine 55
La Danse de la Fontaine Émergente 189
Luxor Obelisk 55
Salvador Dalí Sundial 163
Tomb of the Unknown Soldier 54
mosques 155
Mouzaïa 115
murals 91, 113, 182-3
museums & galleries 13, 25
59 Rivoli 76
Auberge Ganne 198
Bourse de Commerce 75
Château d'Auvers 199
Cité de l'architecture et du patrimoine 45
Fluctuart 149
Fondation Louis Vuitton 43
French National Library – Site Richelieu 76
Galerie Itinerrance 190
Galerie Kamel Mennour 177
Galerie Thaddaeus Ropac 91
Grande Galerie de l'Évolution 159

museums & galleries *continued*
- Halle Saint-Pierre 100
- Institut du Monde Arabe 155
- La Cinémathèque 134
- La Fab 191
- L'Atelier des Lumières 134
- Le Quai de la photo 149
- Les Douches la Galerie 99
- Louvre 68-71
- Maison de Balzac 46
- Maison de Van Gogh 199
- Maison Européenne de la Photographie (MEP) 119
- Manufacture des Gobelins 191
- Monnaie de Paris 177
- Musée Baccarat 46
- Musée Carnavalet 109
- Musée Cognacq-Jay 119
- Musée d'Art Moderne de Paris (MAM) 45
- Musée de Cluny 157
- Musée de la Chasse et de la Nature 119
- Musée de la Contrefaçon 46
- Musée de la Libération de Paris 191
- Musée de la Vie romantique 100
- Musée de Montmartre 86
- Musée d'Ennery 46
- Musée des Arts Décoratifs (MAD) 76
- Musée d'Orsay 173
- Musée du Luxembourg 177
- Musée du quai Branly – Jacques Chirac 46
- Musée Guimet 45
- Musée Jacquemart-André 63
- Musée Marmottan Monet 46
- Musée national de l'histoire de l'immigration 125
- Musée Rodin 177
- Musée Yves Saint Laurent Paris 46
- Muséum National d'Histoire Naturelle 159
- Museum of Art & History of Judaism 110
- Palais de Tokyo 45
- Palais Galliera 45
- Petit Palais 54-5
- Poush 199
- Shoah Memorial 111
- Villa des Brillants 203

music 30, 89, 135, 149

music festivals 18, 22, 24

N

Nogent-sur-Marne 201

northern Paris 78-101, **80-1**
- activities 90-1
- drinking & nightlife 82-5, 92-3, 100, 101
- entertainment 84, 88-9, 101
- food 84, 93, 95, 98-9, 100, 101
- planning 80-1
- shopping 88-9, 95, 101

Notre Dame 142-3

O

opening hours 6, 28, 219

opera houses, *see* theatres

P

palaces & castles 196-7, 205

Pantin 91

parks & gardens 16, 27
- Bassin de l'Arsenal 135
- Bois de Boulogne 42-3
- Champs de Mars 39
- Château de Fontainebleau 205
- Coulée verte René-Dumont 124-5
- Fontainebleau 199, 204-5
- Forêt domaniale de Meudon 203
- Gardens of the National Archives 118
- Grandes Serres 159
- Green Line, the 124-5
- Jardin de Reuilly 125
- Jardin des Plantes 159
- Jardin des Rosiers – Joseph Migneret 118
- Jardin des Serres d'Auteuil 47
- Jardin des Tuileries 55
- Jardin du Luxembourg 171
- Jardin du Palais Royal 72-3
- Parc André Citroën 191
- Parc de Bagatelle 43
- Parc de Belleville 113
- Parc de Bercy 135
- Parc des Buttes-Chaumont 90-1
- Parc Georges Brassens 191
- Parc Montsouris 191
- Petite Ceinture 93
- Pierre Emmanuel Natural Garden 118
- Square Charles Péguy 135
- Square du Vert-Galant 147

Père Lachaise 116-17

Pernety 185

pharmacies 214

Pigalle 82-5

Pletzl 110-11

podcasts 30

public art 73, 91, 113, 182-3

public holidays 21, 24, 25

public transport 29

000 Map pages

R

RER travel 210, 211
responsible travel 216-17
rideshares 209, 210
Rive Gauche 172-3
Rodin, Auguste 203

S

Sacré-Cœur 100
safe travel 214
Saint-Antoine 128-9
Seine, the 14-15, 38, 148-9
shopping 40-1, *see also individual locations,* markets, vintage clothing
shopping malls, department stores & arcades 61, 75, 77, 175
SIM cards 208
smoking 219
southern Paris 178-91, **180-1**
  drinking & nightlife 191
  food 185, 188-9, 190
  planning 180-1
  shopping 185, 189
souvenirs 40-1
squares
  place Dalida 87
  place Dauphine 141
  place de la Catalogne 127
  Place de la Concorde 55
  place des Vosges 108
  place Vendôme 61
  Square Charles Péguy 125
  Square des Peupliers 185
statues, *see* monuments & statues
St-Germain des Prés 164-77, **166-7**
  drinking & nightlife 177
  food 173, 174-5, 176-7
  planning 166-7
  shopping 168-9, 173, 175, 177
  walking tours 170-1, **171**
street art 73, 91, 113, 182-3
street protests 214
swimming 47, 190
synagogues 111

T

tap water 28
taxes 215
taxis 209, 210
telephone services 219
television 31
temples 189
tennis 25
theatres
  Odéon-Théâtre de l'Europe 171
  Opéra 56-7
  Opéra Bastille 126
  Opéra Comique 63
  Palais Garnier 56-7
theft 214
tipping 215
toilets 219
tourist information 9, 31, 69, 217, 218
train travel 209
transport 29
travel beyond Paris 192-205
travel seasons 18-25
travel to/from Paris 208-9
travel within Paris 29, 210-11

U

urban farms 126-7

V

Valadon, Suzanne 86
Van Gogh, Vincent 199
vegetarian & vegan travellers 77
Versailles 196-7
viewpoints 17
  Arc de Triomphe 54
  Belleville 112-13
  Hôtel Dame des Arts 177
  Le Perchoir 17
  Meudon Observatory 203
  Montparnasse Tower 17
  Sacré-Cœur 100
  Tour Denecourt 205
vintage clothing 88-9, 101, 147, 163, 169, *see also* markets

W

walks, *see also* hiking
  Bastille 128-9, **129**
  eastern Paris 128-9, **129**
  Île de la Cité 140-1, **141**
  Île Saint Louis 140-1, **141**
  St-Germain des Prés 170-1, **171**
water 28
water sports 200-1, *see also* boat trips
weather 18-25
Weber, Louise 86-7
western Paris 32-47, **34-5**
  accommodation 47
  drinking & nightlife 47
  food 38-9, 45, 46-7
  planning 34-5
  shopping 47
wi-fi 208, 219
wine 21, 61, 135, 145, 177, 191

'Once my birdwatcher daughter and I spotted a brilliant blue kingfisher in Parc Montsouris – a haven of biodiversity smack dab in central Paris.'

MARY WINSTON NICKLIN

'That time I nerded out in the Musée des Plans-Reliefs, filled with 17th-century models of French towns. Scientists found real bones hidden in the 'cemetery' of the mini Mont Saint Michel!'

MARY WINSTON NICKLIN

THIS BOOK

Destination Editor
Annemarie McCarthy

Production Editor
Saralinda Turner

Book Designer
Virginia Moreno

Cartographer
Rachel Imeson

Assisting Editors
Andrew Bain, Peter Cruttenden, Melanie Dankel, Clare Healy, Lauren O'Connell, Graham O'Neill

Cover Researcher
Marc Backwell

Thanks
Ronan Abayawickrema, Karen Henderson, Darren O'Connell